Perspectives on
WOODY ALLEN

Perspectives on
FILM

RONALD GOTTESMAN
University of Southern California
and
HARRY M. GEDULD
Indiana University

Series Editors

❖

Perspectives on
WOODY ALLEN

❖

edited by

RENÉE R. CURRY

G. K. Hall & Co.
An Imprint of Simon & Schuster Macmillan
New York

Prentice Hall International
London • Mexico City • New Delhi • Singapore • Sydney • Toronto

G.K. Hall & Co.
An Imprint of Simon & Schuster Macmillan
1633 Broadway
New York, NY 10019

Library of Congress Catalog Card Number: 95-48095

Printed in the United States of America

Printing number

1 2 3 4 5 6 7 8 9 10

Library of Congress Cataloging-in-Publication Data

Perspectives on Woody Allen / edited by Renée R. Curry.
    p.   cm. — (Perspectives on film)
  Includes bibliographical references and index.
  ISBN 0-8161-1615-6 (alk. paper)
  1. Allen, Woody—Criticism and interpretation.   I.   Curry, Renée R.,
1955–   . II. Series.
PN1998.3.A45P47   1996
791.43'092—dc20   95-48095
                                     CIP

In loving appreciation of our friendship,
this volume is dedicated to
Cathy Bradeen Knox

Contents

ESSAYS

Series Editors' Note

This series is devoted to supplying comprehensive coverage of several topics: directors, individual films, national film traditions, film genres, and other categories that scholars have devised for organizing the rich history of film as expressive form, cultural force, and industrial and technological enterprise. Each volume essentially brings together two kinds of critical and historical material: first, previously published reviews, interviews, written and pictorial documents, essays, and other forms of commentary and interpretation; and, second, commissioned writings designed to provide fresh perspectives. Each volume is edited by a film scholar and contains a substantial introduction that traces and interprets the history of the critical response to the subject and indicates its current status among specialists. As appropriate, volumes will also provide production credits, filmographies, selective annotated bibliographies, indexes, and other reference materials. Titles in this series will thus combine the virtues of an interpretive archive and a reference guide. The success of each volume should be measured against this objective.

That Woody Allen is a versatile and talented writer, performer, and director is generally acknowledged. For many readers he ranks with Rabelais, Swift, Mark Twain, Henry Miller, Dorothy Parker, and H. L. Mencken as a comic writer who can cause major laughter even when read in private. As a television stand-up comedian early in his career Woody Allen also achieved considerable success, and even those film critics who have misgivings about the quality of his *oeuvre* typically find favorable things to say about one or more specific films—especially *Annie Hall, Zelig, Hannah and Her Sisters, The Purple Rose of Cairo,* and *Radio Days*.

Still, there is little critical consensus about the now considerable body of films Allen has written, directed, and/or acted in. Indeed, Woody Allen's achievement is probably more vigorously contested than is the work of any of his American contemporaries and peers. His place—if any—in the Pantheon is by no means certain. Nor does it seem likely that a clear consensus will soon emerge. The continuing publicity concerning his relations with Mia Farrow and her children will doubtless divert Allen's energies—which often resist focus anyway—and encourage tabloid speculation at least as much as it will encourage serious analysis and criticism in or out of the academy.

Professor Curry rightly argues that Woody Allen is a hard worker who steadily seeks to perfect his craft, but the uneven quality of Allen's large body of films as a writer, director, and actor also makes him a special case. Some critics have argued, in fact, that his compulsion to produce so much gets in the way of his achievement of quality, that for Allen more is less. He is at once one of the most intellectual of American directors and one of the least morally resonant; he is one of the most experimental and self-reflexive of directors, yet one of the least willing to take real risks with film form; he is undoubtedly a clever and perceptive social satirist, but compared, say, to Stanley Kubrick or to his shadow-self, John Cassavettes, Allen's perspective is, as the late Gerald Mast observed, flip rather than profound. Allen is notoriously autobiographical, but his exposures of his fears of death, of sexual adequacy, of his competence to endure in a hostile and uncertain world, and of his profound ambivalences about personal and family relationships somehow conceal as much as they reveal—about himself as well as his characters. Woody Allen is a skilled psycho-comedian, but his deepest instinct seems to be to keep the inner life of his personae on a leash. In sum, his central subject is middle-class urban neurosis, not the naked forked animal.

For all of these reasons and more, Professor Curry's decision to present the whole range of perspectives on Allen is the right one. The careful arrangement of the reviews and essays she has selected and commissioned provide a 360-degree tracking shot of Allen's provocative career. By vivifying the tensions in Woody Allen's creative life and by offering a full panoply of responses to it, Professor Curry has made it more nearly possible for the rest of us to come to a decision about the equivocal nature of this prolific career still very much in process.

Ronald Gottesman
Harry M. Geduld

Publisher's Note

Producing a volume that contains both newly commissioned and reprinted material presents the publisher with the challenge of balancing the desire to achieve stylistic consistency with the need to preserve the integrity of works first published elsewhere. In the Perspectives series, essays commissioned especially for a particular volume are edited to be consistent with G. K. Hall's house style; reprinted essays appear in the style in which they were first published, with only typographical errors corrected. Consequently, shifts in style from one essay to another are the result of our efforts to be faithful to each text as it was originally published.

Acknowledgments

Without the impeccable eye for detail, patience, and good humor of Cathy Cucinella, I would never have sanely completed this volume. Judy Stagg, Dominique Rousseau, and Garrett Collins also helped prepare this text in its early stages. The Woody Allen film class students at California State University, San Marcos, provided an unending source of wit and inspiration. Terry Allison kindly collaborated with me. Patty Seleski provided gourmet meals and friendly ears day after day. Bart Lewis encouraged me to take on the project. My family, Harry, Carole, and Debi Curry, and Devin and Curt Hood, listened to periodic Woody Allen progress reports. Of course, there are Ben and Murphy. And for all those many years of devoted companionship, I thank Tux.

Contributors of Essays

Terry L. Allison is the Collections Librarian at California State University San Marcos. He is completing his doctorate in Comparative Literature at University of California, San Diego. He is the author of several papers in librarianship, gender studies, and popular culture.

Gregg Bachman is the Chair of the Department of Communication at the University of Tampa, where he teaches screenwriting, film criticism and history, and film production. He publishes short fiction and is an award-winning video producer. He is presently working on a manuscript on silent film audiences.

Mashey Bernstein lectures on Composition and Film at the University of California, Santa Barbara. He has written extensively on aspects of Jewish identity vís-a-vís film. He received the Simon Rockower Award for excellence in Jewish journalism.

Mark E. Bleiweiss is a Jewish educator and administrator.

William Brigham is a sociologist specializing in the study of mass communication, focusing on analysis of commercial film. In addition to serving as a Lecturer at California State University San Marcos, he is a regular columnist in the *San Diego Review*.

Renée R. Curry is Associate Professor of Literature and Writing at California State University San Marcos where she teaches American literature, women's studies, and film studies. With Terry L. Allison, she edited *Stages of Rage: Emotional Eruption, Violence and Social Change*. Her publications cover film directors John Waters, Hanif Kureishi, Stephen Frears, Julie Dash, Tim Hunter, Errol Morris, and Woody Allen.

Samuel H. Dresner is a professor of Jewish studies. He is the author of a study of the biblical Rachel.

Richard Feldstein is Associate Professor of English at Rhode Island College in Providence. He often writes on feminism, film, and psychoanalysis.

Ronald D. LeBlanc is Associate Professor of Russian at the University of New Hampshire in Durham. He has written on the treatment of food in works by the likes of Tolstoy and Gogol.

Ronald S. Librach has written about *Mean Streets* and *Raging Bull*, as well as the role of narration in film and literary texts.

Ruth Perlmutter teaches Film History at the Philadelphia College of Art and the Tyler School of Art at Temple University. She has written extensively on film parody, feminism, film/literature, and German films.

Arnold W. Preussner is Associate Professor of English at Northeast Missouri State University in Kirksville, Missouri. He has published on comic film and theater from the Renaissance to the present.

Marc S. Reisch has published on such American figures as Walt Whitman and Woody Allen.

Beth Wishnick is a doctoral candidate at the University of Maryland. Her dissertation is a psychoanalytic study of Woody Allen's image in the media. Her major theoretical concerns center on psychoanalysis, film, and media studies.

INTRODUCTION

Woody Allen: The Artist as Worker

RENÉE R. CURRY

SINCE 1951 Woody Allen has worked to entertain audiences with humorous one-liners, stand-up routines, comic prose, playscripts, screenplays, acting roles, and film direction. The present volume, *Perspectives on Woody Allen*, gathers a selection of significant reviews and critical essays that provide a complex rendering of a hardworking, multi-faceted artist. The general reaction to Woody Allen and to his artistic output changes through time, but from early on he was deemed both by popular reception and by critical response as someone to contend with as a comedic force. His reputation has ranged throughout his career from that of zany slapstick comedian to that of America's "most important comedic director" (Canby in Girgus, 1). The durability and the appeal of Woody Allen's works, particularly those that include his persona, rests in what Annette Wernblad refers to as his ability to look like "a walking apology for himself" (Wernblad, 16). Allen worked in a deliberate way to craft a *persona*, a term that literally means mask, and that also connotes a second self created by an author of a text. These second-selves—whether they are designed for stand-up or for film—afford him both the opportunity to present a public self to the world and to secure a private self for his personal life. Maurice Yacowar tells us that "Allen based his career upon the candid exposure of a sensitive, frightened, and warmly representative modern soul, the Allen image or persona" (Yacowar, 5).

Allan Stewart Konigsberg, born 1 December 1935 in Brooklyn, New York, self-consciously created the Woody Allen persona (the angst-ridden, hypochondriac, little man ever in search of the "perfect" female lover) before he began participating in the world of comedy entertainment at the age of sixteen. The comic one-liners purchased by columnists Walter Winchell and Earl Wilson led eventually to a job as a comedy writer for NBC when Allen was eighteen. He continued writing jokes and routines for other comedians until Jack Rollins and Charles Joffe encouraged him to perform stand-up in 1961.

As the story goes, Woody Allen did not sweep the stand-up world by storm. His performances, awkward at best, gradually improved because Allen, the ardent worker, persistently groomed them with particular attention to further developing the Allen persona. Critics discuss the Woody Allen persona in a variety of ways, but the predominant readings portray him either as Yiddish schlemiel or as traditional comic little-man. Although the schlemiel is typically thought of as a born loser, in fact he or she more often causes, rather than suffers, bad luck (Wernblad, 18). The Allen persona accommodates both of these interpretations: his is the schlemiel as little man.

In 1964 Charles Feldman asked Woody Allen to write the script for *What's New Pussycat?* This film, an artistic embarrassment yet financial success, served as an important step toward his career as screenwriter, playwright, actor, and filmmaker. During the mid-to-late sixties, Allen also began writing humorous essays for the *New Yorker*, the *Kenyon Review*, the *New Republic*, *Playboy*, the *New York Times*, and other publications. Many of these essays he subsequently collected in three volumes: *Getting Even* (1971), *Without Feathers* (1975), and *Side Effects* (1980). Since the mid-sixties Woody Allen has written and directed, on the average, one film each year.

If a single phrase could capture the essence of Woody Allen, it might be the phrase "working man." Woody Allen has been a working man his entire life, and he loves to work. Eric Lax describes Allen as a "digger ant" (Lax 1991, 3) who knows nothing else but work, a man who on vacation in Stockholm wrote the screenplay for *Crimes and Misdemeanors* on a batch of hotel stationery, a man for whom "a vacation without work is a vacation without pleasure" (Lax 1991, 4). Once Allen had achieved a good deal of fame, he determined to direct films yearly in order to provide consistent work for his loyal crew. Like many working people, Allen experienced, and continues to experience, successes and failures. Although his creative output may seem inconsistent when appraised as independent pieces of art, the collective product points to a consistent worker, to a man determined to practice his art day in and day out.

To work with Woody Allen means exactly that: to work. Allen's set is not a jocular one. "There is no laugh-a-minute ambience on his movie sets, but there is an aura of trust and some levity. . . . He [Allen] is pure business even though most of his crew have been with him for ten years or longer" (Lax 1991, 45). Allen's reputation for securing warm and provocative performances from his female leads has little to do with Allen's own warmth or his sense of humor: "Woody's reserve can be disconcerting to one who has not worked with him before; he is physically present to everyone but, except for specific direction, personally available to no one" (Lax 1991, 45). In fact, it appears more likely that Allen wants to complete a job with the actors, not develop a relationship with them. Lax provides a significant observation from Meryl Streep, who, after having performed in *Manhattan* (1979), said, "'I don't think Woody Allen even remembers me. I went to see *Manhattan* and I felt like I wasn't even in it. . . . I only worked on the film for three days, and I didn't get to know Woody. Who gets to know Woody?'" (Lax 1991, 46).

Woody Allen has worked and continues to work daily, not toward off-screen bonhomie, which he claims is "irrelevant" (Lax 1991, 46) to making good movies, but rather toward making people laugh at his movies. Although he has matured in his ability to depict comic characters, situations, and narrative devices, he remains wedded to an early sense that the success of a comedy directly relates to the laughs it incurs:

> "When it comes down to survival, it's laughs that a comedy has to have. There's no way out of it. There's a route that everybody in the world who does comedy takes to try to get around that because laughs are so hard to get. It's not hard to get one or two, but it's hard to get ninety minutes of laughter at a quick enough pace that people aren't bored. It's so difficult that you try everything else. Guys are always saying that what you have to have are some interesting characters so that they go with the story. And yes, of course, you definitely want them, all that's wonderful—if the laughs are there. But if the laughs aren't there, then all that stuff just doesn't mean anything. Whereas if all that stuff's not there but the laughs are, then you've got a good chance for a winner. In the end it's just a pragmatic thing that laughs are the heart and blood of a comedy." (Lax 1975, 75)

Woody Allen has worked hard to draw many laughs from many viewers. His comedy is a truly labored art form, one that he has studied from childhood and one that continues to absorb him. Some viewers laugh in response to the schlemiel/little-man and his hypochondria, his battle with despair, his victimization, his Jewish guilt, his neurosis, his displacement, his relationships with women, his physical dishevelment. Some laugh nervously in response to Woody Allen's uncanny ability to portray realistic personal relationship obsessions, such as the love relationship, the parent-child relationship, the work relationship, one's relationship to God, one's relationship to art, and the relationship with the self. Others laugh at his way with words—his puns, his asides, his comic references to high culture and its major texts, his New York pronunciations.

The laughs, however, come at a cost for Woody Allen the director. Incredibly self-aware, Allen admits that each film he releases leaves him dissatisfied, and that this dissatisfaction stimulates him to work on the next film: "'I'm not saying my work is degenerate or insulting to the intelligence, it's just less than what I wanted it to be" (Lax 1991, 280). To critics, the body of films created by Woody Allen proves far more satisfactory than dissatisfactory, and they find some of his films to be superior pieces of art. The work defies easy categorization; however, the early films, from *What's New Pussycat?* (1965) through *Love and Death* (1975), do seem similarly fragmented, zany, and slapstick. The films from *Annie Hall* (1977) through *Hannah and Her Sisters* (1986) might serve as examples of a peak period in which Allen achieves unique integration of story, form, tone, and technique in each film. The later films, from *September* (1987) through *Bullets over Broadway* (1994), add sophisticated, somber overtones to the comedy. Such a phasic structure, while allowing for a certain amount of developmental analysis, also belies the sophistication of the early fragments that construct *Everything You Always Wanted to Know about Sex* (1972), the latent somberness of the comedy in *Purple Rose of Cairo* (1985), and the totality of form frequently achieved in gems such as *Husbands and Wives* (1992). Allen's work does not, however, progress in a linear way from immaturity to maturity, solemnity, and polish. The work develops and regresses in delirious and unpredictable ways as Allen works his art according to the terms of his own personal and private artistic impulses.

The critical response to Woody Allen's work has also had its phases. In the seventies, critics examined Allen's output in terms of his genius, his total artistry, and the relationship between his personal life and his films. But perhaps critic Maurice Yacowar best captured the Woody Allen of the seventies in *Loser Take All: The Comic Art of Woody Allen* (1979). Yacowar describes this Woody Allen as not "just a comedian," but rather as "a serious, probing artist with a consistent and distinctive vision" (1). With this thesis, Yacowar argues that Woody Allen did not simply become a fine artist at the moment of *Annie Hall* (1977), but that he had always been an impeccable artist and diligent worker. To Yacowar, the critical failure to recognize Woody Allen's artistry stemmed from the general disrespect that people have for comedy as an art form, a disrespect as old as Aristotle's attitude toward the genre, which he expressed in the *Poetics*.

In particular, Yacowar claims that Allen's intellectual concerns have been present from the earliest of his films, and not just evidenced in the peak period films: "Both *What's New Pussycat?* and *Manhattan* explore the difficulty of reconciling one's self with a desired image, and the greater tension between the urge to assert one's individuality and the need to immerse oneself in some larger identification, whether through art, religion, or romance" (Yacowar, 3). Other concerns prevalent throughout Allen's work, according to Yacowar, include an ongoing representation of the anxieties of a modern urban sensibility; the double emotional affliction of lust and inadequacy; the problem of vulnerability and connection; and a discussion of psychoanalysis and identification of the self. Yacowar's Woody Allen uses comedic film as a tool to engage audiences in a dialogue (albeit unspoken) about the "Everyman terrified by the prospect of life" (Yacowar, 151).

In the eighties, the critical response to Woody Allen's work centered around issues of religion and the interplay between an artist's life and his creative output, but commentary also shifted to consideration of Allen as an auteur and as an authority on the American character, Jewish identity, and religion. Nancy Pogel most thoroughly captures the Woody Allen of the eighties in *Woody Allen* (1987). She celebrates him as "one of America's most important humorists and filmmakers" who "participates in a definable tradition of American literary and film comedy" (1). Most importantly, Pogel outlines Allen's persistent work at continuing the little-man tradition in film. Allen's little-man figures, based on Charlie Chaplin's little tramp, have changed throughout the course of his work; however, they are always steeped in rebellion and innocence: "They are childlike, fantasizing, destructive, eccentric, neurotic—filled with updated versions of the modern anxieties that plagued the little men characters of the 1920s. . . . Their childlike demeanor, fallibility, and humanity serve as contrasts to the dehumanizing pressures they inevitably encounter" (Pogel, 10–11).

With his schlemiel/little man persona, Woody Allen maintained a popularity among the comedy club crowd throughout the early sixties, among television audiences that he attracted as the decade progressed, and among film audiences for the last three decades. Pogel notes that Allen does not allow the little-man character to remain a static type. As Allen changes, so does the little-man; in fact, he becomes less appealing in the eighties, and more a vehicle for instigating feelings of alienation between the audience and the film rather than a vehicle for questioning the role of alienation in life. As Pogel notes: "Although the little man had been gradually becoming a less humble, more self-conscious, and more blemished central figure, in *Stardust Memories*, Allen drives his inquiries further. In presenting a still less appealing little-man, who often feels alienated from fans, Allen threatens to cut audiences away from their familiar lines of identification with the main character and to leave viewers with additional uncertainty" (Pogel, 134). Pogel suggests that we witness a more ruthless side of Allen's humor in the eighties, a more confrontational humor that reflects mature concerns "about the probability for attaining meaning in the face of contemporary fragmentation, alienation, and instability" (Pogel, 150).

After working year in and year out for four decades, Woody Allen has become a comic tradition unto himself, and Sam B. Girgus reminds us that current criticism of Woody Allen's work must contend with the mythic and legendary status of the Woody Allen figure:

> The myth of Woody Allen developed concomitantly with the growing reality of his success and fame. Indeed, the myth emerged as a complicated mixture of cinematic image, publicity, and self-serving biography. . . . The ultimate American in his awareness and representation of the world around and within him, he has become a major cultural symbol of a mind-set and a way of life. The quintessential New Yorker, he is our Gatsby looking out, not at Long Island, but at the city itself with the persistent wonder and awe that, in America, all things are still possible and all transformations can still occur. (Girgus, 4, 8)

Woody Allen's mythic status as well as his creative output, particularly his films, has attracted an incredible outpouring of critical response. This book aims to further the recognition of Allen as a complex and dominant figure in comedic filmmaking.

The book is divided into two parts. Part One, "Reviews," gathers together thirteen significant responses to the films at the time of their release. The reviewers chosen are those who maintained an interest in Allen's films throughout his career. Part Two, "The Essays," presents thirteen essays selected to represent the broad range of Allen criticism; of the thirteen, five are published here for the first time.

Part One, "Reviews," begins with Robert Hatch's review of *What's New Pussycat?* for the *Nation*. This review accurately locates three problems that will recur throughout the early film criticism of Woody Allen: a sense of too much physical laboring to get laughs, an inability to differentiate between stand-up routines and narrative force, and a lack of regard for the audience. Although Clive Donner directed this project, Hatch specifically names Allen's writing as the chief flaw of the film: "Part of the problem is with the so-called script by Woody Allen, a television hysteric who plays second clown to Peter Sellers. He has tried to offset a basic lack of situation invention by proliferating old gags. . . ." This lack of story is named again as a problem in Stanley Kauffmann's review for the *New Republic* of *Take the Money and Run* (1969), which Allen cowrote, starred in, and directed, as well as in Kauffmann's tangential comments about *Play It Again, Sam*.

In his review of *Take the Money and Run*, Kauffmann writes, "Allen . . . is a witty man, but he is a stand-up comedian, a performer whose basic method is that of the fisherman: he comes out and casts his lines a number of times, trying to catch as many laughs as possible. After a while, he quits, hoping that his average has been high." Unlike Hatch, however, Kauffmann does find Allen consistently and calculatedly funny. He even notes that Allen has "clever schemes" about filmmaking and that his direction seems "competent enough." Although the problem about narrative recurs whether Allen stands behind the camera or not, Kauffmann's review of *Take the Money and Run* offers some reasons for attending to Allen's work.

About two years later, at the time of *Bananas* (1971), Kauffmann has run out of encouragement. Again he comments on the lack of acting in a narrative structure: "The trouble with Woody Allen's films—which he writes, directs, and stars in—is quite simple. He is a very funny writer and (on TV) a fairly funny stand-up comic. As a teacher and actor, his talent is absolutely zero." Furthermore, Kauffmann finds no cleverness nor competence in Allen's direction of *Bananas*: "Incessantly he photographs from odd angles—once even through the corner of his eyeglasses—instead of relaxing, not worrying about proving he's intellectual, and just telling a

story." After years of Allen's filmmaking and involvement in six projects—
What's New Pussycat?, *What's Up, Tiger Lily?* (1966), *Casino Royale*
(1967), *Don't Drink the Water* (1969), *Take the Money and Run*, and
Bananas—and even some success at the box office, Hatch and Kauffmann
still find Allen's work amateurish and wanting.

In 1975 Robert Hatch reviews *Love and Death* with the knowledge that
audiences seem to think Allen is funny, but with the determined sense that
Allen continues to work too hard for the laughs. In fact, Hatch is convinced that the audience laughs because they can sense how much Allen
wants them to laugh: "When a nice fellow like that goes to so much trouble and expense to be amusing, it seems ungracious not to be amused. It's
like being in a TV audience—when that ingratiating chap holds up the
'laugh sign,' you laugh." Two of the critical issues in 1975 are the same
ones he noted in 1965, no organic narrative and a disrespect for the audience. To Hatch, the performers seem to be having more fun than the audience, and Allen seems to perceive the audience as robots capable of being
programmed to laugh. On the positive side, Hatch does note the exciting
beginnings of a chemistry between Diane Keaton and Woody Allen: "A
pleasant innovation in this film is the habit of Allen and Keaton, in
moments of high emotion or imminent danger, to escape into an
exchange of semantic locutions that defy comprehension and shrewdly
ape a current pomposity." Hatch wants more of this type of "astuteness,"
but he does not get it in this film. For astuteness and chemistry, he must
wait for *Annie Hall*.

Although Hatch's review of *Annie Hall* does not unequivocally praise
the film, it notes a remarkable change on the part of Woody Allen: "There
was a time when I thought Woody Allen was caught in the trap, as I saw it,
of being the smartest, runtiest aleck in the neighborhood. But after *The
Front*, and after *Annie Hall*, I suspect he's on to more important things.
He's now 40, he tells us; he has time, he has quick eyes and ears and a sardonic turn of mind. And Lord knows he has energy." Hatch particularly
praises Allen's ability to manage "successive incidents" this time around
and to allow the audience to relate to those incidents. He does point out,
however, that Allen maintains an amateurish addiction to the prolonged
gag and to the heavy-handed cleverness of camera techniques such as subtitles and split images, but overall, these regressive acts seem to be fading
from the films.

With the release of *Interiors* (1978), Woody Allen exhibits a movement
toward the noncomedic film. Two later films, *Another Woman* (1988) and
September (1987), will follow in this tradition. Ironically, his first foray
into drama attracts an unequivocally positive review from Colin L.
Westerbeck, writing for *Commonweal*. In particular, Westerbeck makes
note of Allen's incredible talent for subtle and unobtrusive interweaving of

emotions throughout the film. Subtlety and unobtrusiveness have not heretofore been Allen trademarks. *Interiors* marks a leap in this direction for Woody Allen. It also marks a change in the type of language used to critique Woody Allen. Westerbeck compares him to Ingmar Bergman, and also describes the opening scene as "a brilliant touch." With this review, Westerbeck leaves behind the critical take on Allen as amateurish and invokes new language to anticipate the Allen films to come.

And the next one to come, *Manhattan* (1979), seduces reviewer Westerbeck with its poetry: "Not since *The Naked City* has there been a film that contained such a beautiful visual poem to New York as Woody Allen's *Manhattan* does." Westerbeck describes in this review the finesse with which Woody Allen depicts a visual narrative that strains against its verbal narration. No longer do reviews concentrate on Allen's inability to tell a story. In *Manhattan*, Westerbeck not only praises the complicated narrative structure, but he also remarks upon the sophistication of the male/female relationship issues as well as the meticulous performances by the three leading women, Diane Keaton, Meryl Streep, and Mariel Hemingway. Allen no longer depends on slapstick physicality and one-liners to simulate a story. Instead he masterfully weaves story, chemistry, camera technique, performance, and emotion into an artful whole. Westerbeck rightfully urges us to attend to all of Allen, but particularly to the silly because it is from the silly in Allen's work that the "genuinely poignant" emerges.

When Colin Westerbeck reviews *Zelig* (1985), he uses definitive language: "*Zelig* is brilliant." Westerbeck takes time in this review to distinguish between the comedy of Charlie Chaplin and the comedy of Buster Keaton; he points out that although audiences may experience more pure bursts of laughter as a result of watching Keaton, Chaplin thinks in terms of an entire comic framework. Therefore Westerbeck names Chaplin the greater genius of the two. Westerbeck goes into detail about these comic icons in order to situate Woody Allen in the appropriate tradition. *Zelig*'s brilliance, with its personal revelations, its "meditation on fame," and its "stunning" technical feats overwhelms this reviewer to such an extent that he finds the movie disconcerting. Westerbeck is disconcerted because *Zelig* proves Allen to be a totally different type of comic than reviewers had previously been led to believe. In other words, since *Annie Hall*, Westerbeck finds Allen to have veered off in a variant comic direction, and with *Zelig* Westerbeck can identify that direction: "I always wanted him to be better at providing those spontaneous touches, the little grace notes of comedy, that make me crack up at a Keaton movie. . . . It was never Keaton he was on his way to becoming, but Chaplin." Westerbeck's review of *Zelig* recognizes Allen's mind as one capable of creating a massive comic universe.

Regarding *Purple Rose of Cairo*, Stanley Kauffmann also comments on Allen's brightness, but he comes down extremely hard on Allen's lack of follow-through: "I remembered the actual new Woody Allen film I had seen, called *The Purple Rose of Cairo*, which begins, as usual, with an arresting idea, new for him (though not new in the history of film); and I remembered that, as usual, he develops it for awhile, then just quits. Quits dead . . . . The theme is just picked up and used for a while, then plunked down as a bright child plunks down a new toy that quickly bores him." Kauffmann goes on in the review to deprecate Allen's productivity—his "learn-while-you-earn" film career—which Kauffman finds exploitative of film audiences. He labels Woody Allen, at the peak of his career, an amateur, a creative person with imagination and skill, but one seriously lacking in "responsibility to his material."

Reviewers of Allen's peak period films not only discuss his success or failure in terms of either responsibility or overall comic ideology, but they also spend significant amounts of time examining his characters, particularly his women characters. Allen's persona still draws an audience, but often it competes with the female characters he designs. Pauline Kael's review of *Hannah and Her Sisters* for the *New Yorker* concentrates on Allen's characterizations as the skillful foundation of the film. Kael finds some of the characters better crafted than others; she complains that Allen misconstrues Mia Farrow's Hannah: "Allen has got her so subdued and idealized that she seems to be floating passively in another world." Kael praises Barbara Hershey's "luscious presence" as Lee, and she notes Dianne Wiest's need to work hard at fulfilling her role as the neurotic Holly. Overall, Kael criticizes Allen's inability "to write enough sides" for any of them to play. She finds fault mainly with his script: "Allen's script, for all its shrewdness about sisterly relations and its considerable finesse, doesn't cut very deep."

Kael admits that Allen's greatest strength in the film lies with characterization, but this time she views Woody Allen's persona character, the hypochondriac Mickey Sachs, as providing the life that the film needs. "It [the film] needs his mopey personality, and it needs his jokes, even though they're throwbacks to earlier gags. . . . The picture needs him desperately, because the other roles are so thin that there's nobody else to draw us into the story." Once Allen develops the ability to create a believable narrative, one not held together by a series of stand-up jokes, flaws in Allen's ability to create in-depth characters become apparent.

In Maurice Yacowar's review of *September* for *Film Quarterly*, he too addresses Woody Allen's ability to create characters, although this time the discussion involves tragic, rather than comic, characters. And once again, like Westerbeck's appreciation of characterization in *Interiors*, Yacowar too finds much to be admired about Allen's creation and development of character in this noncomedic film: "The film's richest pleasure derives from Allen's subtle and touching revelation of his characters. . . . Without or despite their words, the characters express their timorous yearnings and fears." Although Woody Allen's dramas perform less well for him at the box office, some of the critics believe that his fullest characterizations occur in these films. In fact, Yacowar thinks that *September* addresses exactly this issue. He claims that Allen reveals his own personal belief that comedy ultimately fails to "fathom the deepest or outermost blues."

But Allen never stays with drama for long, and sometimes he tries to revive an earlier type of comedy. Upon one such occasion, that of the short film *Oedipus Wrecks*, Pauline Kael finds that he has lost his touch. She finds that not only are most of the characters too waxlike and cartoonish, but that "it has been a while since Allen directed out-and-out comedy, and here and there his timing is off." The film predominantly lacks excitement, according to Kael, but strangely enough, she finds that Allen progresses in his ability to finesse female characterization: "Woody Allen has written the role that Julie Kavner deserves: she's the cartoon Jewish woman redeemed, and she plays it superbly—she's a Yiddish Olive Oyl, a hopeless involuntary comic." Ironically, the character that Kael finds appealing is not really a character, but rather a character type—a cartoon figure.

The last review in Part One of *Perspectives on Woody Allen* is one in which the issue of character takes on many connotations, as discussed by Stuart Klawans. In his review of *Husbands and Wives* for the *Nation*, Klawans finds the film a reprehensible piece of work from the standpoint of cinematic technique and character design and development, and he particularly takes issue with the arrogance of Allen, the auteur. He refers to *Husbands and Wives* as a "mess," a "disarray," and a racist, elitist, solipsistic portrayal of Manhattan; Klawans finds these attributes unforgivable. He views and reviews the film with an abhorrence for what he believes to be Allen's sheltered existence: "He's been shielded from the ruder shocks of commerce, thanks to producers who have been content with prestige more often than profit. Of the major American filmmakers, only Woody Allen has been so protected." Klawans suggests that Allen's sheltered and skewed view of the world might ultimately be the ruin of him, and that the ruin of this phase of Woody Allen might not constitute a great loss.

But the ruin of Woody Allen does not occur. He goes on to direct two more films, *Manhattan Murder Mystery* (1993) and *Bullets over Broadway* (1994) in which he continues the pursuit of strong female characters, although often only attaining character types. Nonetheless he produces enjoyable, although not always intense, comic narrative structures.

Part Two, "Essays," begins with Beth Wishnick's essay on "receptivity"— the term used in literary theory to refer to the various ways in which audiences receive and react to information. "That Obscure Object of Analysis" serves as an objective introduction to the critical biases towards Allen. In the essay written for this volume, Wishnick employs the "psychoanalytical notions of projection and transference," to explore the media blitz surrounding *Husbands and Wives*. She argues that this media pastiche attempts to intertwine the off-screen drama of Woody Allen's and Mia Farrow's separation with the on-screen drama depicted in the film, and in this attempt, it mimics the psychoanalytic notion of the multiple and simultaneous believable truths that make up any psyche: "The media explosion swirling around *Husbands and Wives* highlights one of the many thematic concerns of the movie—namely, the irony of any single version of truth." The author meticulously discusses both the technology of Allen's filmmaking as well as the social construction of the scandal by the media.

Richard Feldstein's "The Dissolution of the Self," provides readers an opportunity to explore a discussion of perspective regarding Woody Allen's work. Feldstein's essay applies Lacanian theory to a single film, *Zelig*. The author argues that Allen advances Lacan's ironic theory of identification when he has "Leonard Zelig not only identify with but actually metamorphose himself into a clone of his desired object." Feldstein meticulously analyzes the numerous transformative interactions between Leonard Zelig and others, particularly his psychoanalyst, Dr. Fletcher, in order to guide the reader to a complex understanding of the "endless duplication" experienced by Zelig and the effect of these transformations on the self. According to Feldstein, the film also works as a "condemnation of capricious societal opinion. First and foremost, Zelig's is a story of one man's hypnotic effect on American spectatorial consciousness." By managing and interweaving these two strains of argument—the self as projector and the self as evaluated by society—Feldstein suggests that Woody Allen prophesies a dissolution of the American self. This dissolution will occur as a result of two pressures: 1) the pressure to mimic, to model one's life after other figures, and 2) the pressure brought about by being gazed at and judged inadequate by other people.

Ruth Perlmutter also examines *Zelig*, but she views the film from a Bakhtinian perspective. The essay reprinted here, "*Zelig* According to Bakhtin," examines Woody Allen's film as a profoundly successful example of Russian literary theorist M. M. Bakhtin's "heteroglossia." Perlmutter paraphrases "heteroglossia" as "an interaction of contending social discourses," an interaction that she claims Allen intentionally works to provide in his film: "Nowhere else in Allen's work do we witness as clearly the intentional counterpoint of multiple systems of discourse (which Bakhtin calls hybridization), that is, the interposition of author with character (Allen is Leonard Zelig); the expectations of comic style and persona from previous films such as his gag structures and erudite intellectual jargon; his ideological framework as a New York Jew converted to psychoanalysis and, particularly, his self-consciousness about movies *and* comedy."

Perlmutter supports her argument with discussions of Allen's comic modes, camera techniques, narrative structures, language styles, belief systems, parodic devices, protagonists, persona, and authorship. *Zelig*, according to Ruth Perlmutter, offers Woody Allen's most enigmatic study of self-categorization; the danger of succumbing to a complicated, beckoning, and pervasive mediocrity; and, the transformative power of cinema.

Arnold W. Preussner also writes about Woody Allen's self-reflection regarding the power of cinema. In the essay reprinted here, "Woody Allen's *The Purple Rose of Cairo* and the Genres of Comedy," Preussner argues for *Purple Rose* to be read as Woody Allen's summary of all his own comic efforts: "The film synthesizes farcical and parodic techniques from Allen's early films with the serious interest in romantic themes that emerge in most of his more recent pictures, thus producing a brief but reasonably comprehensive overview of his career as a comic filmmaker." Furthermore, Preussner believes that *Purple Rose* summarizes Allen's comedy film career to date by exploring the various types of comedy as outlined by Northrop Frye in "The Argument of Comedy" (1949). Preussner supports this argument with analyses of Cecilia's seductive power as an Aristophanic "bright idea," of Tom and Gil as representatives of Roman New Comedy, and of Woody Allen's silver screen as the "'green' world of Shakespeare." Although Woody Allen pays homage to each of these comic genres, Preussner makes it clear that Allen "qualifies" both the patterns and the end results of these genres. In particular, Allen exudes an ironic sensibility regarding the power of comic cinema to offer a substantial escape for viewers. The best that film can offer may be a momentary "surrogate reality."

In the essay William Brigham contributes to this volume, "Home, Hearth, and Hannah: Family in the Films of Woody Allen," Brigham also discusses Allen's concerns with the relationship between cinema and escapism. He argues that although Allen does create seemingly "nostalgic and romanticized" views of people's lives, "these nostalgic detours are just that; temporary oases from a world which Allen does not try to escape because he does want to understand it." In particular Brigham addresses Allen's desire to understand the American family. By analyzing the "borderless" families in *Hannah and Her Sisters* and the subsequent films against a backdrop of thoroughly researched patterns of family depiction in film, Brigham brings attention to a "circularity" apparent in Allen's view of the family. Although, according to Brigham, Allen views the family as an institution that harms its members, he also portrays it as a structure for which adults continuously search in order to "alleviate the pain caused by the first family."

My colleague, Terry Allison, and I wrote "Frame Breaking and Code Breaking in Woody Allen's Relationship Films" for this collection. This essay echoes Brigham's sociological interpretation. In it we analyze *Manhattan*, *Hannah and Her Sisters*, and *Manhattan Murder Mystery* as

films that permit Allen to play in the field of late-twentieth-century relationships between men and men; women and men; and women and
women. Specifically, Woody Allen toys with "breaking the frame" of cinematic screen space for men and for women while he also breaks codes of
prescribed gender behavior. The risks that Allen takes by situating relationship narrative as the primary focus of his work invite a variety of theoretical interpretations guided by feminist, cultural studies, and gender studies
analyses. In particular, the works of Inez Hedges, Larry May and Robert A.
Strikwerda, and Eve Kosofsky Sedgwick provide interesting lenses through
which to focus on the sexual politics of Woody Allen's films.

Marc S. Reisch, in the reprint of "Woody Allen: American Prose
Humorist," nominates Woody Allen as "the most successful comic writer
and actor today." Reisch offers insightful observations into Allen's "reshap-
ing of the comic tradition." He argues that Woody Allen, as nihilist, existential humorist, and as writer of the absurd proposes identity and transcendence as the "constant problem" of being human. In particular, Reisch
deftly analyzes the identity of the "little man" character that Allen often
personifies and parodies in his prose as that "neurotic persona" destined
to try and make sense of a world that simply does not make any sense.

Ronald D. LeBlanc's "*Love and Death* and Food: Woody Allen's Comic
Use of Gastronomy," offers a close analysis of Allen's use of humor in contrast to humor in the literary tradition. This essay points out the detailed
ways in which Woody Allen incorporates his thorough knowledge of
Russian writers into *Love and Death* (1975). LeBlanc argues that while the
film's artistry pays homage to Dostoyevski and Tolstoy, the film's bathos
"deflates and reduces the film's serious, elevated ideas" in a way similar to
that of the comic Russian writer Nikolai Gogol. In particular, LeBlanc calls
attention to Allen's use of food imagery as a way of paying homage to
Gogol: "One of the primary roles that food imagery plays in his films is to
remind us—amidst all the lofty philosophical speculation engendered by
abstractions such as 'love' and 'death,' 'war' and 'peace,' 'crime' and 'punishment'—of immediate physical sensations and instinctual urges. The act
of eating, by returning us to our bodies, helps to affirm the *élan vital* of
human life." LeBlanc supports his argument with numerous well-chosen
examples from the film, particularly Boris's and Sonja's discussions of
food. The essay ends with Woody Allen's own use of gastronomic
metaphor as a tool for explaining his comic art: "'Drama is like a plate of
meat and potatoes,'" while "'comedy is rather the dessert, a bit like
meringue.'"

The reprint of Ronald S. Librach's "A Portrait of the Artist as a Neurotic:
Studies in Interior Distancing in the Films of Woody Allen" discusses
Allen's philosophical overview in less whimsical terms than does LeBlanc's
essay. Librach provides a thorough discussion of the paradox of the intellectual or uncomic comic. This essay views Allen's meticulous develop-

ment of the neurotic character in *Annie Hall*, *Interiors*, and *Manhattan* as part of Allen's desire to justify his own personal philosophy of whining: "Allen knows well enough that even the greatest of philosophical systems are basically elaborate, self-willed rationalizations for the philosopher's temperament or mood and he himself is honest enough to remind us that his own philosophical overview derives in large part from a sincere and therapeutic analysis of his own psychological problems—namely, the fact that he tends to whine too much." The essay reveals Allen's persona in both *Annie Hall* and *Manhattan* as representative of a neurotic worldview. Librach discusses the absence of persona in *Interiors* as significant because it affords Allen an opportunity to study the neurotic rather than play the role: "In *Interiors*, Allen simply documents his characters' lives and their world. He does not displace them in that whimsical world which would have been necessary if he were going to objectify his own persona." Librach argues that Allen recognizes that "neuroticism inevitably entails a certain moral failure—namely, the failure of the courage to be honest." Librach's extraordinary essay finds a more courageous, honest filmmaker awaiting his audience at the end of the making of *Manhattan*.

"Neither Here nor There," Gregg Bachman's essay written for this book, redefines Woody Allen's moral laziness as a reaction characteristic of many first- and second-generation Jewish-Americans. In a deeply personal, yet critical, essay, Bachman names two roads for Jewish-Americans to take: that of the "keepers of the faith," and that of the "true American." Woody Allen's films deftly and repetitively depict the moral and social struggle experienced by those Jews living at the fork in the road. His essay traces the development of this struggle throughout the course of Allen's film ouevre. Interlaced with personal remembrances of seeing the films as a child, the essay provides important critical commentary regarding the pressure put upon the individual Jewish-American to choose a way of life rather than to blend two ways of living. Bachman names Allen as the artist who best portrays the biases that surround this concept of the Jewish comic.

Samuel H. Dresner also addresses the Jewish comic in his essay "Woody Allen and the Jews," reprinted in this volume. His work offers one extreme of the bias, condemning Allen as the self-hating Jew. Dresner warns against adoration of the artist: "My concern is rather with his adoring audience, especially his Jewish audience. For that audience, by its adoration, and even by its neutrality, has ipso facto betrayed its faith and its people." Dresner too delves into the issues surrounding the separation of Mia Farrow and Allen and the ensuing debate regarding Allen's actions as being immoral, illegal, or both. In pointing out that incestuous overtones have lurked in Allen's work for quite a while, Dresner cites the Allen essay "Retribution" from *Side Effects*, and the films *Love and Death*, *Hannah and Her Sisters*, *Manhattan*, *Annie Hall*, and *Husbands and Wives*.

Dresner finds these filmic elements, as well as Allen's real-life amorous troubles, particularly problematic for Jewish audiences because Allen confirms, both on- and off-screen, "the vicious stereotype of the Jew as hypocrite, devil, despoiler of morality, and corruptor of culture."

Mark E. Bleiweiss provides a counterargument to Dresner. He answers the previous essay's accusations and arrives at the conclusion that Allen is merely complacent in his approach to Judaism. The author argues that Allen undermines Jews and Jewish traditions. In particular, "Self-Deprecation and the Jewish Humor of Woody Allen," reprinted in this book, analyzes Allen's use of traditions in Jewish humor. Bleiweiss begins the essay with a discussion of Jewish humor as defined by Sigmund Freud's *Jokes and Their Relation to the Unconscious,* and continues from that point with an emphasis on self-deprecation as "the most prevalent feature in Jewish humor." Bleiweiss offers a synopsis of major scholars on Jewish humor such as Theodor Reik, Dan Ben-Amos, Avner Ziv, Martin Grotjahn, and Heda Jason as a foundation for his critique of Woody Allen's Jewish humor. Bleiweiss uses this foundation to underscore what he sees as Allen's distortion of the self-deprecation theme: the self-deprecating Jew in Allen's films does not emerge from moments of expressed self-hatred into a flurry of bettering himself or into establishing connections with his community as is common in Jewish humor. Bleiweiss does not come down as hard on Allen as does Dresner, but Bleiweiss makes clear that "Allen's humor, far from revealing an admirable moral strength, actually supplements Allen's otherwise morally lazy actions."

And finally, Mashey Bernstein's essay written for this book offers a framework for the debate over Allen's treatment of Judaism in his films. Bernstein explores multiple sides of the controversy and relates these different approaches to Allen's use of comedy as a critical force in his films. In "'My Worst Fears Realized': Woody Allen and the Holocaust," Bernstein argues that Allen's curiosity and interest in his own Jewishness as well as in the Holocaust is influential in and representative of a growing cynicism on the part of Woody Allen: "As his world view has darkened, Allen's reference to and use of the Holocaust has become more pronounced, resulting in not just one movie that has looked at the event, but a consistent body of work that has unflinchingly probed it, providing philosophical speculation far beyond the norm in American movies." To support his argument, Bernstein cites Allen's "dour" essay "Random Reflections of a Second-Rate Mind," and he examines *Shadows and Fog* and *Crimes and Misdemeanors* as Allen's contemplations on the absent God who allowed the Holocaust to occur. In the end, Bernstein finds Allen to be trying out, albeit quite cynically, the idea that each individual must become a spiritually autonomous God and act as though hope might activate a believable all-powerful godliness in the world.

Perspectives on Woody Allen thus offers a variety of responses to the massive oeuvre of Woody Allen. The book serves as a resource with which to begin or to rekindle a critical interest in Woody Allen and his work. Many subsequent collections will surely contribute to Allen studies, for this collection demonstrates that although much has been said, much remains to be said about the artist as worker.

Works Cited

Allen, Woody. *Getting Even.* New York: Random House, 1971.

———. *Side Effects.* New York: Random House, 1980.

———. *Without Feathers.* New York: Random House, 1980.

Girgus, Sam B. *The Films of Woody Allen.* Cambridge: Cambridge University Press, 1993.

Lax, Eric. *On Being Funny: Woody Allen and Comedy.* New York: Charterhouse, 1975.

———. *Woody Allen.* New York: Alfred Knopf, 1991.

Pogel, Nancy. *Woody Allen.* Boston: Twayne, 1987.

Wernblad, Annette. *Brooklyn Is Not Expanding: Woody Allen's Comic Universe.* London: Associated University Presses, 1992.

Yacowar, Maurice. *Loser Take All: The Comic Art of Woody Allen.* New York: Frederick Ungar, 1979.

REVIEWS

What's New Pussycat?

ROBERT HATCH

AFTER *The Knack*, *What's New Pussycat?*, set in Paris and the country-side, but also on the theme of exigent sex, seems labored, physically exhausted, a little grimy. Part of the trouble is with the so-called script by Woody Allen, a television hysteric who also plays second clown to Peter Sellers. He has tried to offset a basic lack of situation invention by prolifer-ating old gags, and he lacks an accurate sense of the dividing line between wackiness and neurosis. A second trouble is Peter O'Toole in the central role of a young man who wants to marry but cannot bring himself to for-sake the implausible availability and confectionary beauty of the young ladies who excite his days and fill his dreams. This requires a sense of friv-olity and a degree of self-mockery—qualities in which Mr. O'Toole is notably lacking. For a man of his surname, he has a surprisingly Germanic view of himself.

Given that weight to push, Sellers (as a sex-mad Viennese psychiatrist in a Renaissance haircut) turns strident, and the extravagantly endowed and motivated girls become sweaty. *What's New Pussycat?* runs into that deadly theatrical situation wherein the performers appear to be entertaining themselves and the audience foots the bill.

Excerpted and reprinted by permission from *The Nation*, vol. 201 (August 2, 1965): 68. Copyright © 1965 by the Nation Company, Inc.

Take the Money and Run

STANLEY KAUFFMANN

SEVERAL REVIEWS of Woody Allen's *Take the Money and Run* have said that it's funny for an hour or so, then runs down. I disagree. It simply runs on. If you came in during the picture and saw the second half first, it would be just as funny as the first half is for those who see it from the beginning. Allen, who is the co-author, director, and star, is a witty man, but he is a stand-up comedian, a performer whose basic method is that of the fisherman: he comes out and casts his lines a number of times, trying to catch as many laughs as possible. After a while, he quits, hoping that his average has been high.

Allen's longer efforts are just larger numbers of tries. This is painfully clear in his current Broadway comedy, *Play It Again, Sam*, which is a revue sketch cancerously overgrown. His film is much better because Allen has clever schemes about the medium itself, where he has none at all about the theater. In fact, if the picture were to be saddled with a theme, it would be the penetration by media-forms into our fantasies: film hits, TV interviews, TV quiz games, TV commercials.

Once again he is the bespectacled shnook, this time the shnook as criminal. We never believe for a moment that Allen *is* a criminal—as we can believe, at least partially, that Keaton is a Confederate railroad engineer—so the fun is all conscious comment. This means that the comment has to keep coming; there is little chance for dramatic understructure in the comedy. And this, plus the fact that Allen doesn't even seem to sense the need for cumulation and growth, makes the picture a series of items, good or less good. But a lot of them are funny.

Janet Margolin is appealing as the doe-eyed Bonnie to this clumsy Clyde. Allen's direction is competent enough; at least the camera always looks where it ought to look in order to get the laugh. My guess is that he owes considerable to Ralph Rosenblum, the film editor, who was "editorial consultant." I think I even saw Rosenblum make a brief appearance, rising through the sidewalk in a freight elevator.

Reprinted by permission from *The New Republic*, vol. 161 (September 6, 1969): 32.
Copyright © 1969 by The New Republic, Inc.

Bananas

STANLEY KAUFFMANN

T HE TROUBLE with Woody Allen's films—which he writes,directs, and stars in—is quite simple. He is a very funny writer and (on TV) a fairly funny stand-up comic. As a teacher and actor, his talent is absolutely zero.

 Bananas is full of hilarious comic ideas and lines, supplied by Allen and his collaborator Mickey Rose; then Allen, the director and actor, murders them. An American weakling gets involved in a Latin-American revolution—something like Harold Lloyd's *Why Worry?* (1923) up to date. There's a lot of smart satire of things worth satirizing, from TV coverage of serious events to facile libertarianism. There is some surprising corn, like Allen stepping out of a car and into an open manhole, or lisping before the word "pith," but generally the script is good. With Dustin Hoffman or Robert Morse, directed by any run-of-the-mill sitcom director from the Disney stable, this might have been a knockout. But see Allen trapped on an exercise machine or at a trial where he is both lawyer and witness, and you'll see the quintessence of Amateur Night. He confuses the ability to write comedy with the ability to perform it.

 His directing is worse. He makes this clear in the first sequence where he wrecks a comic assassination; the shooting is too real for comedy. Incessantly he photographs from odd angles—once even through the corner of his eyeglasses—instead of relaxing, not worrying about proving he's intellectual, and just telling a story. On the rocks of his acting and direction *Bananas* splits.

Reprinted by permission from *The New Republic*, vol. 164 (May 22, 1971): 24. Copyright © 1971 by The New Republic, Inc.

Love and Death

ROBERT HATCH

M Y PERSONAL joke about Woody Allen's style of comedy is that I keep going to his pictures in the vain hope of discovering what induces all the happy laughter. Like almost everyone, I admire my own sense of humor, but in the case of Allen it fails me—the best I can do is recognize that humor is intended.

Perhaps the trouble is that Allen's persona is one that irritates me. He's the smart-aleck kid who compensates for runtiness with a drumbeat of insults and a pretense of gimcrack cynicism, and who evades the consequences by insistently calling attention to his own deficiencies. Like Chaplin's tramp, Allen's smart kid is small, but he is not charming, elegant or lovable. In fact, neither are real tramps, but Chaplin made a figure of universal appeal and fun out of unpromising material. Allen plays his brat as brat, and my impulse is not to beam but to move out of the neighborhood.

Then, too, it strikes me that Allen's pictures never gain a life of their own, never take off on a parabola of skewed logic or generate any internal momentum of chain-reactive extravagance. Behind his screen I seem to see a conference room strewn with crumpled notes and empty coffee containers, where gags and effects were hammered out in exhausting sessions of brainstorming. The films look like hard work; they seem composite, not organic.

I recall a big scene from the current *Love and Death* in which fifty or so coffins standing in ranks and files upon a field open to disclose a corps of aproned waiters, who form couples and waltz. People laughed—I think because they supposed that Woody hoped they would. Then there is a passage during the Battle of Borodino when Allen takes refuge in the mouth of a cannon, which implement rolls downhill to the great danger of Russian (or French?) limbs and then fires, propelling our hero uninjured into a headquarters tent. The episode is expensive, but it lacks spontaneity or surprise.

As the preceding makes evident, *Love and Death* concerns the adventures of one Boris Grushenko (Allen) in the field against Napoleon and in the ballrooms, opera houses and bedrooms of the Russian aristocracy. (He also attempts to assassinate Bonaparte, but the pistol self-destructs—a not unusual sort of slapstick catastrophe). There is the standard sexy flimflam

Reprinted by permission from *The Nation*, vol. 220 (June 28, 1975): 797–8. Copyright © 1975 by The Nation Company, Inc.

with Diane Keaton and other enticers. Under that sort of stimulation, Allen behaves somewhat like Bobby Clark, the principal difference being that Clark's enormous spectacles were painted on with grease pencil and that he was howlingly outrageous. Allen takes liberties with a thought to the family audience. A few funny lines are planted with a good deal of deliberation in the dough of the dialogue, but the standard line of joke is the delicatessen anachronism—a reference to herring being a sure-fire sidesplitter in the context of the Napoleonic invasion (or any other context for that matter: herring is universally acknowledged to be risible—like pastrami, Yonkers, brassieres, or Calvin Coolidge).

A pleasant innovation in this film is the habit of Allen and Keaton, in moments of high emotion or imminent danger, to escape into an exchange of semantic locutions that defy comprehension and shrewdly ape a current pomposity. They do it perhaps too often, but I wish the film could have maintained a level that astute.

Why then does Allen succeed so well, captivating everyone but me and a handful of fellow unbelievers? In part, I think, it is because when he drops out of character, as he frequently does, he seems a thoroughly nice fellow (many of those he emulates and imitates—W.C. Fields and Groucho Marx, for example—seem anything but nice, in character or out). So when a nice fellow like that goes to so much obvious trouble and expense to be amusing, it seems ungracious not to be amused. It's like being in a TV audience—when that ingratiating chap holds up the "laugh" sign, you laugh.

Then Allen is a very "in" comedian; his text is full of up-to-date allusions and one guffaws to show that one reads the right periodicals. And, like the bulk of his audience, he is a bit liberal, so his targets are congenial. It is all perfectly friendly, never stupid, rarely vulgar, extremely animated and entirely professional. Indeed, I think that is how one might define Allen—a skillful performer whose profession is humor. It is not the same thing as being funny—not like Harpo Marx honking his horn and leering, but then no one ever accused Harpo of seeming to be a nice fellow, though his friends say he was.

Annie Hall

ROBERT HATCH

THE FIRST two or three times a fellow named Alvy Singer was mentioned in Woody Allen's *Annie Hall* I blinked, wondering who the devil he was. It took me a while to catch on that he was the character Allen was playing, since it seemed so obvious that Allen was playing himself. To be sure, he describes the film, which he also directed and wrote (with Marshall Brickman), as a "romantic comedy about a contemporary neurotic," so we mustn't assume it to be autobiographical. But that's an assumption hard to sustain: the picture opens with a rather extended monologue in which it seems that Allen (we haven't yet heard of Singer) gives us a quick rundown on his life to date and some reassuring words about his present health. Then from time to time, he addresses us directly on developments in the story, is seen briefly in the tape of a Dick Cavett show and in general frequents the places and pals around with the people where and with whom one might expect to find Woody Allen. And is it so improbable that he sees himself as a contemporary urban neurotic? Pages from the life of Woody Allen, as "adapted by" Allen and Brickman; that might come close.

Annie Hall is a movie about "relationships"—with women, that is. Singer, as I shall call him, is a man of ingratiating vulnerability who finds them only too easy to form, but impossible to maintain. And though he ruminates a good deal about why this should be so, both to us and to his psychiatrist, it never dawns on him that the ease on the one hand may relate to the impossibility on the other. Allen, who otherwise resembles him only in stature, is like Chaplin in that what he shows you about the quality of contemporary life is marvelous, but his attempts to tell you what it all means is a bit dumb. You want to watch what he does and not listen too carefully to what he tells you. *Annie Hall* is made delicious by a succession of incidents whose wit derives from their precise but slightly heightened evocation of experiences we have all had ("we" in this case being especially those familiar with the upper middle class, Upper East Side sixties of Manhattan).

Singer displays Jewish paranoia, grins at *New York Review* sophistication, has achieved the high-status goal of playing off-season tennis in a plastic bubble (he doesn't shop at Zabar's, which surprises me). Standing in a Third Avenue movie queue, Alvy is driven mad by a loudmouth behind him

Printed by permission from *The Nation* (April 30, 1977): 540. Copyright © 1977 by The Nation Company, Inc.

who pontificates second-hand ideas on the aesthetics of film. Allen spoils that jest, though, by producing Marshall McLuhan himself from behind a lobby billboard to prick the bore's balloon. The gag is too studied; it pricks the excellence of the observation. Other japes occasionally fail—there is a joke about Kissinger and Harvard that hasn't been viable for at least five years—and invariably they are examples of Allen plotting to be clever instead of trusting his instincts to get him where he wants to go. He also uses camera technique—split images, subtitles—to reveal what's on the characters' minds when they are saying or doing something else. That's a bit heavy-handed for knockabout comedy (more Eugene O'Neill's sort of thing), and is anyhow unnecessary for an actor/director who knows well enough how to make clear what he and his fellow players are thinking without hanging up signs. (Note his face when a young woman asks him if a crazy remark he's just made is supposed to be funny.) Then, at the end, Allen appears again in monologue to tell the (deliberately) old yarn about the man who complains that his brother thinks himself a chicken. When asked why he doesn't have the unhappy lunatic put away, he says he would, "except that I need the eggs." It's that way about relationships, says Allen in conclusion; "we keep on having them because we need the eggs." When you've finished laughing, ask yourself what that's supposed to mean.

Yet *Annie Hall*, for all its vagaries, is a funny, often touching, sometimes astute picture. It is about the desperate race to stay ahead of anonymity. Singer and his relationships jump into bed as readily as they jump into taxis, and then find that in fact they want to go different ways. Annie, the girl of the title (Diane Keaton), comes closest to traveling along with him. Recently in town from the Middle West, she has that affliction of the painfully shy of carrying on hysterical dialogues with herself in a hopeless attempt to correct any unfortunate remark that she may have made to the person facing her. The effect is to make shyness epidemic. But Alvy himself is not without tics; they are symptoms of his steel-tempered and ever available inferiority complex. (Fifteen years in analysis, he is quick to tell anyone who looks to be getting the upper hand.) When Annie sees how that works, she speaks straight enough and Alvy is on his own again. I don't buy talk about egg-laying relationships, but I understand what Allen shows me about an ego looking for a place to put its little head. It gives substance to a film that is otherwise a shrewd putdown of success, Fun City style. There was a time when I thought Woody Allen was caught in the trap, as I saw it, of being the smartest, runtiest aleck in the neighborhood. But after *The Front*, and after *Annie Hall*, I suspect he's on to more important things. He's now 40, he tells us; he has time, he has quick eyes and ears and a sardonic turn of mind. And Lord knows he has energy.

Interiors

COLIN L. WESTERBECK, JR.

F OR YEARS Woody Allen has made comedies out of the same neuroses, anxiety and despair which are found in Ingmar Bergman's films. Now, with *Interiors*, Allen has made a film that Bergman might almost have made himself. Allen has made a film which is perhaps even better than the film Bergman might have made from the same material, for while Allen is less powerful as an artist, he may also be more human. Indeed, with material of this sort, maybe it is in the end an advantage not to have quite so all-encompassing a formal and aesthetic vision as Bergman would. The experiences that both directors try to deal with—emotional experiences that have no objective content, experiences that are purely, as Allen's title says, "interior"—are so elusive that the more tentative art with which Allen approaches them comes nearer the truth than does the completeness, the aesthetic elaboration, of a Bergman film. Certainly *Interiors* is a film that works as drama at least as well and painfully as Bergman's *Scenes from a Marriage* did.

Interiors ends in a situation very like the ending of *Scenes*, in fact (or like the ending of O'Neill's *Long Day's Journey into Night*, which also has its obvious affinities with Bergman). The central characters are together, yet utterly alone, in a dark house in the middle of the night. The house, which is on the beach in the Hamptons, belongs to Arthur (E.G. Marshall), a wealthy lawyer who has recently left his wife Eve (Geraldine Page). On this particular night he has remarried, with his daughters and their husbands in attendance. After everyone else has gone to bed, the one daughter still up, Joey (Mary Beth Hurt), thinks she sees Eve, who was of course not invited, standing in the shadows on the veranda. From the unlighted sitting room, Joey begins to speak to her mother outside. But Allen never shows us the two of them in the same shot. Eve doesn't speak; and when we do see her, it looks as if Joey isn't there at all, inside the doors where we thought she was. Is Joey only imagining her mother to be present, and in reality talking to herself? Or is it she who is the figment of Eve's imagination?

This evanescence of the characters, as if each existed only inside the head of another, is hinted at again a few minutes later. When one member of the family attempts suicide, another nearly dies in the rescue effort. And while all this is going on out on the beach, Allen at two points cuts back to

Reprinted by permission from *Commonweal*, vol. 105 (September 29, 1978): 630–2. Copyright © 1978 by The Commonweal Foundation.

the remaining members of the family asleep in their beds inside. At the moment when the would-be rescuer is herself being revived, Arthur and the two daughters still in their beds stir into wakefulness briefly, emerging from sleep as those outside do from the ocean—as if the sea of troubles in which the family is really drowning is its own sleep and dreams. The implication here is that the emotional connections among them are almost physiological. Their conflicts with each other are like the conflicted feelings inside some one person. What makes this moment effective is that it is only a moment. It is only a fleeting glimpse of what lies beyond all explanation here, a whiff of the power feelings can have greater than even the suicide suggests. The sleepers don't come fully awake with some hokey premonition. They bestir themselves for the instant, and then lapse back into sleep. It is the momentariness of this crystallization of their feelings, its briefness and faintness, which makes it affecting.

The effectiveness of this moment derives, too, from the fact that Allen has been making the suggestion contained in it all through the film, but making it always just as slightly and unobtrusively as here. At the heart of this film is the notion that a woman's children, having come literally from inside her body, remain in their emotions the visible interior of their mother. While Renata (Diane Keaton) is asleep in bed during the suicide attempt, earlier she was out on the beach alone, staring miserably at the waves as if *she* might drown herself. The truth is that the attempt of one member of the family to kill herself is a composite of the actions and reactions of all the other members. Everything that happens in the film has this tenuous web of connectedness to it.

The only symbolization that the human condition gets here is so close to being literal, and not displaced or symbolic at all, that it is a note as lightly played as the others I've been talking about. I am referring to the fact that the interiors in this movie, besides being the interior experience of the characters, are the interiors of the rooms in which they live their lives. Eve is a decorator, and we are made acutely aware of the decor of all the exquisite rooms in which the film is set. Whenever anything goes wrong, Eve is likely to ask that the windows be closed because barely audible noises from the street outside are "unnerving." Then, the first time she tries to kill herself, Allen opens the scene with close-ups of her hands as they tape the windows shut before turning on the gas; and the sound of the tape being unreeled truly is unnerving—sharp and distinct and louder than life. It's a brilliant touch.

Again, though, what makes this movie compelling is the way Allen can use the same sort of material in a very low-key, almost incidental way. There is another scene in which Eve is riding in a car with Joey, and rolls up the window. That's the whole scene, just rolling up the window—a simple, natural gesture of self-immurement. It is in moments like this that the true, sustained quality of the film lies. Woody Allen is a remarkable man. He is a man who has tried a number of very radical ways to mediate feeling. He has been through psychoanalysis, which is one way, and he has been a nightclub monologist and director of schlock comedies, which are another way. These are both very rough ways to try to deal with feeling; yet Allen has come through them with an extraordinary sense of how obscure and precarious true feeling is. This is what, in *Interiors*, adds a whole new dimension to his career.

A Visual Poem to New York City
(Review of *Manhattan*)

COLIN L. WESTERBECK, JR.

NOT SINCE *The Naked City* has there been a film that contained such a beautiful visual poem to New York as Woody Allen's *Manhattan* does. Like Dassin's film, which was the one to pioneer location shooting in New York back in the late 1940s, Allen's current black-and-white hit opens with a montage of images which are run against a voice-over commentary. A neon sign spells out "Manhattan" on the side of a building in the dawn light. A panorama of the skyline is seen from across the park under lowering skies at dusk. A fireworks display against the same skyline explodes its showers of sparks over the city in perfect time to the closing chords of Gershwin's "Rhapsody in Blue."

The commentary that is read against these images isn't quite so rhapsodic, however. The voice we hear is Allen's own in his role as Isaac, the film's hero, who is trying to get started on the novel he wants to write. "Chapter One," he says, ". . . He romanticized New York all out of proportion. . . ." But again he breaks off, rebuking himself, "No, no . . . too corny . . . got to be more profound." Once more he tries, "He adored New York City. To him it was a metaphor for the decay of contemporary culture . . . no, too preachy. We wanna make some money on this book." And so it goes, the city sounding worse and worse with each new attempt despite the fact that, in the images flashed on the screen, New York looks more and more beautiful. This opening is a perfect little overture to the movie that follows. What it suggests is a film in which the images and the words are going to work in counterpoint, one where certain visual drama will be played under a lot of funny dialogue. To keep what we see and what we hear separate so that the film can function in this way, Allen has thought out his shots carefully and made a highly stylized film. Sometimes an entire scene is done in a long shot from a fixed camera set-up, thus creating a disproportion between the way the scene looks and the way it sounds. We hear the characters as if they were right next to us, but see them as distant. It makes us feel as if our relationship with them is both intimate and estranged at the same time.

Reprinted by permission from *Commonweal*, vol. 106 (August 3, 1979): 438–9. Copyright © 1979 by The Commonweal Foundation.

At other times, Isaac seems to take a verbal pratfall right off the screen. He moves out of camera range before he delivers the punchline toward which the scene has been working. After he chats with Mary (Diane Keaton) at a lunch counter, they both move off-camera while she asks him about his writing. From beyond the edge of the empty frame we hear him tell her as they walk away, "The first story I wrote was called 'The Castrating Zionist.' It's about my mother." A variation on this device is for lines to be delivered from the total black-out of the frame. A good deal of Isaac and Mary's relationship seems to take place in the dark. On a date they go to the Hayden Planetarium and wander around in a giant model of the solar system, drifting aimlessly against a background of intergalactic void. It's the ideal setting for their love affair.

Taking advantage of the latitude which his approach affords, Allen begins using the composition of his shots to put a little English on the emotions in his film, letting the laughter fall silent from time to time. While Isaac's best friend Yale (Michael Murphy) is having an affair with Mary, Isaac scrupulously avoids getting involved with her. But as soon as she and Yale break up, Isaac allows himself to fall in love. Then Yale calls up Mary on the sly to lure her back. During this phone conversation Allen frames the shots of Yale, Mary and Isaac so that each character appears at the extreme edge of the screen. This unbalanced framing introduces tension into the scene. It makes visible the disruptive quality of what Yale is doing. Yet in a film where we have been laughing at lines spoken off the screen altogether, we don't feel manipulated to see the same characters crowd back on again at the edge—clinging to the side of our perception as if to the wall of a building where they have just stepped out on a window ledge unsure of their own intentions. In a way Yale's phone call is just another of those off-camera voices in Isaac's life. Yet because of Allen's rendering of the scene, we can't help all of a sudden taking these people more seriously.

As the film goes on, Allen composes certain scenes alike in order to make them clack against each other in our minds. We feel the earlier scene resonating in the later one and enforcing its emotion. When Isaac has an afternoon out with his son by his second marriage, for instance, he stops in front of F.A.O. Schwartz's window to point out a little sailboat to the boy, who insistently starts pointing out a much larger one to him. The musical score for this silent comedy is "Lady Be Good." Then later, as Isaac happens to be walking by a bookstore at some seaside resort, where there are real sailboats in the background, a similar shot through the store window shows him doing a double-take. He has just spotted there on display a book his ex-wife (Meryl Streep) has written about their divorce. Again the musical accompaniment is "Lady Be Good."

In a sub rosa way, relationships like these between the scenes inform Isaac's relationships with the women in his life. Before Mary there's Tracy

(Mariel Hemingway), a seventeen-year-old with whom Isaac is having an affair when the film opens. One of those scenes done completely in long shot is an early one where Isaac, disturbed by the difference in their ages, tries to warn Tracy not to become too attached him. The scene is not only done in long shot, but in silhouette and a kind of semi-darkness that are mimicked a little later by the scene where Isaac and Mary first begin to fall for one another. We see Isaac and Mary sitting together on a park bench now just as we saw Isaac and Tracy on the couch in his apartment earlier. Coming together and splitting up look much the same here. There is a certain confusion in Isaac's emotions, an indecisiveness, which Allen's montage expresses. We get the feeling that his relationships with women are interchangeable, and therefore always doomed.

Woody Allen has us all at his mercy. He sees through our collective neuroses so readily that we realize none of us is safe around him. "My first wife," Isaac explains with the typical understatement which one of those long shots provides, "was a kindergarten teacher who got heavily into drugs. She went to San Francisco, was EST for awhile, then became a Moony. Now she's with the William Morris Agency." No one could prevail against this kind of wit. There isn't anybody Allen couldn't devastate. What makes his pitiless attack on us enjoyable, though, is his willingness to aim the worst of it at himself. That's why we trust him with all our secrets. No analyst could inspire such complete confidence from us. Allen's insight into himself is what makes him funny, but also what makes him serious. He's so pathetic it's laughable—*so* pathetic, in fact, that it's pathetic.

In this film Allen's way of keeping his sense of humor about himself, his perspective on his life, is finally provided by Tracy. This seventeen-year-old is more stable than Isaac, Mary and Yale put together. Tracy is the only one who won't play musical chairs with her emotions the way they do. "Don't be so mature," Isaac pleads with her when she's reluctant to take him back after he's hurt her, and even he has to smile, weakly, at how puerile his own feelings are compared to hers. It's all so silly, and so genuinely poignant, too.

The Invisible Man: You Are What You Meet
(Review of *Zelig*)

COLIN L. WESTERBECK, JR.

A DIFFERENCE BETWEEN Charlie Chaplin and Buster Keaton is that only the latter makes you burst out laughing. Dwight MacDonald pointed this out years ago. There are little moments in a Keaton film, surprising and fleeting gestures of accommodation, that make us laugh at the sheer humanity of the character he portrays. My favorite is when he boards an antiquated train in *Our Hospitality* wearing a stovepipe hat that won't fit under the coach's low ceiling. Decorously, and with glances of apology both to other passengers and to history for his tonsorial anachronism, he replaces the stovepipe with his familiar porkpie. I just can't help guffawing. The finest moments in Chaplin's films—Adenoid Hinckle's ballet with the globe of the world in *The Great Dictator*, or Little Fellow being fed through the glass of a monstrous machine in *Modern Times*—don't strike me with the same immediacy.

The truth is that Chaplin is the greater genius. His idea of comedy is larger than Keaton's, his insight into humanity more piercing. But the points in his movies where you recognize this are not ones that bring tears of laughter to your eyes. Instead, you sigh with satisfaction at the rightness of the image before you. That's brilliant, you murmur to yourself.

Zelig is brilliant, too. The film is a meditation on fame, on the emptiness of it. The title character, Leonard Zelig, is a man famous for being famous. Wherever the rich, the noted, the newsworthy gather, Zelig is there. He is the grandest impostor of all time. At a party in a Chicago speakeasy, he hobnobs with reputed gangsters, then sits in on clarinet with the Negro jazz band. Woody Allen's movie is a documentary about a fictitious character who was a phenomenon in the 1920s, but is now forgotten. The film's first master stroke is to be set in the twenties, which was the age that invented modern phenomena of this sort. In an era of flagpole sitters, a man celebrated for being a gate-crasher is completely credible. In the first glimpse we get of him, Zelig is being awarded the brightest honor that period could bestow; a ticker tape parade. He's Charles Lindbergh, the quintessential twenties figure, someone who becomes the

Reprinted by permission from *Commonweal*, vol. 110 (September 9, 1983): 468–9. Copyright © 1983 by The Commonweal Foundation.

most famous of them all simply by being such a modest, unassuming likable guy.

Zelig is Woody Allen's most personal film since *Annie Hall*. It is, for one thing, an in-joke that Allen and his current girlfriend, Mia Farrow, are playing on his co-star in *Annie Hall*, Diane Keaton, who was his girl then. *Zelig* is a parody of *Reds*, Keaton's big hit with her new boyfriend, Warren Beatty. But *Zelig* is not just whimsy. While lovers come and go, the abiding problem in Allen's life, the one that won't go away, is his own celebrity.

Zelig is the meditation on fame that Allen attempted, but botched, in *Stardust Memories*. The new film gets to the heart of the paradox that celebrity contains for Allen. The movie sees the modern celebrity as a kind of Everyman figure—someone who is all things to all people, and a nobody to himself. Leonard Zelig is a zero, a cipher. Left alone in a room, he would have an identity crisis. To be a Zelig you'd have to be incredibly famous, instantly recognizable the whole world over, and at the same time painfully shy, nervous, insecure—as Woody Allen is. *Stardust Memories* was a resentful film. It was angry and confused. In *Zelig* Allen achieves an insight into his predicament that eluded him in the earlier movie. He becomes more objective about himself. He is dispassionate.

Just as a technical feat, *Zelig* is stunning. Matte shots, where one image is overlaid on another, have become extremely sophisticated in recent years because of space epics like *Star Wars*. Allen makes ingenious new use of this technique by inserting Zelig not only in still photographs, but in motion sequences. Much credit has to go to director of photography, Gordon Willis, for the trick here was to balance the light between the new footage and the wavering, scratchy look of old newsreels. Willis has literally made Zelig into the face in the crowd Allen wants him to be. He's the batter on deck while Ruth is at the plate, the storm trooper milling with other Brown Shirts in the street behind Hitler. Willis makes all the footage of Allen and Farrow alone compatible with the old black-and-white stock. They move with the same brittle jerkiness as everyone else. And Allen adds the finishing touch to the film's bogus authenticity in the form of interviews with contemporary intellectuals—Susan Sontag, Irving Howe, Saul Bellow—who comment ponderously on Zelig's place in history.

Zelig's is a personality that can split itself into a hundred different people. He is, as they used to say, a suitable case for treatment. The documentary focuses on the attempts made by his psychiatrist, Dr. Eudora Fletcher (Farrow), to cure him of his compulsive adaptability. The psychiatric interviews between doctor and patient are the funniest routine in the film. The first thing Dr. Fletcher has to do is disabuse Zelig of his delusion, whenever he's with her, that he's also a psychiatrist. What makes these scenes funny is that the loquacious, neurotic Woody we all know and love momentarily appears. He emerges from the somewhat black humor of his Zelig character like the sun from an overcast sky. Aside from these few minutes, however, Allen doesn't allow himself to do his familiar *schtick*. Laughter of the sort that provokes is not what he's after here. A higher amusement is. He keeps himself, as a comedian, out of it. He remains true to Zelig's character, which is to have no character, to be a chameleon.

The result of all this, as I said before, is brilliant. If I find the movie disconcerting, that is only because brilliance sheds an eerie kind of light—a cool blue light that ultimately leaves us more *be*mused than *a*mused. *Zelig* is a cerebral comedy. The pure originality of Allen's idea, the clarity of his conception, is what succeeds here. Through all the years of Allen's straight comedies, from *Take the Money and Run* to *Sleeper*, I criticized him for not being Keatonesque enough. I always wanted him to be better at providing those spontaneous touches, the little grace notes of comedy, that make me crack up at a Keaton movie. But with *Annie Hall*, his work turned in a different direction altogether. It was never Keaton he was on his way to becoming, but Chaplin. Allen's occasional cynicism is just another form of Chaplin's sentimentality. Allen's Zelig is a reincarnation of Chaplin's Tramp. *Zelig* is Allen's *Modern Times*.

A Midwinter Night's Dream
(Review of *The Purple Rose of Cairo*)

STANLEY KAUFFMANN

HERE'S A dream that was worth dreaming. I dreamed that I saw a Woody Allen film—a new one, called *The Purple Rose of Cairo*—and that it began, as usual, with an inviting premise which, as usual, was different from anything he had done before. The time is the Depression, the scene a small town. Mia Farrow, the browbeaten young wife of an unemployed workman, has a job as a hash-house waitress and spends all her spare time in the local movie theater. Her husband is a soft-soaping brute who is too busy loafing with the boys and sponging on her and fooling with other women to pay her much marital attention. She suffers it all, somewhat dopily, partially compensated by her fantasies at and after the movies. The current item at the local theater is *The Purple Rose of Cairo*, which she has seen often. In the cast is a rising young actor played by Jeff Daniels. One night Farrow is watching the film yet again when Daniels, crossing the screen in a certain scene as always, suddenly stops, faces the audience, and addresses Farrow. He says that he has noted her faithful presence and is attracted to her; he comes down off the screen in the pith helmet and tropical clothes of his part, and sits next to her. In short order, they leave the theater together.

Up on the screen the other members of the cast are dismayed and implore him to come back so that they can finish the story as usual. The audience in the movie house is very upset, too: they paid their money to see the whole, uninterrupted movie.

Outside the theater, wandering about town, Farrow and Daniels develop a romance in innocent Filmland strophes. He refuses to go back to the screen without her, and she hides him in various places while she goes home to take care of her husband. Meanwhile the theater manager has complained to the film's producer in Hollywood about the interruption. Hollywood is shaken: producer and entourage descend on the town. Also involved is the actor of the Daniels role, also played by Daniels of course, because the anarchic behavior of a character he has played may wreck his blossoming career. He, too, wants his character to return to the screen. But the anarchy is spreading: several other cities report that the Daniels

Reprinted by permission from *The New Republic*, vol. 192 (April 1, 1985): 26–7. Copyright © 1985 by The New Republic, Inc.

character has stepped out of *The Purple Rose of Cairo* in various theaters and has disappeared.

From here on—in my dream—Woody Allen's film develops this premise in one or more engrossing ways. It explores the quasi-mystical fact that an actor's performance in a film—with his person and personality and voice—has a life completely independent of the actor's own person and personality and voice that gave it being. This is true, with such completeness, in no other art except TV, which, in this regard, is film, too. The idea of a character threatening his creator who is himself in every physical detail beats any sci-fi concoction of look-alike humanoids because the mystery is around us all the time in everyday experience, a mystery that is part of our lives. And Allen illuminates this common, ignored mystery simply by focusing on it and by pursuing it to a comic-scary metaphysical point.

Or: the character himself, taken alone as an Ariel liberated from a script's bondage to roam as he will, is a fantasy that all of us have indulged from childhood. Who has not had private conversations and adventures and romances with appealing screen characters, experiences that had nothing to do with stories in which we met them, everything to do with what we alone can see in them and they in us? This vein of daydream is explored by Allen to conclusions that put definitions of reality in strong, ironic opposition, that dramatize how much better designed a well-created character is compared to people in the real world, who are created only by the bunglings of genes and by social circumstance.

Or—possibly the most poignant and powerful aspect of all—Allen pursues to fulfillment his major theme: the sovereignty of fantasy even in the humblest. Farrow's fantasy about the Daniels character is so strong that it penetrates the texture of the film to distract the character and draw him out of ordained behavior into independent life with her, a life in which he reciprocates her feelings. Her fantasy is so strong that it affects everyone else in the film because the Daniels character doesn't split like a stock movie ghost and leave his shell up there; he comes out complete. That's power, a discovery of power in herself! More, her fantasy is so completely reified that it touches the lives of other people: the audience, the manager, the producer, the original actor of the film role, and some other images of the role in prints of the film elsewhere. All because of Farrow's fantasizing deep in her small browbeaten being. "My mind to me a kingdom is," said Edward Dyer. Anyone's mind, says Woody Allen, is a cosmological empire—no, an emperor who can reshape absolutely everything; and Allen follows this concept to a thematic-dramatic conclusion, showing how, used this side of sanity, that force may be the best truth.

Then I awoke. And I remembered the actual new Woody Allen film I had seen, called *The Purple Rose of Cairo*, which begins, as usual, with an arresting idea, new for him (though not new in the history of film); and I remembered that, as usual, he develops it for a while, then just quits.

Quits dead. After Allen gets 84 minutes out of his premise, just enough footage to call the film a feature, he sends the errant film-character back up on the screen, sends all the Hollywood folk back to the Coast, sends Farrow back to her husband. Nothing culminates, in any of the three ways sketched above or in any other way. The theme is just picked up and used for a while, then plunked down as a bright child plunks down a new toy that quickly bores him.

It's also a bit uncomfortable that Allen sentences Farrow to return to her oafish husband, and now she's probably worse off than she was before because she has to recant her declarations about leaving. Allen has tried to soften this with some hints beforehand that all is not absolutely awful between them, but that doesn't much assuage our feeling that she is going back to dreariness and abuse, recurrently narcotized by film. (It's Fred Astaire and Ginger Rogers next time.) Farrow doesn't even seem to have any awareness of what her fantasy had accomplished in the lives of others: she treats the whole episode as if no one knew about it but herself. One needn't delve into theories of solipsism about it: this ending simply doesn't fit the facts of the film as given. Why aren't people in her town going to point at her in the street and say: "There's the woman who brought a film actor down off the screen and upset dozens of people"? No hint of any of this.

The film is well enough made, one more step in Allen's learn-while-you-earn film career. His direction here doesn't have any of the grace that he showed in A *Midsummer Night's Sex Comedy*, but it's succinct and controlled. Gordon Willis, the cinematographic wizard of *Zelig*, makes sufficient distinction between the small town in color and the screen action in black-and-white without belaboring the point. The cast is good. Farrow is so drastically mousy, abetted by Jeffrey Kurland's clothes, that it underscores the power of her fantasy, her ability to make a dashing screen figure come down into the audience and fall for her. Danny Aiello, the husband, here controls his customary proletarian churlishness so that he is bearably unbearable. Jeff Daniels, who was the young husband in *Terms of Endearment*, is not an overwhelming screen dynamo, but he is a reassuringly competent actor, quite pleasant. The distinctions he makes between the movie character and the actor who played him are as clear and unlabored as Willis's camera work. Allen does not appear in the film himself, which must be counted a plus.

The ritual comments are in order about Allen's writing and direction. He is the most active personal director in America today, a man of unique intelligence, true wit, and fertile imagination. But he is also fundamentally an amateur, if by a professional we mean someone who not only knows how to make a film (which Allen has learned) but also has a sense of responsibility to his material. Godard, through much of his career, seemed to get bored with films before he finished them, but with Godard, I felt that it was because he was probing the borders of filmmaking itself that he became impatient with the instrument in hand, and wanted to fashion another to probe more deeply. No such motive is apparent in Allen. He gets bright ideas, juggles them in a while, then—unprofessionally, in the sense described—simply abandons them.

Hannah and Her Sisters

PAULINE KAEL

WOODY ALLEN'S "Hannah and Her Sisters" is an agreeably skillful movie, a new canto in his ongoing poem to love and New York City which includes "Annie Hall" and "Manhattan." The principal characters are members of a show-business family, with the stable, dependable Hannah (Mia Farrow), a successful actress who manages a career and children with equal serenity, as the pivotal figure. At the start, the whole clan gathers at her sprawling upper-West Side apartment for Thanksgiving dinner. It includes her two flailing-about sisters: the wildly insecure cocaine-nut Holly (Dianne Wiest), whose acting career has never taken off, and the unsure-of-herself Lee (Barbara Hershey), who goes to A.A. and turns to men she can look up to. It includes the three sisters' bickering show-business-veteran parents: their boozy, habitually flirtatious mother (Maureen O'Sullivan) and their affable, but underconfident father (Lloyd Nolan). And it includes Hannah's financial-consultant husband (Michael Caine), who is swooning with passion for Lee, and an assortment of friends and relatives. Not in attendance is Lee's artist lover (Max von Sydow), who has no patience for sociable chatter. The movie ends at another Thanksgiving celebration, two years later; by then, Holly has pulled herself together, Hannah's husband has had his fling with Lee, and Hannah's ex-husband, Mickey Sachs (Woody Allen), a TV writer-producer, has rejoined the clan. And things are rosier. Like Ingmar Bergman's "Fanny and Alexander," which was also about a theatrical family, the film is full of cultured people and it has a comfortable, positive tone. Bergman's central character, Alexander, was clearly based on Bergman as a child; Allen's heroine is clearly based on Mia Farrow. And, like Bergman, whose cast included old friends, an ex-wife, an ex-lover, and a few of his children, Allen uses several actors he has worked with before, has Mia Farrow's mother playing Hannah's mother, and uses Farrow's actual apartment and seven of her eight children.

Hannah is meant to be the still center of the film, but mute would be more like it. Casting Mia Farrow as an ideal creative, nurturing woman in demure, plain-Jane dresses, Allen turns her into an Earth-Mother symbol and disembodies her. Most of the time Hannah the Madonna seems barely animate. Allen has got her so subdued and idealized that she seems to be floating passively in another world. Barbara Hershey has a luscious presence here. She has a sexual vibrancy about her, and she fits her role—it's easy to believe that her brother-in-law would become obsessed with her. But Allen hasn't written enough sides for her—or for anyone else—to play. Dianne Wiest does all she can with her role—she makes a style out of neurosis. Her Holly is so fouled up that she's always angry at herself and everybody else, too. Her nerves aquiver, she seems to be holding back either screams or tears; she lives in a tizzy. (And she's so completely lacking in confidence that she's bound to match up with the Woody Allen character.) But Allen's script, for all its shrewdness about sisterly relations and its considerable finesse, doesn't cut very deep. There's a basic, bland unadventurousness about the picture: it never makes us wonder about anything. Hangups are there to be got through: the characters are like patients in the hands of a benevolent, godlike therapist.

"Hannah and Her Sisters" would be lifeless without Woody Allen's presence as Mickey Sachs, who is convinced he has a fatal disease. It needs his mopey personality, and it needs his jokes, even though they're throwbacks to earlier gags. It's a funny thing about Woody Allen: the characters he plays learn to accept life and get on with it, but then he starts a new picture and his character is back at square one. Mickey is a hypochondriac, terrified of dying and obsessed with the same old Woody Allen question: If there's no God and no afterlife, what's the point of living? Mickey takes a year off from his work in TV to ponder the meaninglessness of everything. He tries to find faith in Catholicism and then, for a moment, in Hare Krishna (because of the sect's belief in reincarnation); he attempts suicide. Then he sees the Marx Brothers in "Duck Soup," and when they sing "Hail Fredonia" he realizes that he wants to enjoy life for as long as he can. He'll settle for romantic love, for a "relationship." But we've been through all this with him before.

Still, the picture needs him desperately, because the other roles are so thin that there's nobody else to draw us into the story. Michael Caine flails around confusedly trying to bring something to a role that's out of bedroom farce but that he seems expected to give other dimensions to. At first, you attribute Caine's discomfort to the character's crush on Lee, but afterward he goes on being ill at ease. Maureen O'Sullivan (who was born in 1911) comes through with a ribald-old-trouper performance that's gutsier than anything she ever did in her M-G-M years. But it's a small role. So is that of Lloyd Nolan (born in 1902), who made his final appearance here; he brings to his part the dapper weariness of a vain man whose wife goads him unconscionably—he may suspect that tormenting him is what keeps her on her toes and beautiful. In a larger role, Max von Sydow has nothing to play but an aspect of the earlier Woody Allen characters: he's a rigid intellectual, a man so devoted to high culture that he's exasperated by other people's delight in pop. He's like the Woody Allen of "Stardust

Memories," and his determination to educate Lee recalls the Woody of "Annie Hall."

This character's gloom and the way he cuts himself off from other people tell us that Woody Allen is saying here that the high arts are not everything—that we also need the ease and relaxation of pop culture, that superficiality isn't all bad. Allen's love for the romantic, "civilized" pop music of the past is expressed throughout the movie, which features Rodgers and Hart songs, a couple of Harry James recordings, and some Count Basie, as well as Gustav Leonhardt playing Bach. Allen draws the line at high-powered rock, though: part of Holly's coming to her senses is her graduating from the downtown life of CBGB's to classical music. Woody Allen can't seem to get rid of a streak of draggy pedantry; he's still something of a cultural commissar. (I could have done without the quick tour of Manhattan's architectural marvels that's included in the movie.)

Like Bergman, Allen shows his intellectuality by dramatizing his quest for meaning and then shows his profundity by exposing the aridity of that quest. This celebration of family is essentially a celebration of sanity and of belonging to a group—of satisfying the need for human connections. It's a tribute to human resilience, a look-we-have-come-through movie, and the people who were deeply moved by "Manhattan" are likely to be still more deeply moved by "Hannah." The infertile Mickey even becomes fertile; the picture goes the traditional like-affirming route. Yet what he has come through to is so lacking in resonance that it feels like nowhere. "Hannah" is very fluid in the way it weaves the characters in and out; Allen's modulated storytelling has a grace to it. The picture is certainly better than three-fourths of the ones that open, and it's likable, but you wish there were more to like. It has some lovely scenes—I was particularly taken with the one in which Holly and a good friend (played by Carrie Fisher) are out in a car with a man (Sam Waterston) whom they're both interested in, and at their last stop before calling it a night they discuss the logistics of which one he should drop off first. Yet, over all, the movie is a little stale, and it suggests the perils of inbreeding. It might be time for Woody Allen to make a film with a whole new set of friends, or, at least, to take a long break from his sentimentalization of New York City. Maybe he'd shed the element of cultural self-approval in the tone of this movie. There's almost a trace of smugness in its narrow concern for family and friends; it's as if the moviemaker has seen through the folly of any wider concern.

Woody Allen has joined a club that will have him, and that may help to explain the awesome advance praise for the film. Like the Robert Benton picture "Kramer vs. Kramer," which also stirred up enormous enthusiasm in the press, "Hannah" evokes the "family/style" pages in the *Times* and all the books and editorials and "Hers" columns about people divorcing and remarrying and searching to find meaning in their lives. It's about people that members of the press can identify with; it's what they imagine themselves to be or would like to be. They're applauding their fantasy of themselves.

All the vital vulgarity of Woody Allen's early movies has been drained away here, as it was in "Interiors," but this time he's made the picture halfway human. People can laugh and feel morally uplifted at the same time. The willed sterility of his style is terrifying to think about, though; the picture is all tasteful touches. He uses style to blot out the rest of New York City. It's a form of repression, and from the look of "Hannah and Her Sisters," repression is what's romantic to him. That's what the press is applauding—the romance of gentrification.

September

MAURICE YACOWAR

As in *A Midsummer Night's Sex Comedy* (1982), in *September* Allen traces the romantic tangles and mangles that beset three (sort of) couples on a country retreat. In the earlier film the tangles were sorted out. The various happy endings were clearly due not to any realistic or psychological resources but to supernatural interventions, a fanciful version of *deus ex machina*. On the level of plot, there was the magic unleashed by the implausibly successful inventor, played by Allen himself. In the larger structure of the film, *auteur* Allen adhered to a kind of external imperative, the pattern of successful romantic conclusion in the classic romantic comedy (*pace* T.S. Eliot's "Tradition and the Individual Talent"), most notably Bergman's *Smiles of a Summer's Night* and the *Midsummer Night's Dream* of both Shakespeare and Mendelssohn. But in *September* there is no even implausible inventor to engineer a happy ending, indeed none of the leavening relief that director Allen usually affords us by stepping his persona down to the world of his mortal characters. There is only the advent of the winter of the heart.

So the tangled lovers go unrequited. The French teacher, Howard (Denholm Elliott), loves the fragile Lane (Mia Farrow), who is in love with her summer tenant, Peter (Sam Waterston), who is in love with her best friend, Stephanie (Dianne Wiest), who returns his love but ultimately decides to stay with her friend and marriage. Across this doomed quadrangle falls the grating presence of Lane's ex-actress mother (Elaine Stritch) and her present husband, Lloyd (Jack Warden). In refusing to resolve his characters' romantic failures, Allen eschews the happy endings he managed for *Hannah and Her Sisters* (1986). In effect, in *September* Allen rejects the romantic resolutions which characterize archetypal comedy.

It is axiomatic that comedy ends in romantic resolution because the genre celebrates the individual's inclusion in a fertile community. In the springtime season of classic comedy, the lovers move from chaos and opposition into the harmonies of a socially sanctioned union. Here lies the larger truth of Chaplin's observation that comedy is long shot and tragedy close-up. For comedy deals with the individual in the social landscape, while tragedy isolates the individual in the confrontation of destiny. Hence, one might add incidentally, the charged tragic pathos in the climactic closing shots of both Chaplin's *City Lights* and Allen's *Manhattan*.

Reprinted by permission from *Film Quarterly*, vol. 42, no. 1 (Fall 1988): 46–9. Copyright © 1988 by the Regents of the University of California.

Hence, too, the wag's observation that comedy ends in a wedding and tragedy starts with one. For the most part Allen has avoided the marital resolution in his comedy. Of his sixteen features, only in four—*Bananas* (1971), *Sleeper* (1973), *Zelig* (1983), and *Hannah and Her Sisters* does Allen close on a note of romantic closure. More commonly he ends with the modernist open-endedness, either resignation to loss or the ambivalence of lovers growing apart. The volume of emotional failure and irresolution in *September* is not just an acknowledgment of the complexities of modern love and anxiety, but an insistence upon the irrelevance of the classic comic format to contemporary life. Marriage or even the temporary solace of an affair no longer (if indeed it ever did) provide the traditional happy ending, but at best an illusory refuge from the underlying chaos. Moreover, in its seasonal setting, its failures and melancholy, *September* denies not just the pleasure of comedy but its force and validity as well. In this film, more profoundly even than in *Interiors* (1978), Allen expresses his seldom noticed but long-held conviction of the superior relevance and importance of the tragic mode over the comic. In addition to the film's power as a realistic and intensely moving human drama, *September* can be viewed as a meditation upon Allen's most familiar metier, the comic form.

Elaine Stritch's character can be taken to personify the comic mode. Her name, Diane, associates her with classical verdure, which she confirms by blithely plucking flowers and strewing them about untended. She also wears bright flowery clothing ("I look like I'm going to a luau"), but after the excoriating events of the film she leaves in a suit of defoliated white ("one of those needy cases"), calmed of mind, all passion spent. She seems more of a force than a person. "Time passes and she's still here," Lane complains. Diane alone has lived a life of blithe fulfillment, transcending or ignoring the tragedies that have ruined the others. "Life is too short to dwell on our tragedies," she concludes. Peter is drawn to the life Lane calls "a frivolous existence," because he sees her as "a survivor," when others (especially Lane) are "annihilated by life's tragedies." Diane is a comedienne in the French sense of actress, as well as for her hedonistic, "playgirl" life, as chronicled in the scandal sheets and now in her memoirs. There is an element of the comic in her association with story-telling. She overflows with fictions, whether autobiographic anecdotes or quips. In contrast, the blocked Peter abandons his attempt to write a novel based on his father (a history professor who survived blacklisting by making his career in gambling, another comedic survivor) because "It's lifeless"; instead he settles on the hack work for Lane's mother.

Most obviously, the comic Diane has most of the film's funny lines. Indeed she is the only character in control of her funny lines. She is the film's one wit. The other characters may have an occasional thigh-slapper but it is usually at their own expense or an unwitting irony. For example, Stephanie confesses that she won't let her radiologist husband take an Xray of her because he'd see things he couldn't understand and be "terribly hurt." This is an extremely witty metaphor for a woman closed against her husband, but only the anxiety, not the wit, is the character's. Diane has the jokes. In these specifics, she differs markedly from the two mother figures in Allen's earlier noncomedy, *Interiors*. Diane combines the vulgarian vitality of Pearl (Maureen Stapleton) with the chilling authority of Eve (Geraldine Page). Despite her humor, though, there is a callousness and cruelty as Stritch performs Diane that perhaps go beyond what Mia Farrow's real-life mother, Maureen O'Sullivan, might comfortably have given in the role as originally cast.

Similarly, by replacing the brashly American Charles Durning with the tonier English Denholm Elliott in the role of Lane's loving neighbor, and casting the gruff Jack Warden instead of Elliott as Diane's husband, Allen shifted the higher-culture lover from the earthy actress to her sensitive and more artistic daughter (Lane is a would-be photographer incapacitated by her negative thinking). The casting changes emphasize the cultural context in which Diane can be read as the comic. The character of Peter was significantly hollowed out, perhaps even demystified, when its presenter was changed from the epic romanticism of Sam Shepard to the moodiness of Christopher Walken, and finally to the reedy infidelity of Sam Waterston substantially repeating his role in *Hannah and Her Sisters*. As Peter shifts from his primary relationship with Lane to a calculated fling with Stephanie and then the pandering relationship with Diane, he shrinks from artist to a figure of comic inadequacy.

As the personification of comedy, Diane is vital energy insensitive to time. Lloyd makes this point metaphorically when he describes their meeting in a shared taxicab: "By the time the meter hit three dollars she had her tongue in my ear." But the comic vision is fatally limited by its inability to deal with the fact of mortality. So Diane is sobered when she checks her make-up in the mirror and notes the absence of any future. Later she considers trying to merge her liver spots into a tan. In a more immediate deficiency, the comic is self-absorbed. Diane does not hear Lane's plans to sell her house, which leads to their climactic quarrel. When Diane decides finally to leave the house to Lane, she inconsistently chases out the prospective buyers. Earlier, Diane referred to Lane's previous lover, Jack, as Jeff, confusing him with a revived memory of her own dates with Jeff Chandler. Lane justly charges her mother with selfishness and insensitivity to others: "Don't you ever listen when I talk?" Her fictioning proves irresponsible when she alternately forces Lane and Peter together and lies to them about each other. We learn even worse when Lane charges that it was her mother who shot her lover; Lane "only said the things the lawyer told me to say." From Diane's stricken look and from her earlier confession over the ouija board to Lane's father ("I'm a tough cookie. I can file and forget. . . . [but] I want her to forgive me.") we can believe Lane's charge. Lane's life was ruined at the age of 14, when she bore her mother's guilt. Like comedy, Diane has only a partial vision even of her own experience; the tragic persists.

In contrast to the raunchy, selfish frivolity of Diane's comedy, Allen implicitly develops an alternative kind of wit, an ironic but compassionate observation of others. The film's richest pleasure derives from Allen's subtle and touching revelation of his characters. The choreographed close-ups as he details the shifting relationships between Stephanie, Lane, and Peter, for example, are both moving and witty. Without or despite their words, the characters express their timorous yearnings and fears. Allen's dramatic ironies make the characters seem trapped and defined beyond their awareness. Thus Lane enters just as her suitor Howard admits to having nothing at home to which to go back. The camera holds tellingly on Stephanie after she admits to Howard that Lane might well have fallen in love with Peter. There is also Allen's usual witty score, the classic tunes speaking wordlessly for the characters. Stephanie's piano medley concludes with "I'm Confessing (That I Love You)" just after Howard has finally expressed his love to Lane and Lloyd has told Peter about his love for Diane. Yet the song also represents Stephanie's having worked around to expressing her love for (if not to) Peter.

In perhaps the film's central statement, Lloyd describes his profession in physics in terms applicable to Allen's mature film-making. For both men, the job involves confronting the ineluctable doom in the universe and in the individual life. Lloyd studies the random nature of existence, knowing that the entire universe will eventually "vanish forever—the universe, all space, all time, it's just a temporary convulsion. And I get paid to prove it." For Allen as for Lloyd, the universe is "haphazard, morally neutral and unimaginably violent." As a consequence Lloyd clings to Diane while he sleeps so he won't dream of photons and quarks. But the comic muse, pure and traditional, holds no such solace for Allen. Just as Lloyd makes this admission, Allen shows Howard quietly rise and leave, having overheard the physicist define in cosmic terms his own profound isolation. Peter's response is more trivial: "Don't say that. I have to sleep alone tonight," he says, but then proceeds to seduce Stephanie. The annihilating force of nature is brought home by the storm, which floods a neighbor's house and which leaves our characters "powerless," lit only by candles for the middle third of the film.

Stephanie faces domestic versions of these cosmic threats but by her own admission can only run from them. When the lights go out she starts to play the piano ("What'll I Do?") and she is still/again playing when the lights and phonograph return to life. Her flirtation and affair with Peter is an attempt to run from her impatience with her husband, expressed at his phone calls. But then she runs from the affair, to recover her friendship with Lane. To Lane she prescribes a life of small consolations, a domestic version of Diane's (the comic) frivolous life: "Tomorrow will come and you'll find distractions . . . a million petty things to keep you going." Of course, none will be able to deal with Lane's rending grief. "I'm so lonely," she weeps, and there is no consolation for her. When she rejects suicide because "That's my problem: I always wanted to live," Lane is defined as a liver manquée, whose spirit and hope were sapped by the indomitable simple-mindedness of her mother, the merely comic spirit.

Of all the nostalgic songs that silently speak for the film's failed lovers, perhaps the dominant one is "Slow Boat to China." The lyrics normally express the lover's desire to be isolated with his beloved, away from threat of rival or other form of loss. But here there is no security in isolation. As Stephanie explains to Lane: "We're all up here, isolated from the world. Unpredictable things happen." But what happened was the collision of emotional needs, the lovers' cushioned version of the Big Bang, dread source of our random and amoral existence. There's one period song that Stephanie does not play. She does not have to play Kurt Weill's classic because Woody Allen's film is his "September Song." It's also about his own artistic choices and the failure of the comic vision to fathom the deepest or outer-most blues.

Oedipus Wrecks, from *New York Stories*

PAULINE KAEL

THERE ARE some genuine laughs in Woody Allen's thirty-nine minute "Oedipus Wrecks." He stars in it as Sheldon Mills, a quiet, dignified lawyer, who, distraught, says to his analyst, "I'm fifty years old . . . and I still haven't resolved my relationship with my mother." When his mother, Mrs. Millstein (Mae Questel), appears, it's clear that nobody could resolve a relationship with this demon. A tiny woman, she seems harmless until you hear her voice: it drills into your skull and sucks out your brains. There is no answer to anything she says. Poor Sheldon, who has tried to escape the hideously familiar sound by de-Jewishing his name and becoming engaged to a Gentile (Mia Farrow), doesn't stand a chance.

His deepest wish is fulfilled: his mother disappears—but only to return in punishing nightmare form, discussing his engagement with crowds of people. Clearly, she understands—as we do—that he'd be afraid of dating a Jewish woman, afraid that she'd turn into his mother. He feels that if he marries his shiksa he'll escape his mother; he'll grow up—he'll gain his dignity.

This is Woody Allen's kind of comedy—the situation harks back to his earlier, funnier films, and the audience is grateful. But what was once peppy and sloppy-spirited has become almost oppressively schematic. This film (with cinematography by Sven Nykvist) is too cleanly made for what it's about. It just doesn't have the organic untidiness that was part of Woody Allen's humor. Even his jokes are clean now, and his malice has been airbrushed out. He can't really revive the kind of comedy he used to do. For one thing, when a man in his thirties is befuddled it can be charming—you figure he'll work it out. But when he's in his fifties even his befuddlement has a weight. The little film itself is too deliberate. It has been a while since Allen directed out-and-out comedy, and here and there his timing is off. (When the magician is on-stage putting swords through the Great Chinese Box that Mother is in, the scene is flabby right up until the cut to Sheldon, in the audience, smiling.) If Allen's pacing were speedier and more casual and erratic maybe we wouldn't get the occasional feeling that we're watching waxworks—that he has already done too much of this. (We especially don't need his sortie into the Chaplinesque; he reaches for high emotion with something so derivative it cancels itself out.)

But even with the wax, the fumbles, and the absence of the kind of movie-making excitement that Scorsese charges us up with, this short-story comedy is very appealing. (It might be more appealing, and it would definitely be messier, if the mother wasn't simply a demon—if maybe she was a likable force of nature, with wit and gusto, but still made Sheldon feel ashamed of being her son.) The movie does take a surprisingly amiable—if somewhat ambiguous—turn. From what we see, Sheldon's relationship with his fiancée is polite and bland; it has no color or warmth—it has no silliness. And he gives no sign that he knows he's missing out on anything. But when, at his therapist's suggestion, he consults a clairvoyant, Treva (Julie Kavner), he finds himself responding to qualities that mark her as the opposite of his fiancée. Treva is like a high priestess of slobbiness. Devoted, caring, anxious, solicitous—and, above all, weepy—she's everything he has been fighting off.

Woody Allen has written the role that Julie Kavner deserves: she's the cartoon Jewish woman redeemed, and she plays it superbly—she's a Yiddish Olive Oyl, a hopeless involuntary comic. And, even in the guise of Sheldon the lawyer in tweeds, Woody Allen recognizes her as his soul mate. The movie is a Freudian vaudeville, worked out with details such as Sheldon's loose, improved sex life during the period of his mother's disappearance. It's just after he acknowledges to his analyst that he's happy without her that everything clamps down on him. Freud was a Jewish comic, too (and his jokes also went on too long).

Husbands and Wives

STUART KLAWANS

"**C**AN I go now? Is this over?" With these words, Woody Allen puts an end to his new film, *Husbands and Wives*, and to the last of his pseudodocumentary interviews within it. From the seat I was occupying, at Loews 84th Street, that plaintive cry already had arisen many times: "Can I go now? Is this over?"

As audience member, movie character and filmmaker, all three of us were begging to be released from different but related tortures. From the mess he put on screen, I'd guess Woody Allen disliked making *Husbands and Wives* as much as I disliked watching it, as much as his character, Gabe, disliked living through a burned-out marriage to Mia Farrow's Judy. But was there a fourth level of horror behind that final plea? Was the writer-director-star thinking of his career when he said, "Can I go now? Is this over?"

Woody Allen has given a lot of people a lot of pleasure over the years, so it gives me no pleasure at all to report, on the basis of present evidence, that his career *should* end, at least as presently constituted. Judging his new film on the basis of its attendant gossip, a viewer might figure that the picture's disarray mirrors that of Allen's almost-marriage. Working from somewhat broader assumptions, you might conclude that it's been Allen's artistic ambitions, and the conditions in which he's realized them, that have brought him to this state.

Having started out as a scuffling autodidact from Brooklyn, Allen succeeded by the late seventies in turning himself into a Manhattan sophisticate. Forget the Academy Awards—he was being published in *The New Yorker*. Someone who had fought less hard for that status might have taken it more lightly. But Allen guarded it by insulating himself, both personally and artistically, with the result that his liveliest films of recent years have been set in fantasies of the past, while his present-day pictures, by and large, have been increasingly wan and self-enclosed. In *Husbands and Wives*, he's portrayed a solipsist's Manhattan, with no working class except for cab drivers, no people of color except for two extras at a concert hall (and of course the Knicks), no same-sexers of any description. Children and the very old are invisible; the young, as we know from the gossip, exist primarily as targets of sexual opportunity. This is, of course, the same

Reprinted by permission from *The Nation*, vol. 255, no. 12 (October 19, 1992): 447. Copyright © 1992 by The Nation Company, Inc.

version of present-day Manhattan that Allen has been giving us, to less and less effect, since *Manhattan*.

He's been able to do so largely because he's been shielded from the ruder shocks of commerce, thanks to producers who have been content with prestige more often than profit. Of the major American filmmakers, only Woody Allen has been so protected. Then came the collapse of Orion Pictures and the need to negotiate a new distribution arrangement (ultimately with TriStar). Rumors circulated that Allen's financing might dry up; some people even said that his backers might welcome an excuse to get out of the next *succès d'estime*. This was the *other* behind-the-scenes divorce being threatened while Allen made *Husbands and Wives*—a commercial divorce in which Allen figured to be the partner who was no longer sexy enough.

That isn't what you see on the screen, of course. Within the ever more circumscribed terms of his art, Allen could allow himself to dramatize only domestic problems within one small corner of Manhattan's intelligentsia. Within that corner, he apparently could envision only one actor-character as being wholly unlovable, and it wasn't himself. Although he does require three of the principals—himself, Judy Davis and Sydney Pollack—to look foolish at times, Pollack also gets to be virile; Davis is endlessly lauded by her fellow actors as beautiful and smart; and Allen is greeted wherever he goes by expressions of respect, offered even by total strangers. (He's playing a short-story writer. Of *course* New York lies at his feet.) And Mia Farrow? Except for the first scene, in which she turns shrill and runs from the room in tears, she frumps her way through the movie, dutifully embodying her writer-director-former boyfriend's notion of an emotional black hole.

Given its double agenda of displacement and revenge, it's no wonder the movie doesn't make sense. Ostensibly, the picture is a documentary, shot in the jerky, hand-held fashion that was the latest thing ten years ago in A.T.& T. commercials. At times, the characters settle down for interviews, performed in front of a longed-for tripod. At other times, the unseen documentarian narrates the action in voiceover. But nobody explains how the documentarian and his shaky-handed cameraman got into the bedroom where Judy Davis and Liam Neeson were making love. I'd like an answer. I'd also like to know why a professional writer—one who's neurotic enough to be played by Woody Allen—would hand somebody the only copy of a manuscript; or why characters who have eaten at an Italian restaurant should later confess they've drunk too many margaritas.

I can only conclude that *Husbands and Wives* is the product of someone who has fallen out of touch with his times, with his surroundings— even with the continuity of his own work-in-progress. Or is it merely coincidence that this ramshackle film, with its running motif of housebreaking, should have been made just when the outside world was threatening to break down Allen's front door? Maybe the scandal surrounding *Husbands and Wives* will rescue the film at the box office, allowing Allen to return to his cozy self-enclosure. For his sake, though, I hope not. It's time for him to make a new start, with a bigger view of the world and a riskier way of making pictures about it; time for those of us who love him to let the old Woody Allen go. It's over.

ESSAYS

That Obscure Object of Analysis

BETH WISHNICK

S OMEWHERE IN the dark recesses of the tabloid press, a lurking version of "the truth" waits to be revealed about Woody Allen. Or so we would like to believe. But whether or not that version has to do with the man or his movies remains to be seen. The on-screen drama of *Husbands and Wives* (1992) sent many of its viewers home with self-conscious reflections about their own lives and loves. But it was the off-screen drama that caught the eye of the public, and gave many of these viewers the impetus to see the film. And it was the off-screen drama that became front-page headlines, from magazines as diverse as *Time* and *Newsweek* to *Vanity Fair*, *Esquire*, *Rolling Stone*, and *People*. The scandal was also covered in the smaller, more elite publications, such as the *New Republic*, *Macleans*, the *Nation*, the *National Review*, and of course, the trademark of mainstream elitism, the *New Yorker*. Plastered on newspapers all over the country, particularly the northeast corridor, where most of his fans reside, Allen's photograph was multiplied and made into a fragment of a larger collage that included photographs of the other participants in his suddenly not-so-private life. Articles next to articles, pictures within pictures—this postmodern media pastiche soon began to resemble the best of Allen's films. For in his most serious and self-conscious moments, Woody Allen's art is all about the multiple enclosures that surround our perceptions of experience. To explain this phenomenon, and show how it relates to Allen's art, I have employed the psychoanalytic notions of projection and transference.

The media explosion swirling around *Husbands and Wives* highlights one of the many thematic concerns of the movie—namely, the irony of any single vision of truth. Stylistically, this point is made through the jittery, hand-held camera that mirrors the emotional chaos at the opening of the movie. This device continues throughout the film, and becomes more pronounced whenever the plot itself portrays shaky and turbulent emotion. While reminding us that we are only seeing part of the truth, this shaky camera also calls attention to the artificial nature of film. The shaky camera, in short, is a self-reflexive device used to break the mimetic illusion. What we are watching is a film, and lest we forget, the filmmaker will remind us.

This essay was written specifically for this volume and is published here for the first time by permission of the author.

Allen also emphasizes the multiplicity of meaning and truth through the formal device of the mock interview. At intermittent moments, most of the principal players appear on screen talking to an unseen, unknown interlocutor who seems to be asking them questions. Is this a filmmaker, therapist, or novelist? Simulating the cinema verité format, with its "realistic" collection of voices and points of view, this technique is actually meant to function as a documentary of the movie Allen is making—which has unwittingly acted as a companion piece to the play within the play going on in the press. Functioning like Chinese nesting boxes that enclose within one another, this subtext of the making of a movie actually becomes part of the text, thereby merging the form and content.

With its abrupt stops and starts, the film style of *Husbands and Wives* mirrors the stops and starts of relationships. It is here that Allen manages to deconstruct the twin conventions of both marriage and art by exposing the artificial nature of both. Allen goes behind the scenes and reminds us that conventions are socially constructed, that they are not a priori assumptions, and that they appear so only when framed. By adjusting the frame, then, Allen unmasks their pretense. The chaos that rushes in is his movie, *Husbands and Wives*, which is self-consciously about the making of a movie—itself. Ironically and eerily, this theme has been reflected in the profusion of reviews about Allen and his film. As a collection, these reviews are really about the making of a story, false frames included. Seen in this light, the "who is Woody Allen?" question dissolves into "who is telling which story?," Woody Allen or his reviewers? This process becomes evident when we turn to the notions of projection and transference.

Woody Allen and his reviewers can be respectively likened to the patient in analysis who transfers feelings from the past onto the figure of the analyst, thus projecting internalized feelings outward. Like the patient who tells his story to the analyst, who then retells that story back to the patient, Woody Allen has been telling his story cinematically and otherwise in the media. The media has told that story back to him through magazine articles, newspaper reviews, and editorials. The result, as in analysis, is a jointly authored tale in which authority flips back and forth between storyteller and audience.

In addition to this dialectic between Allen and the press, there is the other dialectic between the media and the consumers of the media. As patients, we have looked to the press as an authority on Allen's life and film. In the transference, however, it is we who have become the authorities. We have pieced together our own story lines and offered interpretation, just like the analyst. And just like the analyst, our interpretations have taken the place of fact. From Allen to screen to media to us, we have internalized this multiple chain of projections, often forgetting that the real object has receded from sight. As in Freud's seduction theory, where a real or imagined event is displaced by affect, here the real or imagined Woody

Allen has been replaced by media-assisted interpretation and projection. The "who is Woody Allen?" question becomes a house of cards, built around shadows, obscured in opinion.

Husbands and Wives opened with a bang because of the hype surrounding Woody Allen and Mia Farrow's personal life. "Discovered" to be involved with his longtime lover's adopted daughter, Soon-Yi Previn, Allen was suddenly catapulted into the public eye and used as a vehicle to explore the roots of moral corruption[1] and the nature of incest.[2] His family saga was laid out next to reportage of the Republican National Convention, whose call to arms was the decline of family values. And for those who were looking to vilify psychoanalysis in the discussion of the national health crisis, his folly was offered up as evidence of the abuse that permeates the mental health profession: "Just how many sessions of psychotherapy should be paid for in the coming national health plan?"[3] This press response is interesting on a number of levels.

Socially, the response is indicative of the way in which Woody Allen is being used as a moral and ethical scapegoat in order to discuss the problems that plague our country. Richard Dyer, in his 1979 book, *Stars*,[4] emphasizes the important hold that celebrities have on our lives, one important enough to generate an intertextual media war on who is actually going to deliver the "goods" on Woody Allen. Psychologically, the response shows just how much we have internalized Woody Allen's own projections, and in turn, project our own life dramas onto his.

In the midst of his troubles, Allen gave a news conference and appeared on "Sixty Minutes." In a prepared statement regarding his relationship with Previn, he summarized his situation: "In the end, the one thing I have been guilty of is falling in love with Miss Farrow's adult daughter at the end of our own years together."[5] This rendition then gives way to analysis, like any good story: "I didn't find any moral dilemmas whatsoever."[6] The flat-out denial here highlights the irony of the situation. Forced to defend himself to a not-so-adoring public, Allen becomes the patient in analysis who justifies his life, gives his version of the story, and employs defense mechanisms to ward off unpleasant feelings. And like the patient/child, he has come to resent that authority: "I never cared, and don't care to this day, if I ever made another film in my life."[7]

What we have here is an act of aggression, mirroring the Hegelian-like struggle between patient and analyst. As the analysand progressively appropriating his/her own life story, Allen can be shown as attempting to rein in his narrative. Roy Schaeffer has written that in analysis "the analysand becomes coauthor of the analysis as he/she becomes a more daring and reliable narrator."[8] Allen as analysand is ironically coauthor and object of analysis here, a situation that highlights the supreme irony of the transference. How can the analyst—in this instance, the media—be more of an authority on Woody Allen than he is himself? And taking the matter one step further, how can we, the audience, really pinpoint the focus of our responses? Is our transference to the man or the media?

For her media version of these events, the more demure Farrow chose an upscale, cosmopolitan magazine known primarily for its interest in the personalities of famous people. The choice of *Vanity Fair* accordingly offers a sharp contrast to the "strictly news" approach of Allen's—one that humanizes her rendition and gives it a softer edge. *Vanity Fair* is also known for its coverage of the latest trends in art, including film, theater, and literature. Farrow's story then, is set within a publication that reinforces the art of her tale, which ironically mirrors the play within the play theme in the press, as well as in Allen's movie.

"Mia's Story" alerts us to the artifice of its subject and construction merely by its title. An obvious fictional construction, since it was written without the benefit of direct quotations from Farrow, this story paints a sympathetic portrait of a woman cruelly wronged by both her daughter and her lover. The ambitious *New York Newsday*, however, managed to acquire a letter that Farrow wrote to a close friend: "I have spent more than a dozen years with a man who would destroy me and corrupt my daughter.... I can think of no crueler way to lose a child or a lover and with them a treasured part of my life."[9] This account lacks the aggression characterizing Allen's clipped, succinct, and tidy narrative. Allen's flat and reductive conceptualization, in fact, stands in sharp contrast to Farrow's version—which suggests strong feeling. Her account is sweeping in its melodrama—and tearfully evokes a vain and wasted past. In short, Farrow's account calls up images of love, loss, and possible revenge, like a romance novel. Her account paints her as the victim of a cruel triangle. Previn, the supposed victim in this sprawling tale, gave her version of events in *Newsweek*. As in Allen and Farrow's choice of magazines, Previn's selection of *Newsweek* makes a statement similar to Allen's. The events should not be clouded with affect and implication: "I'm not a retarded underage flower who was raped, molested and spoiled by some evil stepfather.... I'm a psychology major at college who fell for a man who happens to be the ex-boyfriend of Mia. I admit it's offbeat, but let's not get hysterical."[10] This rather flippant account represents Previn in the transference as a patient attempting to appropriate her life story from the media, like Allen. And like Allen's, it is an account that appears designed to reduce an inherently complex situation into a linear, simple narrative. Her protestations come across as hostile and aggressive. Implications of incest are ignored. Her current lover is referred to not as her siblings' father, but as her mother's ex-boyfriend. Nonetheless, this rendition is still a rendition. Whatever the tone, whatever the angle, it is just one more piece of the entire picture—which can be judged neither in isolation nor at face value.

It is here that we see how context becomes just as important as content. It becomes, in fact, part of the content—and illustrates how placement becomes part of the meaning. What I refer to is the actual layout of the article. Previn's version appears as a news item in a news magazine, on the page following an interview with Allen. It is framed within a collagelike assortment of pictures—a current photo of herself, a baby picture, a photo of her mother, and one of Allen. Above her statement there is a chronological rendition of events entitled "The Days of Their Lives." This pictorial media collage acts as a mirror to the familial collage of the principal players. It reinforces the drama of the situation by presenting itself as a constructed work of art in which linearity and simultaneity exist side by side. And most importantly, it brings the Freudian romance to life.

Again and again we have intertextual references to other lives and other shows (television as well as movies). Again and again we have the play within the play echoing Allen's self-reflexive cinematic preoccupation. And like Allen's growing repertoire of films, which are redefined each time a new film is made, each voice in this drama accents and speaks to every other voice. We can say, in fact, that Previn's statement is like a repository, her voice containing traces of everyone else's voice, her statement rising to prominence only in relation to the other lines of the principal players.

Previn's story is not without reverberations. One family acquaintance, in fact, refuses to believe that Soon-Yi knew what she was saying in the comments in *Newsweek*: "Soon-Yi doesn't know half those words, what they mean."[11] The obvious target, of course, is Allen, who is indirectly being accused of ventriloquism. Is Soon-Yi the dummy? And if so, why has Allen stolen her voice?

Whatever the answers to these questions, we must remember that they, as well as the questions, have been presented to us by the media for our unscrambling. The implications that we draw, the pictures that we put together have not much to do with the stated object of analysis. We ourselves become the "dummy" when we take the press versions as authentic mirrors of the situation. Thus, the speculation on whether Previn could have possibly known what she was saying becomes unimportant, highlighting the more important fact that this intertextual banter has everything to do with the construction of a good story.

When Previn's tutor is quoted as saying that Soon-Yi "misinterprets situations,"[12] the inference that situations exist for interpretation deconstructs the tutor's argument. It is here that the poststructural emphasis on self-reflexivity becomes a useful lens. Jacques Derrida and his following come to mind in the discussion of texts that call their own realities into question. The content of these dialogues is not the issue, but instead the simple fact that these dialogues have been published as accurate mirrors. Rather than renditions that reveal and refer outwards, these renditions conceal their reference points and refer back to themselves; they are steeped in paradox because they betray a belief in an outside, stable truth, while at the same time revealing skepticism. These renditions have long ago ceased to be about Woody Allen, Mia Farrow, and Soon-Yi Previn. As a collection, they tell their own story, and form accounts caught in the cross fire of mimesis—an aggressive battle, a lost cause.

One of the points I have been trying to emphasize here is the conflation that has gone on in the press between Allen the man and his art. Over and over, countless reviewers have refused to make the distinction that Allen has said he wants to be made. Asked about how the turbulent events of his life may have related to the script of *Husbands and Wives*, Allen flatly denied any real connection. "People tend to think these things reflect my life in some way.... But basically, they don't reflect my life."[13] Yet, most of the reviewers have compared the on-screen failing marriage of Gabe and Judy Roth in *Husbands and Wives* to the off-screen failed relationship of Allen and Farrow. Take, for example, a review of the movie in *New York* magazine: "The scenes between Woody Allen and Mia Farrow lack the minimal degree of illusion necessary for fiction.... Farrow looks beaten, her head down, her shoulders turned in." Eluding this reviewer is the fact that even reportage of the "facts" is itself created. There is no way to know whether "Farrow was attempting to portray a depressed woman or was genuinely depressed."[14] Reportage is always filtered.

The philosophical concern thus begging to be explored here has to do with the epistemology of knowledge. How do we know what we know? From Kant to Derrida, this question has been defined as one that is inseparable from the act of interpretation. For Kant, all knowledge is itself interpretation. With Derrida, we go one step further. Reacting against all forms of rationality, reflecting the nihilism and relativity of our century, all truth is reduced to fiction.

It is exactly at this point that the search for "truth" regarding Woody Allen becomes important. Whether we agree with the Kantian notion that all is interpretation, or the more extreme Derridian one of fiction, the fact remains that we are left with mediation. Even the Kantian notion itself, or "noumena," is interpretation. Trapped within the double representations of language and media, we are left with what philosophers call the hermeneutic circle—meaning that we can never escape from interpretation. Concentration on the "truth" of the real-life events surrounding *Husbands and Wives*, therefore, has been a red herring, a tantalizing displacement of a focus that belongs elsewhere—namely, on the act of interpretation itself.

As in most spectacles, the real focus of this media-propagated event has been obscured. Accordingly, Allen's character has been scrupulously dissected in the press, and picked over for answers. And interest in his sex life has given this sought-for nakedness an added visual dimension. From accusations of child abuse to speculations on the details of his conduct with Previn, newspaper headlines have attempted to lay Allen bare. Take the *New York Post*'s headline: "DYLAN: I WATCHED AS DADDY AND

SOON-YI HAD SEX."[15] Aside from being an example of a false search for Kant's notion of noumena, this is also a wonderful example of voyeuristic, sexual curiosity—a Freudian bedroom scene. Says an outraged Allen, "I've had to actually go on television myself and talk about my private life, and really the sexual part of my private life."[16]

What we have here is yet another example of the way in which the media has colluded and continues to collude in the interpretation that has posed as truth. And we can also see the impact of poststructuralism in the way textuality and intertextuality have pervaded this whole affair. The 31 August 1992 issue of *Time* magazine offers a brilliant example of this postmodern Derridean phenomenon.

Time cunningly makes reference to Allen's 1989 film with the mini-headline "Hollywood Babylon: Crimes and Misdemeanors," contained within a larger, more glaring headline, "Scenes from a Breakup," which is itself contained inside the magazine's front cover, "Cries and Whispers," with its obvious reference to Allen's mentor Ingmar Bergman. The layout alone is a visual example of the chaos pervading the content of events. And the articles within articles also echo the mirroring that occurs in Allen's films. Also emphasized in the layout are the multidimensional points of view, reinforced by the many stories included within the one, overarching story.

The article compares Allen to Charlie Chaplin, Errol Flynn, Fatty Arbuckle, and Roman Polanski, who were all involved in sexual scandals. And like the Freudian repetition compulsion, this drawing of parallels points to the unconscious desire for sameness on the part of the reviewers. It is also a good illustration of Derrida's notion of difference, which claims that no concept can ever be understood in isolation. Since *Time* is a mainstream, pop magazine, we see just how pervasive the themes of poststructuralism really are.

The *Time* article is a postmodern pastiche in both form and content. The form is collagelike in its seemingly haphazard arrangement of pictures and stories. In content, it deconstructs by making reference to other constructed tales. The opening of the article is itself catchy and familiar, like fiction: "Woody and Mia. No last names, please, for the king and queen of Manhattan's glitterati. For a decade they were the wax-doll couple atop a cake at the wedding of popular art and social responsibility." The wording evokes visual landscapes, as well as moral concerns. And it employs many intertextual references, among them the television show "The Brady Bunch." Like most fiction, it looks for conclusions and implications: "The moral: Never believe in the fairy tales movie people create.... Another moral: Don't always heed what you read...the facts are hard to determine, let alone the truth."[17] By making reference to "fairy tales," this article is immediately seen in relation to other fictions. By stating the indeterminate nature of truth, these words throw their own status into question.

A year later, *Rolling Stone* magazine responds to the *Time* article by picking up on the aspect dealing with Allen's tarnished sexual image. *Rolling Stone* also claims to have sorted out the facts from fiction, a claim that immediately throws this version into suspicion. "From being perceived, along with Mia Farrow, as half of the perfect modern couple...Allen was suddenly a tabloid sensation, no longer being compared with Ingmar Bergman but Roman Polanski and Fatty Arbuckle. The more lurid aspects of the story have resolved into cold facts."[18]

By responding to a year-old story in another magazine, by claiming to have discovered the "cold facts," *Rolling Stone* offers another example of the pervasive nature of poststructural intertextuality. The article contains an interview with Allen himself, and seems to be an extended footnote of a 1992 *Rolling Stone* review of *Husbands and Wives*. This in itself is interesting, because it shows an intertextual dialogue in which reference to another publication is made within a publication, reinforcing the artifice of both as constructions. It is also interesting because the magazine seems to be having a dialogue with itself.

Whereas the 1993 article seems more authentic because it is an interview, the 1992 article is more of an obvious construction. Like most of the film reviews, the 1992 review conflates the man with his movie. The reviewer is also very judgmental, and seems to be under the illusion that he himself has discovered the truth behind the film's dialogue. Combining film analysis with some speculative psychoanalysis, the 1992 author says of the scenes between Allen and Farrow, "The wrenching intimacy must have been hard on them. But anyone can understand the pain of releasing long-suppressed feelings." The end of this article attempts unsuccessfully to separate Allen from his work: "Allen may have blown it as a parental role model but not as an artist. He's still pushing into perilous frontiers."[19]

This conflation between Allen and his work has marked all of the reviews of *Husbands and Wives*. The events of Allen's life have added interest and intrigue to the way in which the movie has been received. Richard Dyer has specifically discussed the importance of publicity in the promotion of a star's image. That notion is applicable here, because Allen's image as a nice, moral, albeit neurotic guy quickly changed when knowledge of his affair with Previn became public, and especially when Farrow accused Allen of molesting their daughter. The resulting publicity thus painted him as an unethical, immoral, and not-so-nice guy. The resulting publicity, in fact, reflected a mad and betrayed public audience. Says Dyer, "The importance of publicity is that, in its apparent or actual escape from the image that Hollywood is trying to promote, it seems more 'authentic'" (Dyer, 69).

Dyer has hit upon a key point. Enmeshed as we are in Kantian phenomenon, it is appealing to think that we are getting the "real thing," something beyond appearances. When the newspapers "exposed" Woody

Allen's conduct to the public, this "exposure" was taken at face value to be the truth, and seemed to offer the public real knowledge of the situation, and the bonus of a personal relationship with Allen. Overlooked was the fact that this gossip, like surface phenomenon, was merely covering, rather than exposing the real truth of the situation.

Christine Gledhill discusses the perceived promise of genuine information about the star's life: "The star promises what mass society and the human sciences—sociology, Marxism, psychoanalysis—throw into question: intimate access to the authentic self."[20] This promise, of course, is an illusion, and one that highlights the appeal of publicity and gossip. Thus, the conflation in the press between Allen and his film serves to emphasize the interpretive nature of reportage. It is impossible to separate the man from his work, just as it is impossible to separate fact from fiction. Where does one end, and the other begin?

Reviews on Allen and his film, therefore, must be read as interpretations—personal visions limited by personal ideologies. Each review reflects both the cultural ideology, as well as the psychology of each reviewer. As a collection of different voices, each review accordingly has a different angle, and a different tone. One thing they all seem to agree on, however, is the similarity between the plot of Allen's life and his movie. Another point of agreement is the way in which the movie reflects our culture—"Life and love in urban America at the end of this very tired, shopworn century."[21] Allen's emotionally charged movie is a good mirror of our "emotionally embattled times."[22] His film, therefore, reflects the chaos and alienation of our society.

While reflecting the existent culture, these reviews are also very psychologically telling. As a whole, most of the reviews have betrayed a real ambivalence toward Allen and his film. The term that best describes this ambivalence is the psychoanalytic notion of *double bind*. A double bind exists when two conflicting ideas are uttered at the same time, thus undermining the ostensible main point. The *Dictionary of Psychotherapy* (1986) defines the double bind as "a secondary injunction which conflicts with the first at the metacommunicative level."[23] The conflation between Allen and his work offers the clearest example of this double bind. Where a reviewer has distinctly stated that Allen's film should not be confused with his life, that same reviewer has also drawn abundant parallels between the two. *Macleans*, for example, spends the bulk of its nine paragraph article discussing the connections between art and life, which "seem to have cruelly mimicked each other" in this case.[24] "At first," says the reviewer, "it is alarming to see the anger engraved on Farrow's face. She looks as if she cannot stand to be in the same shot as Allen." After stating more of these connections between the film and life, this reviewer ends his article lauding Allen as a great filmmaker: "Fortunately art has a longer shelf life than gossip." But does it? Clearly, gossip has colored this reviewer's opinion of art. And clearly, rather than "serving as evidence that an artist should not be confused with his work," the reviewer seems to say that the artist is integrally bound with his product. This is the sentiment shared by nearly all of the reviewers of *Husbands and Wives*.

The next clearest example of the double bind can be found in the reviews that are overtly negative, yet positive at the metacommunication level. An article in *Commonweal* offers a good illustration: "Monotonous in visual style, predictable in its plot, catering too exclusively to urban sophisticates who want to laugh affectionately at themselves,...*Husbands and Wives* isn't satisfying. Yet Woody Allen has made an interesting movie that at least deserves to outlive the scandal-sheet headlines that now serve as its unofficial advertising."[25] For this reviewer then, the movie is a disappointment. Interestingly enough, there is an implied expectation here that Allen fails to meet. Instead, his film is too narrowly targeted and banal to be interesting. At the same time, however, it is worthwhile and deserves attention. Surely, the film cannot be that bad if it deserves to outlive the surrounding scandal.

Two more examples of ambiguity illustrate this double bind. In the *Nation*, Stuart Klawans begins his article with reference to the last lines of Allen's film: "Can I go now? Is this over?"[26] One wonders why this reviewer bothered to watch the whole movie. "As audience member, movie character and filmmaker, all three of us were begging to be released from different but related tortures." Is this reviewer masochistic, or does the film possess some redeeming qualities that he neglects to mention?

The next example, and perhaps the best illustration of this secondary injunction, can be found in the review by John Simon in the *National Review*: "Is there much point in reviewing *Husbands and Wives*, Woody Allen's latest?" After four pages on a film that apparently deserves no mention, the author of this article ends his "pointless" review with some reflections on Allen's interview technique. "What TV show even is low enough to want to interview these characters about their dreary relationships? Well, you say, Woody thought them worthy of a whole movie about them."[27] Obviously, the author of this review thought them worthy of a whole article. The overt negative tone of these reviews, undermined by their verbal ambiguity, leads us back to the notion explored at the beginning of this paper, namely, transference. *The Dictionary of Psychotherapy* defines transference as "the process whereby the patient displaces on to the therapist feelings, attitudes and attributes which properly belong to a significant attachment figure of the past, usually a parent" (Walrond-Skinner, 364–65). This complex of emotions, involving both love and hate, allows for the repetition of childhood scripts to emerge and play themselves out. Peter Brooks describes the process as "an acting out of past events as if they were present."[28] The role of the therapist in this regard is to help the patient remember his past, by making what is unconscious

conscious. Says Freud, "We overcome the transference by pointing out to the patient that his feelings do not arise from the present situation and do not apply to the person of the doctor, but that they are repeating something that happened to him earlier. In this way we oblige him to transform his repetition into a memory."[29] There are two pertinent points here. First, the transference is not confined within the four walls of analysis. This is an assertion Freud made more than once. The phenomenon "is merely uncovered and isolated by analysis. It is a universal phenomenon of the human mind...and in fact dominates the whole of each person's relationships to his human environment."[30] In the case of Woody Allen it is important to remember this point when reading the reviews/interpretations of the movie/man because these reviews are always going to be colored by the individual psychologies of the reviewers. And like the literary text, these reviews contain all of the behavioral propensities and defense mechanisms that characterize the psyche. The fierce interest in Woody Allen's personal life, therefore, becomes explainable when we realize that all of these responses are coming from transference. The intense opinions, the moralizing, the anger, and the disappointment are childhood scripts being projected onto the figure of Allen. All of these feelings have nothing to do with the real man, since as already discussed, the real Woody Allen is a tantalizing displacement for the more somber hermeneutic circle from which we cannot escape.

The second point to remember is the existence of two kinds of transference. Freud distinguishes between the positive and the negative, "the transference of affectionate feelings from that of hostile ones."[31] The negative transference, with its accompanying hostility, is "as much an indication of an emotional tie as the affectionate ones" (Freud 1920, 443). This negative transference exists "side by side with the affectionate transference, often directed simultaneously towards the same person" (Freud 1912, 106).

The widespread ambivalence found in the host of reviews of *Husbands and Wives* is a strong indication of both positive and negative transference. As the patient in analysis reenacts the past by staging a play of feelings that replays old scripts of love and hate, the numerous reviews can also be said to be staging a play. They are also reviving old loves and hates, and old modes of response. In "The Dynamics of Transference," Freud notes that each person has acquired specific methods of conduct that they continue to repeat throughout their lives. This is a point picked up by Norman Holland in his psychoanalytic literary theory, which is based upon Heinz Lichenstein's theories of identity.

For Holland, meaning comes from a mingling of self and other. There is no objectivity. In "Unity Identity Text Self," he says that "any individual shapes the materials the literary work offers him—including its author—to give him what he characteristically both wishes and fears."[32] Holland continues: "Each reader groups the details of the play into themes that he thinks important, and if he chooses to press on to a highly condensed central theme it will surely be something that matters to him." This is a point that must be remembered when we read the numerous responses to Woody Allen. It becomes evident that "the highly condensed central theme" of each review is most certainly an individual concern of the reviewer's own life.

As Brooks has noted, the transference is "an acting out of the past as if it were present" (Brooks, 342). The "as if" here is a key issue, because while the transference revives the past, it is still a replica. The repressed material, therefore, that is repeated in behavior is both authentic and unauthentic. It is authentic in that it is a clear "play" of the past. It is unauthentic in that it is still a play taking place in the present. This mixture of the past and present creates a situation in which "all the patient's symptoms abandon their original meaning and take on a new sense" (Freud 1920, 444). What this "new sense" calls for is interpretation. And it is this process of interpretation that allows both patient and analyst to collude in their attempt to make sense of the past, which is now placed in the present.

Knowledge of the patient's life, therefore, is nothing more than the interpretation of both patient and analyst in the attempt to make meaning out of the patient's random wording. Like the patient and analyst engaged in the creation of a life story, the literary interpreter is engaged in the attempt to make coherence of the text. In *Narrative Truth and Historical Truth*, Donald P. Spence makes this point: "Just as the analyst must listen constructively and actively much of the time, supplying his own meaning to a large part of the analytic 'conversation,' so the outside reader must supply many of his own assumptions when he tries to understand the transcribed text of an hour or read a published report of a case."[33] The result is an ordering of events that can be likened to fiction.

This point is made by Freud more than once. *The Interpretation of Dreams* is all about sorting through the various distortions that occur to our thoughts at night, and relating them to consciousness. His case histories involve the search for plausible explanations of behavior. They involve the selection and ordering of vast amounts of past material. Thus selected, the material becomes the framework through which the individual life is viewed. The resulting construction, however, is tricky in that it is neither just the past nor just the present. Says Robert S. Wallerstein, "Once we have decided on that particular construction, we come to see and we in fact determine the past in a particular manner—so that, pushed to its logical extreme, the verbal construction that we create not only shapes (our view of) the past, but indeed, it, a creation of the present, becomes the past."[34]

By mixing chronologies, the life story becomes an amalgamation of past and present, just like transference. Dora, the case history in which Freud claims to have discovered transference is, in fact, written like a story. Even the subtitle of his work, *Fragment of an Analysis of a Case of Hysteria*, attests to the subjective and incomplete nature of this clinical rendition. Because Dora did not complete her analysis, Freud was left with filling in the blank spaces himself. "I have restored what is missing, taking the best models known to me from other analyses; but like a conscientious archaeologist I have not omitted to mention in each case where the authentic parts end and my constructions begin."[35] Says Freud at the end of his analysis, "Dora came to see me again: to finish her story" (Freud 1963, 142).

The emphasis on story here is a good way to view the press explosion on Woody Allen. In sorting out the press reviews, it becomes evident that these reviews are not as much mimetic reflections, as they are collections of subjective voices. It also becomes clear that I am dealing with not one story, but with multiple stories and multiple projections. The many versions of this media scandal, therefore, are no less murky when we compare them to the endless tellings and retellings within the psychoanalytic dialogue, with all of its slippages and nuances. We are left with an obscured object of analysis. Woody Allen, the media, ourselves—where does one end and the other begin?

Notes

1. *Time*, 21 September 1992, p. 64.
2. *Time*, 31 August 1992, pp. 54–61.
3. *New York Times*, 18 April 1992, p. 6.
4. *New York Newsday*, 19 August 1992, p. 5.
5. Richard Dyer, *Stars* (London: British Film Institute, 1979); hereafter cited in text.
6. *Time*, 31 August 1992, p. 60.
7. *The Philadelphia Inquirer*, Sunday, 22 August 1992, p. G8.
8. Roy Schafer, "Narration in the Psychoanalytic Dialogue," in *On Narrative*, ed. W. J. T. Mitchell. (Chicago: University of Chicago Press, 1980), p. 34.
9. *New York Newsday*, 20 August 1992, p. 6.
10. *Newsweek*, 31 August 1992, p. 57.
11. *Vanity Fair*, November 1992, p. 295.
12. *Vanity Fair*, November 1992, p. 295.
13. *Philadelphia Inquirer*, Sunday, 22 August 1993, p. G8.
14. *New York*, 21 September 1992, p. 60.
15. *New York Post*, 13 January 1993, p. 5.
16. *Philadelphia Inquirer*, Sunday, 22 August 1993, p. G8.
17. *Time*, 31 August 1992, p. 55.
18. *Rolling Stone*, 16 September 1993, p. 45.
19. *Rolling Stone*, 1 October 1992, p. 72.
20. Christine Gledhill, "Signs of Melodrama." In *Stardom*, ed. Christine Gledhill. (New York: Routledge, 1991), p. 213.
21. *America*, 10 October 1992, p. 255.
22. *Rolling Stone*, 1 October 1992, p. 72.
23. Sue Walrond-Skinner, *The Dictionary of Psychotherapy* (New York: Routledge and Kegan Paul, 1986), p. 102; hereafter cited in text.
24. *Macleans*, 21 September 1992, p. 53.
25. *Commonweal*, 23 October 1992, p. 18.

26. *Nation*, 19 October 1992, p. 447.

27. *The National Review*, 19 October 1992, p. 57.

28. Peter Brooks, "The Idea of a Psychoanalytic Literary Criticism," *Critical Inquiry*, vol. 13 (Winter 1987), p. 2; hereafter cited in text.

29. Sigmund Freud, "The Dynamics of Transference," (London: Hogarth Press, 1958), *Standard Edition*, vol. 12 (1912), p. 106. (Trans. by James Strachey).

30. "An Autobiographical Study," (London: Hogarth Press, 1959), *Standard Edition*, vol. 20 (1924), p. 42.

31. Sigmund Freud, "The Dynamics of Transference." *Standard Edition*, vol. 12 (1912), p. 106.

32. Norman Holland, "Unity Identity Text Self," in *Reader-Response Criticism*, edited by Jane Tompkins (Baltimore: Johns Hopkins University Press, 1980), p. 125.

33. Donald P. Spence, *Narrative Truth and Historical Truth*, (New York: W. W. Norton, 1982), p. 30.

34. Robert S. Wallerstein, "Forward," in *Narrative Truth and Historical Truth*, Donald P. Spence, (New York: W. W. Norton, 1982), p. 11.

35. Sigmund Freud, *Dora: Fragment of an Analysis of a Case of Hysteria* (New York: Macmillan, 1963), p. 27; hereafter cited in text.

The Dissolution of the Self in *Zelig*

RICHARD FELDSTEIN

THOSE ACQUAINTED with contemporary critical thought know of Jacques Lacan's reinterpretation of Freudian theory. Perhaps the central revision of French Freud comes in Lacan's famous essay on the "Mirror Stage," which posits that when a child peers into the looking-glass for the first time, s/he sees an inverted image and falsely takes this reflection as the first illustration of a unified self-concept (Laplanche 250–252). In this process of identification, the child experiences itself as a unity, and this perceptual transformation, brought about through the visual projection of the self, is but an approximation that establishes a false value system based on a notion of the self as individuated entity. In other words, Lacan thinks instances of self-discovery and self-recovery are ironic acts because the child, whose motor incapacity and fragmented, disjointed self-image dominate the first 6 to 18 months, finds in its reflection a fictional totality based on an idealization whose boundaries are filled in by the process of projective formulation. Moreover, the irony of this first illusion is that it colors, in the biased light of projection, all subsequent experiences because it casts the self in terms of the other. Thus, from this first fictional moment of primary identification, the child can never know itself as inseparable from others, as s/he is bound to a mirroring self-reflexivity indivisible from culturally mediated images.

With Lacan's theory in mind we can see that Woody Allen, long known for recreating psychoanalytic motifs in his films, takes a Lacanian perspective when having the central character of his 1984 movie, *Zelig*, use the process of identification to ape the other. But Allen takes Lacan's ironic concept a step further when he has Leonard Zelig not only identify with but actually metamorphose himself into a clone of his desired object. Tabbed "the changing man," Zelig becomes, among other things, a Frenchman when surrounded by two Frenchmen, an Oriental when in Chinatown, a fat man when in the company of those who are overweight, and a bearded replica of a Rabbi when with Orthodox Jews. In one fictional account, F. Scott Fitzgerald notes that an aristocrat by the name of "Leon Sellwin or Zellman" spoke adoringly "in an upper class Bostonian accent" of Calvin Coolidge and the Republicans; an hour later Fitzgerald is flabbergasted to find the same man professing to be a Democrat while speaking with the kitchen help in the "coarse accent" of the man in the street. Watching Zelig's magical metamorphosis, the American novelist is for once at a loss for words. In another account of the "human chameleon," a black waiter named Calvin Turner explains how he spotted a tough-looking white gangster, a stranger who had never frequented this speakeasy in Chicago, mysteriously disappear just when his double, a black trumpet player, appears on stage and begins "playing black." At the end of Turner's account, the screen is split by two pictures of Zelig: one of a cleanshaven, white gangster and the other of a black musician with a moustache.

The most extended example of Zelig's fantastic powers comes in his analysis with Eudora Fletcher, his psychoanalyst. Together they explore his prehistory and the resulting repercussions from the unique mental disorder that developed during his childhood. We learn that Zelig is the product of a broken marriage, and this disruptive circumstance causes him to readjust to life with a stepmother whom he detests and a father who tells him on his deathbed that "life is a meaningless nightmare of suffering, and [his] only advice . . . is to save string." While alive, however, Zelig's sadistic parents enjoy persecuting their children: "when anti-Semites bully Leonard, his parents invariably take the side of his anti-Semitic tormentors." If Leonard should disobey them, he is thrown into a darkened closet; "when [his parents] are really angry, they get into the closet with him." Leonard's brother beats him, Leonard's sister beats his brother, and eventually brother Jack has a nervous breakdown and sister Ruth becomes a shoplifter and alcoholic. Only Leonard seems to escape unscathed, but then he begins reacting to potentially threatening situations by transforming himself in trance states he cannot recall once awake.

Given this psychobiography, Dr. Fletcher is faced with finding a cure for a man who "distorted himself beyond measure" when becoming "a cipher, a nonperson, a performing freak" in order to "fit in, to belong, to go unseen, to be loved." In Zelig's analysis, he mimes his analyst, pretends Dr. Fletcher is the analysand, and forces her to revise her strategy. Thereupon she comes upon the brilliant technique of forcing Zelig to see himself while in a trance state. By mirroring Zelig's most prominent trait to him—his use of the identificatory process—Fletcher enables Zelig to mime a self-image from which he has sought escape. Because Fletcher tells Zelig that she is a charlatan, a quack pretending to be a psychoanalyst, he recognizes himself in her depiction of a *poseur*. Equally as important, he accomplishes this feat while in the trance state. In this manner Fletcher helps Zelig join dissociated aspects of himself, and because of this breakthrough he is more cooperative with his doctor, who is finally able to hypnotize her patient with little resistance from him. Able to penetrate below the seething surface of consciousness to the mainstream of unconscious representation, Zelig finally acknowledges why he had become the "changing man": "It is safe to be like others," he states. "I want to be liked." While in this hypnotic state, however, an unexpected development occurs when Leonard declares his love for Eudora Fletcher. Although this first gesture of endearment brings no like response, eventually doctor and patient do marry. In a wry summarizing statement on the conclusion of Zelig's analysis, F. Scott Fitzgerald ignores the adeptness of Fletcher's therapeutic strategies while focusing instead on the interpersonal relationship between doctor and patient: "In the end it was not the approbations of many, but the love of one woman that changed his life" and allowed Zelig to overcome his psycho-physical malady.

From a Lacanian perspective, Zelig's problem originates in the *meconnaissance* experienced when perceiving in his mirror image an other who reflects back a sense of permanence, substantiality, and identity ("Aggressivity" 15). For in the mirror stage, out of a shifting field of *gestalten* emerges an icon of the ego's unity, which allows for a feeling of satisfaction from the ego's integration of the fragmented self associated with the symbiotic, pre-narcissistic phase of development. But this satisfaction is based on an idealized model of integration, a primary identification that serves as a basis for all secondary identifications. In this primary identification, when the specular I conceives itself as a social I, the object of human desire becomes essentially an object desired by someone else (Lacan, "Mirror" 5). This mediation image is the illusion Zelig mistakes as real, for in subsequent secondary identifications, he confesses repeatedly his resolve to avoid rivalries with others by introjecting their images and chameleonically replicating himself. These secondary identifications with the rival, then, "are prepared for . . . by a primary identification [in the mirror stage] that structures the subject as a rival with himself" ("Aggressivity" 22).

Lacan's ideas on the identificatory process were anticipated by G.W.F. Hegel in *The Phenomenology of Spirit*. In this treatise he explains that "self-consciousness is faced by another self-consciousness [that] . . . has come *out of itself*" (Hegel's emphasis, 111). Moreover, Hegel notes a twofold significance associated with his notion of alienation and self-consciousness: "First, it has lost itself, for it finds itself as an other being; secondly, in doing so it has superseded the other, for it does not see the other as an essential being but in the other sees its own self" (111). This narcissistic tendency of seeing the other as a simulacrum indissociable from the self is the malady that leads to an endless reduplication from which Zelig's hybrid is constituted. Consequently, Leonard discounts himself and takes the ego of the other as the locus of truth while simultaneously directing his desire toward a nonbeing, "another Desire, another greedy emptiness, another I" (Kojeve 39–40). In this way he indissociably entwines himself with the other and seeks to learn, through the process of identification, its desired object so that he can even imitate it.[1] In time, however, most of us must renounce this tactic because of the paternal prohibition associated with the Oedipal phase, when the "law" is introjected. But as Eudora Fletcher finds out, Zelig has remained arrested in a regressed state of object relations since his habitual reaction to conflict has been so extreme: to enjoin himself ineffectually to others in a series of fantastic materializations. Thus, Zelig's case seems irremediable until Dr. Fletcher discovers a means of yoking fragments and transforming this repository of diverse personae from a toady who accommodates others by becoming a microcosm of the mimicked object to a being with a discernible historical dimension.[2]

THE VARIABILITY OF SOCIETAL OPINION

Taking place in the Jazz Age, Woody Allen's *Zelig* is not only a fantastic story of one man's metamorphoses, but also a condemnation of capricious societal opinion. First and foremost, Zelig's is a story of one man's hypnotic effect on American spectatorial consciousness. In the beginning of his documentary, when Zelig is brought to Manhattan Hospital for observation, he instantly becomes a curiosity piece. In a later stage of the film, when Ruth Zelig, Leonard's half-sister, and Martin Geist, her lover and an ex-carnival promoter, remove Zelig from the hospital to begin a series of tours, he is billed as "the phenomenon of the ages" and becomes grist for the publicity mill that Geist puts into motion. Promoted by this consummate capitalist, Zelig finds the public buying pens, charms, dolls, clocks, toys and earmuffs, all of which sport his image. Even a new Charleston-like dance craze called "The Chameleon" entrances the public, who buy such hit records as "You May Be Six People But I Love You," "Leonard the Lizard," and "Reptile Eyes." Aware of people's insatiable appetite for any promotional gimmick associated with "The Changing Man," Geist arranges an endless series of exhibitions that take the tour, among other places, to Hollywood, the White House, and the Continent, where L'Homme Cameleon charms the fascinated French public. The tour ends only when Martin Geist kills Ruth Zelig and her lover, Louis Martinez, before turning the gun on himself.

After the dissolution of this love triangle, Zelig disappears for an extended period before he is found imitating a clergyman on a balcony with Pope Pious XI. Outraged Italian authorities waste little time in extraditing the impostor to America, where he is readmitted to Manhattan Hospital before being re-entrusted to Dr. Fletcher's care at her house in the country; there, doctor and patient begin the famous "White Room Sessions" which eventually lead to Zelig's cure and his declaration of love for Fletcher. No longer beset with a psycho-physical malady, Zelig publicly acknowledges his debt to his psychoanalyst and both are celebrated nationally—given the key to New York City, invited to a special banquet where Fletcher exchanges ideas with the medical elite and taken to San

Simeon at the request of newspaper mogul William Randolph Hearst to enjoy the company of, among others, Jimmy Walker, Delores Del Rio and Charlie Chaplin. Explaining this red-carpet treatment, John Morton Blum, historian and author of the fictitious book *Interpreting Zelig*, notes that the American public found in him a "symbol of possibility, of self-improvement, of self fulfillment." In other words, America, the great melting pot, fell in love with a man who projected an image of its own desire for transformation. Lacan speaks about this phenomenon in "The Freudian Thing" when remarking on the "cultural ahistoricism peculiar to the United States of America," a position against which he rails because it produces a societal stance split off from its own historicity (115). Americans throw accolades at Zelig because he mirrors their desire to escape from obsessions that bind them to predictable behavioral patterns. Above all, besides happiness in matters of love, Americans long for upper mobility, fame, and fortune. By being the quintessential symbol of adaptability, Zelig helps to perpetuate the notion that the American dream is achievable.

As long as Zelig is unsuccessful in his endeavors, he projects himself as an icon with a temporal dimension indicating the possibility of changing one's circumstances. But once Zelig fails to live up to Judeo-Christian moral standards he meets with the same approbation as did Richard Nixon, who was alternately prized and spurned by an American public that preferred not to be confronted with the image of itself as an unethical society. Zelig tumbles from power when Lita Fox steps forth to accuse him publicly of having married her and abandoned her and their baby. As soon as a precedent is set, others come forward to divulge that Leonard Zelig, while in a dissociated trance state, libeled himself for acts of bigamy, adultery, automobile accidents, household and/or property damages, negligence, plagiarism and "unnecessary dental extractions." For these actions he is sued and must take to the air waves to apologize to his many victims. To the Tropman family in Detroit he explains, "I never delivered a baby before in my life, and I just thought that ice tongs was the way to do it."

Feeling betrayed that Zelig has become a sign of dissolution, the American public dispossesses him. Like the body rejects unwanted toxins, he is cast off on a propellent of vituperative prose:

> America is a moral country; it's a God-fearing country. We don't condone scandals, scandals of fraud and polygamy. In keeping with a pure society, I say lynch the little Hebe.

At this stage in the film, Zelig represents an image of dissolution in several ways: as the "termination or destruction by breaking down" of the subject in the process of identification and as the "loss of restraint, esp. in moral behavior" (*Webster's* 657) Because he has become a symbol of excess and its defiance of the "law," the public feels uneasy with his projection of corporeal boundarilessness, or, in other words, with the lack of socio-cultural limits set on the possibilities for transformation. Whereas previously the public wanted only release from quotidian circumstances, now, taking into consideration Zelig's unchecked immoral proclivities, they busy themselves delineating the boundaries of self and other and thereby disengaging and distinguishing themselves from the uncanny images of Zelig with which they once identified.

Unable to accept being thought of as a social pariah, Zelig disappears again, this time for a period of such duration that the public all but forgets him. Eudora Fletcher, however, continues to search for him, and, after much time and effort, she discovers the "little Hebe" in a movie newsreel featuring pictures of Hitler and members of the Nationalist Socialist Party in Germany. According to Saul Bellow, when Zelig was faced with the American public's outrage for his immoral behavior, he sought "immersion in the mass anonymity, and Fascism offered Zelig that kind of opportunity so that he could make something anonymous of himself by belonging to the Nazi movement." Just as he had become a papist after his first mysterious disappearance from public view, so now Zelig identifies with the aggressor when positioning himself within Hitler's inner circle. According to Lacan, this type of identification can be traced to the mirror stage and a behavioral pattern called "transitivism," in which "the child who strikes another says that he has been struck; the child who sees another fall, cries" ("Aggressivity" 19). Because of the fusion Zelig experiences in this regressed, trance stage, he can become a Nazi and treat himself as if he were his own enemy; in this manner, Zelig simultaneously denies his own existence while expressing the masochistic transference of the "slave" from a sadistic position of the "master." Only when he actually sees Eudora Fletcher in the hall where Hitler is speaking does he awaken from his trance state and the dissociation that produced his Nazi personality.

As quickly as Zelig is branded an anathema, he is forgiven by mainstream America, which delights in his having embarrassed Hitler on stage, evaded an S.S. battalion who were unhappy with his display of "*schweinhund Israeli* behavior," and commandeered a plane to escape Nazi Germany with Eudora Fletcher. When she faints, commanding a stolen aircraft, Zelig pilots the plane to a transatlantic speed record while flying upside down. Commenting on the inconstancy of American public opinion at this point in Zelig's history, Irving Howe remembers that "For a time everyone loved him and then people stopped loving him; and then he did this stunt, you know, with the airplane, and then everyone loved him again; and that is what the 20s were like and when you think about it, has America changed so much." While being awarded the Medal of Honor by the President of the United States for his patriotism, Zelig himself exclaims proudly, "But I had never flown before and it shows just exactly what you can do if you're a total psychotic." Yet we must keep in mind that no matter which commentator voices an opinion in the film, all are fictitious mouthpieces who lip-synch Woody Allen's script. Even the documentary itself is an elaborate imitation done in black and white to simulate a typical documentary of the twenties and thirties. Technically speaking, *Zelig* is a mock replica which doubles the main character's use of the identificatory process; given this context, the host of commentators—Sontag, Fitzgerald, Turner, Bell, Bellow, Howe, Fletcher or Zelig—finally present a composite picture of events that calls attention to itself as a metalinguistic play between view and viewed and invites, as the screen of our projections, our own *meconnaissance*.

Notes

1. He would emulate the child's solution to loving the mother: "The demand for love can only suffer from a desire whose signifier is alien to it. If the desire of the mother *is* the phallus, then the child wishes to be the phallus so as to satisfy this desire" (Lacan, Feminine 83).

2. For a detailed discussion on Hegel and Lacan see both Edward S. Casey's and J. Melvin Woody's "Hegel, Heidegger, Lacan: The Dialectic of Desire" and Wilfried Ver Eecke's "Hegel as Lacan's Source for Necessity in Psychoanalytic Theory," which appear in *Interpreting Lacan*.

Works Cited

Allen, Woody, screenwriter, *Zelig*. Orion, 1984.

Gove, Philip Babcock, ed. *Webster's Third New International Dictionary of Language*. Massachusetts: G. & C. Merriam, 1976.

Heel, G.W.F. *The Phenomenology of Spirit* (1807). Trans. A.V. Miller. Oxford: Oxford UP, 1977.

Kojeve, A. *Introduction to the Reading of Hegel: Lectures on "The Phenomenology of Spirit."* Ed. Allan Bloom. Ithaca: Cornell UP, 1980.

Lacan, Jacques. "Aggressivity in Psychoanalysis," *Ecrits: A Selection*. Trans: Alan Sheridan. New York: Norton, 1977.

Lacan, Jacques. "The Freudian Thing," *Ecrits: A Selection*. Trans. Alan Sheridan. New York: Norton, 1977.

Lacan Jacques. "The Mirror Stage as Formative of the Function of the I," *Ecrits: A Selection*. Trans. Alan Sheridan. New York: Norton, 1977.

Lacan, Jacques. *Feminine Sexuality*. Trans. Jacqueline Rose. Eds. Juliet Mitchell and Jacqueline Rose. New York: Norton, 1982.

Laplanche, J., and J.B. Pontalis. *The Language of Psycho-Analysis*. Trans. Donald Nicholson-Smith. New York: Norton, 1973.

Smith, Joseph H., and William Kerrigan, eds. *Interpreting Lacan*. New Haven: Yale UP, 1983.

Zelig According to Bakhtin

RUTH PERLMUTTER

ACCORDING TO Russian literary theorist M. M. Bakhtin, parody's primary target, the disruption of accepted social dicta, is accomplished by heteroglossia, an interaction of contending social discourses—the languages, ideologies, and individual speech types that characterize different social classes, occupations, belief systems, and geographic regions. To Bakhtin, the most effective dialogic discourse is autocritique performed by a character who lives according to literature (e.g., Don Quixote and Madame Bovary) or who, like Proust, is writing a novel within a novel, thus exposing both the process of making fiction and the reality pretensions of single-line fiction.[1]

In its appropriation of other cinematic texts and modes, in its transgression of their sacred intent, and in its translation of heroes and heroic acts into a demythifying parody of the Hollywood star complex and the viewer, Woody Allen's *Zelig* exemplifies Bakhtin's views on autocritical parody. A reflection on author-to-character-to-viewer relationship, *Zelig* is *within* and *about* cinematic mythology—the audience's need for heroes (stars) and for transparent filmic "as if" reality. Nowhere else in Allen's work do we witness as clearly the intentional counterpoint of multiple systems of discourse (which Bakhtin calls hybridization), that is, the interposition of author with character (Allen is Leonard Zelig); the expectations of comic style and persona from previous films such as his gag structures and erudite intellectual jargon; his ideological framework as a New York Jew converted to psychoanalysis and, particularly, his self-consciousness about movies *and* comedy.[2] Allen's protagonists (mostly played by himself) are also typically from show biz and/or movies. Thus, as a comic star, author, or agent, and always an insatiable movie buff who plunders and parodies previous comics, he is forever playing with what Bakhtin calls the author's "as if" relationship to the "represented event" he stands outside of while at the same time representing it. He also makes his presence felt with "tangential" authorial asides (sequence changes, outlandish stories, inside jokes) that elicit active decoding by viewers.[3]

His most consistent reflexive strategy has been the tension between his self-berating position as a schlemiel, his star status (in and out of his films), and the autocritique of this status. He expresses it in *Zelig* by assuming the role of Leonard Zelig, a freakstar of the 1920s, whose celebrity status depends on his ability to transform himself and whose metamorphic nature permits him to parody himself and real events through different styles and voices.[4]

A film about a media freak, *Zelig* reactualizes multiple media modes,[5] like newsreels, home movies, the documentary, Hollywood melodrama, movie-fan crazes, and the 1920s-style song and dance clichés of vaudeville and musical theater.[6] Structure and character thus not only serve a dual interactive narrative function, to dialogize real and invented selves within embedded reflexive forms, but they also reveal the essence of Allen's struggle with author as character as star.

The narrative structure, plot, comic action, and editing principles of *Zelig* rest on the changeability of its principal (imaginary) figure, Leonard Zelig. As a "schlemelion," Zelig incarnates Bakhtin's notion of double-voiced style. He moves facilely among numerous voice, speech, and image zones. He is not just the auteur playing an ordinary fictional character; he is inserted into actual events and accounts of the 1920s: F. Scott Fitzgerald writes about him, contemporary cultural moguls like Sontag, Bellow, and Bettelheim recall him as a familiar icon of that age. He is integrated into popular songs ("You're the tops, you're Leonard Zelig," by Cole Porter) and dances (the "Chameleon" dance), is edited into actual newsreels, and parodying the crazes associated with Chaplin, he is the inspiration for lunatic fads and paternity/libel suits.[7] An incarnation of dialogism, his body accommodates to different belief systems and societal hierarchies. He can change color, time, space, and dialect. True to an essential comic mode grounded in double-voiced discourse—metamorphosis—Zelig embodies the comic's ability to defy natural and physical laws with his body distortions. He can swell, dislocate, and forever adapt.[8]

Zelig's changes reveal the underlying dematerialization anxieties that first prompted his contortions. These stem in part from a pandemic sexual crisis: to prove masculinity, he must surmount his single-voiced state, hysteria-ridden narcissism, and onanistic sexual preoccupations (note the references to masturbation) by becoming multiple *male* subjects.[9] When he finally falls in love with his psychiatrist, he sheds his many incarnations and free-floating (mal)adaptability and moves toward a societally more acceptable single identity, heterosexual monogamy, that is, so-called normality.

In Bakhtinian terms, the guilts and moral consciousness that promote Zelig's multiple personalities and male crisis are resolved when he achieves the Hollywood happy ending. In other words, when he marries the shiksa who is also, handily, his psychiatrist, there is both narrative harmony (the dialogic voices of Zelig are stilled into a single-voiced unity) and sexual resolution, which presumably solves his masturbatory inclinations and defuses the ethnic guilt of assimilation.[10]

The dialogic principle of *Zelig* rests on its accumulation of parodic speech types and irreverent language styles, which Bakhtin calls the heteroglossic exposure of the ceremonious and pompous tones of the "professional," such as academic and medical jargon.[11] The unreal Zelig is authenticated by interviews with real intellectuals such as Saul Bellow and Susan Sontag. These scholars represent Allen's pantheon of household gods, his personal Sanhedrin, called from Mount Zion to witness Zelig's authenticity, and as is their wont, they deliver problematic testimony. They describe him by parodying their own scholarly predilections. Sontag, a noted modernist, characteristically describes him as an aesthetic triumph, while Irving Howe, a scholar of Jewish life, considers him an "extreme product of assimilation in the American Jewish experience."

True to Bakhtin's notion that parody provides release from the self-congratulatory unctuousness to which the professional elite are prone, the medical establishment gets its share of ridicule. Diagnoses are derided when the pompous doctor who announces that Zelig will die of a brain tumor is himself struck down by one. Zelig's and Fletcher's swapping of psychiatrist-patient roles blurs while mocking psychiatrists' cherished distinction between therapist and neurotic. In fact, Zelig adopts the mannerisms of psychiatry so successfully that Dr. Fletcher mistakes him for a doctor. "He had such a professional demeanor," she states. The parody of the empty pretensions of officialdom deepens not only when Fletcher pretends to be his patient, suffering his ailment, but also when some ordinary citizen says in a street interview, "I wish I could be Leonard Zelig." Thus, role exchanges, character doublings, and the ability or the desire to be someone else provide endless satiric involutions of the banality of academic vanity as well as character logic in a nonfiction fiction. Zelig appropriates institutional discourse while critiquing its duplicity and filmic conventionality.

As a part of the heteroglossic parody of "authentic" as well as "official" voices, it would seem significant that the first time we actually hear Zelig's voice is in a taped interview, where he refers to himself as a psychiatrist. Until then, his character is described in newsreels, in songs, and by others. The fact that his voice is not heard directly until half the movie is over, and, again, pretending to be a psychiatrist, making jokes about fees and his advanced course in masturbation, reinforces his "ghostly" metamorphic sensibility as a fantasy and as an impostor.

While the ideological voices throughout the film paradoxically document the existence of a fantasy, they simultaneously undermine the traditional mechanisms for the authentication of real events and people. The use of an offscreen commentator in the style of a Movietone News narration and the mixture of actual newsreels and interviews along with staged interviews that span the 1920s to the 1980s create "a conscious anachronism or conscious incorporation of a stylized world with the contemporary," one of Bakhtin's ways of describing parodic stylization.[12] The effect is to put into question the authority and the ideological premises of the "truth" genres: the talk show interview, the "documentation" of history on film, the authenticity of newsreel footage. In effect, Allen is altering what Bakhtin calls the "horizon of expectations" of a genre. In restaging the talk show interview in its audacity at "inventing" a public personality, he reexamines the entire realm of the artifice of cinema/television and radio before it. The preinvented characters in *Zelig* are interviewed in color in 1983 looking back at the time they made "news" in the 1920s in grainy black-and-white newsreel format. Dr. Fletcher's mother, in an interview, criticizes her own husband and daughter, thus reversing celebrity pretensions to a glamorous life-style, while exposing the fraudulence of the staged realism of talk show programs and of *Zelig* itself.

Underlying the critique of multiple modes, professional languages, and hallowed belief systems is a specific parody of Warren Beatty's *Reds*, the Hollywood saga of John Reed, the American eyewitness reporter of the Russian Revolution. In Bakhtin's terms, *Reds* is mainly a unitary and canonized form of discourse. In its one parodic innovation—the appearances of aging leftists as corroborators of Reed's existence—"real" people are talking about a "real" person they knew. The interviewees in *Zelig*, however, dialogically validate the reality and reputation of Zelig by talking about an invented character as if real, while also parodying their own rhetorical styles.

Allen's assault on *Reds* reaches virulent proportions in the embedded parody of an overblown Hollywood melodrama that replays Zelig's life. Called *The Changing Man* (1935, Warners Bros.), it mimics the attempt in *Reds* with its blend of live interviews and melodramatic love story, to make fiction look like history. Moreover, the sequence in *The Changing Man* where the Dr. Fletcher character scours the world in search of the missing Zelig, mocks the excessive nature of Louise Bryant's frantic trek across the ice in Finland in search of John Reed. It could be assumed that Allen's submerged rivalry with Beatty, who appropriated his girl friend, Diane Keaton, for his own bedmate and co-star and who, with *Reds*, took almost all the Academy Awards in 1981 (as *Annie Hall* did in 1977), influenced the conception of *The Changing Man*. The parody of *Reds*, both as fictional documentary and historical melodrama, indicates how much Allen, in Bakhtinian terms, refracts his personal interests "through another's speech in another's language,"[13] thereby exposing the paradox of invention and the "factitious" nature of pretensions to "truth" in movies.

Zelig's parodies of the "truth" genres—documentary reporting and the fictionalizing of history in melodrama—reaccentuate (Bakhtin's word for textual innovation and restatement) the process in classical film construction of creating a plausible "as if" real world. Through an excessive manipulation of continuity editing logic and through refraction (the passage of a voice through various speech or ideological zones) of a character into multiple registers, *Zelig* both embodies and ironically defies the notion that a central consciousness can singly carry and instigate the course of events.

The apparent moral center of the film, moving from self-doubt to self-revelation and the resolution of his fictive credibility, Zelig only exists by the manipulations of montage. Modally and metaphorically, Zelig slides across the frame as a multiple signifier of the banality of cinematic reconstitution. Literally "built" through editing, Zelig is *the* motivated line, *the* carrier of motion and emotion, *the* example of how a character becomes a metonymic linear structuring device in classical movies (since their inception).

On one hand, Zelig's uncanny ubiquity challenges the foolish consistency of trapping a central figure within a single-line discourse. The film thus interrogates the classical method of wooing the audience with the logic of sequential flow, progress toward closure, and other structures that propel invested characters along a narrative trajectory.[14] On the other hand, the redistribution of this omniscience, not only among posited authors (newscasters, interviewees) who attest to Zelig's magical existence, but also in the assumed shapes that he verifies before our eyes, reveals an underlying motivation: the use of such distortions as a device for self-protection from betrayal by the fickle idolatry of the viewer. Shedding his own substance in an *apparently* involuntary accommodation to the public's desire for and identification with a hero and/or star, Zelig *becomes* its monstrous product. By assuming all the ridiculous roles dictated by the viewer, he pillories the insidious power of public acclaim. This strikes at the heart of Hollywood's most enduring myth—the Pygmalionesque creation/construction of the hero/star—and thereby interrogates the Frankensteinian nature of viewer involvement in movies, the phenomenon of the monster that is controlled or ultimately destroyed by its creator.[15]

Zelig's passage through stages of angst, self-doubt, and miraculous "heroic" feats, all of Zelig's adventures—attending a Hitler rally, crossing the Atlantic upside down, not to mention his body magic skills—are mock-heroic: the epitome of Bakhtin's descriptions of the way the comic novel desacralizes and repositions the traditional pieties of the heroic ordeal. Cinematically, Zeligism *is* refraction in the sense that a divided and reflected existence reaccents the star-crazed "hysteria" that underlies the classical text.

Beneath this formal restatement of Hollywood's "dogmatic pretensions to lead a real life"[16] are the syllogistic reversals (stars and viewers are all freaks) that were already evident in the parodic involutions of *Stardust Memories*. Both *Zelig* and *Stardust Memories* revile viewers for their blindness to the magical qualities of film and the sanctity of the Holy Fools that make them.

Long before *Zelig* (even in his first film, *What's Up Tiger Lily*, where Allen plays a Sherlock, Jr.-like projectionist whose shadow making love on screen interferes with the image track), the idea of Zeligism provided Allen with a major parodic device for escaping fictional containment within the cinematic frame.[17] He yearns to "be" like someone else (Bogey), to be elsewhere (Kugelmass), to be a revolutionary (*Bananas*), and, literally, to get out of his own skin. *Zelig* itself compounds its Zeligism: in an effort to cure the changing man, Dr. Fletcher pretends to be Leonard's patient, with his ailment. In a public television interview, a man on the street wistfully says, "I wish I could be Leonard Zelig." Echoing these Zelig-like anxieties in the preface to his autobiographical play, *The Floating Light Bulb*, Allen flatly states that the author's "one regret in life is that he is not someone else."[18]

The whimsy of his vicarious longings allows Allen as Zelig to critique cinema from within—as a "filmic" man who is created by the invention of self and film. As in Bakhtin's view of autocritique, Zeligism exposes the limitations of character/actor and author/narrator status within a film. A creation of the editing room, Zelig defies spatial logic and continuity as well as his own reality. His changeability is a reflection of the dreamlike quality of film. Like Keaton's Sherlock, Jr., and Vertov's the "Man with a Movie Camera," Zelig's transports into many fantasized selves represent an autocritical demonstration of the artifice in staging the illusion of reality.

The overdeterminism of Zelig—his presence as the epitome of narrative excess—derives in part from his "Bovarism,"[19] which creates realms of parody from the infinite regression of self-consciousness. Just as in Allen's short story "The Kugelmass Episode," where the protagonist wishes himself into Emma Bovary's salon, Zelig's interventions reveal the deception of fictional logic. The shifts between Zelig as a comic performer (sic: freak) and as a literalization of Allen's dematerialization anxieties are true to Bakhtin's view of "double-accented double-styled hybrid construction,"[20] where the author's views are merged with his character's belief system while also reflecting the novel's collective voice, the "ideological world of speaking persons."[21] This explains why it is significant that long before we hear Zelig's voice, even indirectly on a tape, we hear about him in the canonized tones of public opinion.[22] The true filmic man, Zelig has dissolved himself into the text, merged with others, and only lives according to the conventions and artifices of cinema.

Zelig according to Bakhtin suggests that Bakhtin's insights about parody are not only relevant but may be central to the modernist mode of cinema. Bakhtin's notions of autocritique, mutually interactive (dialogic) texts, and the "carnivalesque" (outrage against official culture) are consonant with modernist themes: the challenging of authority from social hierarchies to textual illusionism itself; the assertion that the reconstituted self is the only reality; that citational works are the only texts and irony the only appropriate contemporary posture.

Zelig's modernism stems from a tension between the regressive narcissism implicit in self-creation and a distinctly adversarial and antinostalgic tonality. What remains is a text that challenges the spectator with an invented compositional protagonist. If Zelig's self-cancellations turn against celebrity cultism and the spectator's credulity in Hollywood's conquest of reality by fantasy, they also mock the heavy-handed terminology of cultist interpretations. The excoriation of spectatorial competence crosses class lines—from the inadequacy of popular culture to satisfy the yearnings of the mass audience for stars and their fantasy life to derision of pronouncements by recognized cultural authorities.

Underlying Zelig's involutional conformities is a condemnation of the insidious results of narcissism and nostalgia, both cinematically and societally. As a formalist exercise in editing, Zelig's endless replacements attack the viewer's gullibilities. As social comment, the film *Zelig* connects self-conscious paranoia with the immorality implicit in accommodation. Zelig's anxiety over the American public's rejection leads him to an outrageous transformation into one of Hitler's claque. Not only is the humor compounded by such an unthinkable role for an American Jew but the tone of mock seriousness camouflages Allen's messianic impulse. Allen himself stated that the film was not a "pleasant fantasy of metamorphosis but about the kind of personality that leads to fascism."[23] This statement itself may be an inflated claim to seriousness in his comedy, but it does demonstrate his continuing preoccupation with guilt about the Holocaust.

Within the film, Bellow, as one of the pundits, interprets Zelig's Nazi switch as a means of satisfying a desire to become "anonymous," to "immerse himself in the mass," even a mass that promises his own destruction. This echoes Allen's implicit attack on the viewer masses that can applaud a "psychotic" act: "It shows you what you can do if you're psychotic," says Zelig, addressing the crowd that gives him ticker tape adulation on his return from Germany—with the implication that the crowd that adulates a psychotic is itself suspect.

Dialogism and autocritique as strategies underlying Zelig's changes and accommodations are extensions of Allen's ideological framework as an American-Jewish comic suffering "the ordeal of civility." As "the changing man," he wanders between guilt about abandoning the Jewish "ethic" for the Protestant "etiquette" and masturbatory self-analysis.[24] He is the Jew who dared to insert himself into culture and discovers that he also inherits a fictive reality and a morally corrupt world.

The dialogic mask of the freak, the exhibitionist, the *apparent* innocent, hides—as Bettelheim suggests in the film—the fact that Zelig is "the ultimate conformist."[25] Underlying his transformations and desire to be like others is Zelig's assimilation anxiety. Eager to be absorbed into the dominant culture, he epitomizes the dilemma of the American Jew who wants to change his ethnic envelope in order to be socially integrated. *Zelig*, then, sums up Allen's notions throughout his career: innocence, romance, nostalgia, morality have been betrayed. As an *apparently* self-hating Jewish comic, the loss of America as a locus of values is also laid at the door of ethnic collision with American consumer culture. Heir to the "immigrant culture shock" comics—Chaplin, the Marx Brothers—Zelig enacts the legacy of rootlessness and loss of patriarchal constraints (domesticity, monogamy, family loyalty) and becomes the victim as well as the perceiver of the contending voices that trouble the Western world.[26]

He uses the safety of the comic—vulgar taste, aggression, and antisocial behavior along with a confusion of genre registers and formal dislocations—to suggest that the crisis of the maker and the spectator to comedy is also the crisis of Jewishness and American culture. In the spirit of Amos who denounced his self-indulgent people as "the kine of Bashan," Allen is reviling Americans and Jews for their bad taste and capitulation to the superficial.

Never at home anywhere, yet struggling to reinvent a home in other shapes and forms, Zelig/Allen personifies Theodore Herzl's view that "an emancipated Jew lives in a ghetto of illusion." A creature ravaged by the pressure to succeed in America and by the impossible attempt to record truth in art or life, *Zelig* is Allen's most radical deconstruction of cinema— an acomedic lament.

The supreme filmic Bakhtinian parodist, Allen has entered Bakhtin's world through Ellis Island. The continuous argument underlying the multivoiced contentiousness of his life's *ordeals* has the structure and flavor of his Talmudic ancestors.

Allen's work can be considered a working-through of two poles of self-categorization. He subverts previous traditions and outmoded conventions of the cinematic canon in order to warn against the real dangers to society of easy accommodations in mediocrity. Yet he incorporates these within a "pleasant fantasy of metamorphosis," accompanied by running gags, movie-buffery, and movie-buffoonery that reveal his view of the malicious absurdity of reality.

In earlier films, his protagonists are like Sherlock, Jr.—innocent voluptuaries of Hollywood "romance," either receiving directives from a revered hero as in *Play It Again, Sam* or as a schlemiel whose self-hating worries covertly expose societal pretensions, as in *Manhattan*. Since 1980, with *Stardust Memories*, Allen's growing self-assurance has allowed him to express his ambivalence about the relationship between his comic muse and the moral turpitude of the public vampire. An investigation into the problematic nature of cinema "magic" interacts with the comic strategies of replacement and Allen's own brand of literalization, his Bovarist wit. Thus, his anachronistic self-insertion into official "sacred cows" blends with cinematic manipulation, the comic's ability to become someone else[27] and to question the nature and benevolence of reality itself.

In the two "rose" films that followed *Zelig* (*Broadway Danny Rose*, 1984; *Purple Rose of Cairo*, 1985),[28] Allen contends in a gentler vein with the public's star-crazes that prompt Zeligism in his protagonists. Pedagogically, he valorizes freaks who live in the grotesquerie of so-called normal reality and fantasize a world with "rose"-colored glasses. Instead of pillorying the process that creates public idols in *Zelig* and *Stardust Memories*, Allen lingers on the more redemptive aspects of literalization and the conquest of reality by cinema: his protagonists either choose a higher life-style as in *Danny* or an ideal narrative in which to be reborn as in *Purple Rose*. The title *Broadway Danny Rose* itself embeds a belief in transformation and the possibility for a modern "Ascension." Danny "Rose" has bloomed in the spiritual desert of Broadway. As a nurturer of many Zeligs yearning to be stars, he imbues his "nobodies" with his scriptural homiletics: "acceptance, forgiveness and love."[29]

Purple Rose makes a more definitive separation between the gloom of the real world and escapes to the simpler inadequacies of Hollywood, where true to the Bakhtinian exposure of cultural pieties, morally culpable stars captured within the screen are counterpointed with contemporary social reality—depression, cruelty, and the victimization of a Chaplinesque heroine. Only thin disguises for other Allen transplants (stand-up comics, theatrical agents, etc.), the character mutations in *Purple Rose* sustain the Allen spirit of the "filmic" comic—movie-buff, conjurer, inventor—who entertains the customers while picking the pockets of their accepted culture. Allen's (and Zelig's) presence flirts around the edges of a screen in which is embedded the paradox that not only are movies an escape from failed romance, deceptions, and harsh realities but they also reveal the sad vicariousness beneath the viewer's narcissistic identification. With a relief born of that sadness, we welcome the heroine's return to the protection of the "magic" movie house.

Zelig's quixotic challenges of societal tyrannies and his questioning of the benevolence of reality are harbingers of the redemptive pedagogy of *Danny Rose* and *Purple Rose*. After *Zelig*, we have no choice but to accompany Allen through Joyce's cracked mirror or Alice's magic mirror and enter the spiritual world of Danny or the magic world of early Hollywood movies, where Bakhtin's voices prevail.

If the persona of Zelig and the essence of Zeligism turn on the irony of accommodation, the film itself reflects on the transformative, ultimately duplicitous nature of film. Zelig, the comic subject, and *Zelig* the film, as metatext, encompass the paradox of parody. They are both self-engendering: Zelig spins identities out of himself like a caterpillar while the film strives to control both the subject, as character/author, *and* the narrative.

They are both also self-transgressive: humor and irony arise out of Zelig's violation of norms while he and the text incorporate and adapt to them.

If the author is both omnipresent and absorbed into the text, so is the viewer. *Zelig*'s hyperbolic editing style mocks our mythologies (Hollywood star-craze) and the modes and fictional universe that form our shared belief systems. In the end, the double-voiced parodic text incorporates us by demanding our competence as decoders of its forebears, while its manipulations and transgressions evaluate, indeed, lead us to question, our cultural mystifications.

Much of the humor in *Zelig* arises from the disruption of canonized formal and social forms. Zelig's shifting identity challenges and acts out the institutional modes of representation in social life and in cinema—at once central subject, hero, star, poseur, exemplar of the crisis of both his masculinity and ethnic assimilation, and, most particularly, the self-denigrating anticomic whose animus is finally directed at the impercipient and cannibalistic viewer.

In this inextricable cinematic embrace between the viewer's distortions and the characters' transformations to escape an unacceptable reality, Bakhtin and *Zelig* are also firmly wedded. The presumption lies in the creation of a character sutured together until whipped into shape in order to survive the culture and the rules of film. Thus, the innate contradiction in Zelig as an adaptive character and one who is trying to wrest control of his own narrative acknowledges and challenges the actorly and fictional traditions of a character contained within a continuity.

This character hybridization—Zelig as both a freak (societal deviant, exceptional man with a unique identity) and a conformist (i.e., one who has lost his identity) fed to the consuming public—reinforces Bakhtin's view that parody functions as a model barometer of the social self. Grounded in a dialogized interrogation of the cinematic mythmaking process—the "framing" of characters in the time and space of a Hollywood romance—*Zelig* exemplifies the parodic link between allusion to primary cinematic texts, formal binding consistencies, and social practices. For one, it disrupts the unity of character through temporal dialogization, à la *Citizen Kane*. An involuted critique of the reconstitution of a character within a parody of the *March of Time* parody of the reconstituted life of Kane, further dialogized in *Zelig* by the reconstitution of "real-life" characters as they would look today (in color) reliving their past relationship to Zelig (in black and white), puts into play the whole notion of the invention of a chronology of a life as-if-real, while it also reflects on the capricious nature of memory and history and their reconstruction. For another, *Zelig* reaccentuates the viewer-parody of Hollywood romance in *Sherlock, Jr.* (a primary text for Allen's parodies, from *What's Up, Tiger Lily* through *Purple Rose*). Zelig as an "impossible" character inserted within self-created "impossible" events and situations ends up catching "the girl of his dreams." The narrative is closed not only with the character's restoration to a single identity but also with a final irony: the proverbial happy ending suggests that "escape" has led to fictional conformity, à la *Sherlock, Jr.*

The film's epilogue plays with the tradition of Hollywood closure with a double entendre joke about endings. At the beginning of the film, Zelig lies about having read *Moby Dick* and suffers his first transformation (multiple self) and, paradoxically, his first wished-for conformity (single self). At the end of the film, it is stated that on his deathbed he confessed that he was in the middle of the book and his only regret was that he could not live long enough to find out how it ended, thereby reopening the Bakhtinian parody of filmic truth and Hollywood endings.

Notes

1. M. M. Bakhtin, *The Dialogic Imagination* (Austin: University of Texas Press, 1981). Bakhtin considers parody not a faddish paradigm but part of the fabric of social intercourse. To Bakhtin, the "most fundamental organizing idea" of the novel since its inception is the testing of heroes (for fidelity, martyrdom, valor, etc.). In parodic novels, the heroic discourse itself is on trial. Superimposed (dialogized) on the class-oriented speech of apparent "truth-bearing" characters (those who speak the "official languages" of the professions—law, church, medicine, etc.) is a parodic subtext of distortions. Thus, the fool's stupidity, the rogue's "gay deception," and the clown's masks question the verities embraced by "sacred" heroes. (Bakhtin, 291, 304, 311, 374, 388.)

2. Bakhtin calls this mechanism of author insertion and absorption among characters "direct authorial narration" (262).

3. When Bakhtin describes the structure of the novel, it is in the language of its making, that is, from the construction of the text *and* within it and its *represented* event. Thus, he describes how the "tangential" author (not represented directly in the diegesis, or as he calls it, in the "chronotype" of the work) makes his presence felt (with chapter headings, sequence changes, beginning/end expectations) to elicit the active creation of the work by its readers. He states, "We might put it as follows; before us are two events—the event that is narrated in the work and the event of narration itself (we ourselves participate in the latter, as listeners or readers)" (255).

4. Bakhtin calls this the stylization of oral everyday material (262).

5. Bakhtin calls this the stylization of written narration, that is, letters, diaries, and so forth, which in cinema extends to modal insertions—letters, signs, photos, paintings, TV screens, other movies, performance codes (262).

6. Linda Hutcheon, *A Theory of Parody* (New York: Methuen, 1985), 18, for her discussion of *Zelig*'s "cross-genre play" as a "cinematic parody of the television documentary and movie newsreel." She also points out that *Zelig* is a parody of *They Might Be Giants* (d. Anthony Harvey, 1971), where the protagonist believes he is Sherlock Holmes and is treated by a female psychiatrist named Dr. Watson. (110) In terms of intertextuality, *Zelig* has a long tradition behind it—of comic transformations and doubles—from Pagliacci, the clown (whom Zelig also becomes at one point), to Keaton's *Playhouse*.

7. See John McCabe, *Charlie Chaplin* (New York: Doubleday, 1978), 79, for a description of the Chaplin mania, such as Chaplin buttons and dances, like the "Chaplin Waddle," as well as similar paternity suits leveled against Chaplin.

8. Raymond Durgnat, *The Crazy Mirror: Hollywood Comedy and the American Image* (New York: Dell Publishing Co., 1969), 69. *Zelig* belongs to this comic tradition: the

"trucage" (trickery) of Melies, the double nature of Chaplin's persona, the defiance of the laws of continuity and spatial logic in the formulaic Hollywood "romance" in *Sherlock, Jr.*, the verbal anarchy of the Marx Brothers and their forebears. These have all thrived on the doubling strategies of mime, pose, mask, and self-display that underly their visual and verbal games of wit. The power of silent comedy derives from comic figures who defy natural and physical laws by virtue of the manipulations of cinema. According to Hutcheon (p. 51), the majority of theorists consider parody a subgenre of the comic because it usually holds its model up to ridicule. In Hutcheon's view, irony more than ridicule is a parodic principle, and especially in modernist metaparody, the tendency is to say something serious, positive (rather than just pejorative), and reverential (rather than just mocking). The strategies in *Zelig* certainly produce irony and serious explorationsof societal customs and institutions. The reverence comes in the homages to the magic of cinema.

9. Zelig can only change into other men. Cross-gendering has not been a parodic device for Allen.

10. Allen is also voicing an autobiographical litany of culpability in succumbing to American culture. He refashions his dependency on psychoanalysis to actual "transference"; he rewrites his real life love affair; he converts his own intermarriage discomfort into malaise about the false consciousness of Hollywood romance. By the outrageous insertion of a Hollywood romantic reunion at a Nazi rally with Zelig as a Nazi cohort, Allen even assuages his American Jewish guilt complex about being spared the Holocaust (c.f., the compulsion to see *The Sorrow and the Pity* over and over again in *Annie Hall*), while impaling both the Mephistophelian seduction of Hollywood and its grotesque offspring, the American dream.

11. See Bakhtin's *Little Dorrit* discussion, ibid., 302.

12. Ibid., 362.

13. Ibid., 324.

14. Bakhtin (p. 32) terms this "the impulse to continue" and "the impulse to end."

15. See William Nestrick, "Coming to Life: *Frankenstein* and the Nature of Film Narrative," *The Endurance of Frankenstein*, ed. George Levine and U. C. Knoepflmacher (Berkeley, Los Angeles, London: University of California Press, 1979), 290–316.

16. Bakhtin's (p. 414) description of the distortions of the classical novel.

17. One wonders if this highly comic device is an inverse reflection of Allen's ethnic discomfort and guilt, as in the scene when he mortifyingly and hilariously sees himself as a Hasid at Annie's grandmother's table.

18. Replacement strategies have been constants in Allen's work, and they extend not only to sexual fantasies but to the resolution of Allen's competition with and for women as well. In *Play It Again, Sam*, he loves his buddy's wife and surrenders her á la *Casablanca*. In *Manhattan*, while excoriating his adulterous buddy's immorality, he plays around with his girlfriend. *Stardust Memories* replays Allen's resentments toward his ex-girlfriend, Diane Keaton. Her persona is recast (by Charlotte Rampling) as an extreme neurotic. In *Broadway Danny Rose*, Danny plays John Alden and wins the girlfriend of his Italian singer client. Even *Hannah and her sisters* play musical beds with the Allen protagonist. He is replaced in his relationship with Hannah by a male who lusts after one of her sisters, while he (the Allen persona) ends up with the third.

19. For a more extensive discussion of Allen's Bovarism, see Maurice Yacowar, *Loser Take All* (New York: Frederick Ungar Publishing Co., 1979), 95.

20. Bakhtin, 304.

21. Bakhtin, 365.

22. The first time we actually hear his voice is in a taped interview, where he refers to himself as someone else, a psychiatrist. Until then, his character is described. His voice is not heard directly until half the movie is over, and there again he pretends to be a psychiatrist, making jokes about fees and his course in advanced masturbation.

23. Caryn James, "Auteur! Auteur!" *New York Times Magazine*, January 19, 1986, 25.

24. This argument is taken from John Murry Cuddihy's *The Ordeal of Civility* (New

York: Dell Publishing Co., 1974). See my discussion of the importance of Jewishness in Allen's works in my article "The Melting Pot and the Humoring of America: Hollywood and the Jew," *Film Reader* 5 (1982): 247–256.

25. In addition to connecting Zelig's physical changes to his desire "to be loved" and "to fit in," Hutcheon (p. 110) points out the ideological connection between his assimilation anxieties and the rise of Hitler and the Holocaust, which was directed against those who did not "fit."

26. Characteristically, Zelig's first changes reflect his assimilation duplicity. They occur because of his intellectual shame—he had to pretend he had read the great American novel, *Moby Dick*—and because he was not wearing green on St. Patrick's Day.

27. With replacement, comics are always becoming someone else—either by changing their body shapes or sexual identity (e.g., the infantilized contortions of Jerry Lewis) or by serving as victim of mechanical objects that run amok (in Buster Keaton's conversation gags, machines overpower him until he uses, indeed, "becomes," them for his survival).

28. The two films that followed *Zelig* also reaffirm the premodernist belief in the self-creative power of the imagination to alter reality. Romanticist devices of illumination—the magic lantern in *Midsummer* and the transmogrifying magic trick in *Floating Light Bulb*—actually mediate between grotesque reality and "lovable" freaks.

29. In terms of the comic strategies of replacement and the desire to enter the mainstream, Danny himself is a dialogic character. Conspicuously wearing a giant gold medallion with the Hebrew letter "chai," he is the Jewish John Alden. He acts as intermediary in his client's romance, and as a result, he not only gets the Italian shiksa but he also "converts" her from cynicism to his essentially religious philosophy. As a consequence, the "deli" ("stage" for the fabulation of Danny; its marquee opens and closes the film) where all the comics hang out, awards Danny his "Oscar." A symbolic testimony to the rewards of assimilation, a Jewish-Italian sandwich will bear his name.

Woody Allen's *The Purple Rose of Cairo* and the Genres of Comedy

ARNOLD W. PREUSSNER

A T FIRST glance, Woody Allen's *The Purple Rose of Cairo* seems like one of his more modest films, especially when placed beside such major film comedies as *Annie Hall*, *Manhattan*, and *Hannah and Her Sisters*. Yet despite its seemingly modest pretensions, *Purple Rose* offers some of Allen's most important reflections on the medium in which he has now been working for the better part of two decades. The film synthesizes farcical and parodic techniques from Allen's early films with the serious interest in romantic themes that emerges in most of his more recent pictures, thus producing a brief but reasonably comprehensive overview of his career as a comic filmmaker. In doing so, *Purple Rose* also conjures up associations with three of the four primary types of comedy identified by Northrop Frye in his influential essay, "The Argument of Comedy"; Aristophanic Old Comedy, Roman New Comedy, and Shakespearean "green world" comedy.[1] Allen first uses a variant of the Aristophanic "bright idea" in endowing the film's heroine, Cecilia (Mia Farrow), with the unconscious ability to lure the movie character Tom Baxter off the screen and into her own realm of existence. The plot then takes a new-comic turn as both Tom and his actor-creator Gil Shepherd (both played by Jeff Daniels) compete for Cecilia's affections. And throughout the film, Allen uses the silver screen itself as a cinematic equivalent of the second or "green" world of Shakespearean "festive" comedy, and furnishes Cecilia with some of the qualities and predicaments of Shakespeare's comic heroines.[2]

To be sure, these generic types overlap at least somewhat: the black-and-white movie, for instance, functions both as one side of an old-comic dialectic or *agon* and as the '30s equivalent of a "festive" holiday environment. And "festive" comedy itself draws on many of the conventions of Roman comedy. Even so, an artificial separation of these three comic strands for purposes of analysis would seem warranted. For such an analysis should enable us to see why *Purple Rose* is not only "one of the best movies about movies ever made,"[3] but also, and more precisely, an extremely thoughtful exploration of the generic possibilities of comedy.

Reprinted by permission from *Literature/Film Quarterly*, vol. 16, no. 1 (1988): 39–43.
Copyright © 1988 by *Literature/Film Quarterly*, Salisbury State University.

Let us begin by focusing on *Purple Rose*'s generic debt to Old Comedy. As Frye has noted, the natural development of this genre is toward fantasy and absurdity. Usually, the comic action is triggered by a character or group of characters who concocts a "bright idea," an outrageous or improbable notion which, when implemented, provides the play with its dramatic momentum.[4] (Examples of such "bright ideas" in Aristophanes range from the separate peace with Sparta arranged by Dikaiopolis in *The Acharnians* to the sex strike in *Lysistrata* to the construction of Cloud-cuckooland in *The Birds*.). In essence, the bright-idea format always posits a ludicrous or implausible "what-if?" situation and then develops the ramifications of that situation to their logical (or illogical) conclusions. As Frye emphasizes, the idea itself, no matter how bizarre or counter-productive, is always cause for comic celebration ("Old and New Comedy" 3).

In *Purple Rose*, Allen's "bright idea" that a screen character can leave his fictional domain and fall in love with a real-life movie fan produces the rapid-fire humor of the film's middle section.[5] Of immediate interest and amusement here are Tom Baxter's comic attempts to deal with a world where his fake movie money will not pay a restaurant tab, autos do not speed away without the assistance of drivers, and romantic episodes do not end with the stock Hollywood kiss and fade-out. In addition, Tom's departure triggers a series of comic debates strongly reminiscent of the Aristophanic *agon*. The remaining screen characters, assuming that Baxter's absence makes it impossible for them to proceed (even though they all agree that his role is decidedly minor), begin to argue first among themselves and then with the theater audience. The audience harangues the theater manager, who in turn places a frantic phone call to the film's producer. Disaster looms for the production studio when it learns that Tom Baxters in several other movie houses are threatening walk-outs. And Gil Shepherd stands to lose his chance at his biggest screen role (Charles Lindbergh) if he cannot bring his current cinematic creation back under control. At a deeper level, *Purple Rose* dramatizes an *agon* between "real" and "reel" life, between the harsh reality of Cecilia's existence and the imaginary world she escapes into night after night at the Jewel theater. As we shall see, this debate takes on added significance when considered from the perspective of "festive" comedy.

Tom's "translation" into real life also produces a series of complications which gives the middle section of *Purple Rose* a definite new-comic pattern. As Frye emphasizes, Latin New Comedy almost always chronicles the efforts of a young man to outwit an opponent and possess the girl of his choice. Often this "opponent" is his own father, who may either want the girl for himself, or want his son to marry elsewhere, or both ("Argument" 58). In Shakespearean comedy, the emphasis falls much more heavily on competitive relationships among the youthful lovers themselves, with a Terentian "heavy father" such as Egeus in A *Midsum-*

mer Night's Dream sometimes providing the impetus for such competition. After an often bewildering series of complications, reversals and recognitions has run its course, the new-comic plot invariably culminates in what Ruth Nevo defines as a "telos of recovery," a resolution in which the protagonists receive "more and better than they bargained for."[6] In addition to the marriages or betrothals of young lovers, such rewards may also include the recovery of lost children, the reunion of entire families (as happens in *The Comedy of Errors*), and the freeing of witty slaves who have helped to produce the comic *catastrophe*. For Frye, such action is symbolic of a "new social integration," a positive restructuring of society itself ("Argument" 61).

Tom's departure from the movie screen leads to several new-comic complications, the first of which features a rivalry between Tom and Cecilia's boorish out-of-work husband, Monk (Danny Aiello). At Tom's urging during their initial conversation, Cecilia slips out on Monk for an evening of merrymaking. Later, Monk confronts Tom and beats him. (Luckily, Tom emerges unscathed due to his imaginary status.) Still later, Tom escorts Cecilia into his silver-screen world and takes her to the Copa, thus inciting the jealousy of torch-singer Kitty Haynes (Karen Akers), the woman for whom Tom "falls" in the regular movie script.

Both of these entanglements (Tom-Cecilia-Monk; Cecilia-Tom-Kitty) serve primarily as foils for the major romantic confrontation of the film, that between Tom and his "creator" Gil Shepherd, who must convince Tom to return to his screen role in order to placate the studio and salvage his career. The complications begin when Cecilia mistakes Gil for Tom in a restaurant. Gil, realizing Cecilia's error, begins to romance her as a means of contacting and manipulating Tom. Eventually, the plot climaxes when Gil demands that Cecilia choose between her two rival suitors as several silver-screen characters offer her competing words of advice. Cecilia succinctly summarizes her predicament, noting that she has gone from being unloved by her husband to being loved by two men, both of whom are, in a sense, "the same two people."

Faced with a choice between the ideal but ephemeral Tom and a character who is both real and, to all outward appearances, highly attractive, Cecilia makes what appears to be an eminently sensible decision in favoring Gil. Her choice sends the defeated Tom back into his native environment (and, presumably, back to Kitty Haynes), thus opening up possibilities for a genuine new-comic conclusion in which Cecilia will receive "more and better" than she had ever hoped for. Not only has the real matinee idol himself replaced his charming but insubstantial counterpart; he has also urged Cecilia to fly off to Hollywood with him. When Gil subsequently deserts Cecilia, we recognize, if we didn't know it already, that both we and Cecilia have been set up, that despite our knowledge of Gil's ulterior motive in courting Cecilia, we may well have allowed generic expectations for a "Hollywood finish" to impair our critical faculties. Allen's new-comic plot thus offers us errors, complications, and romantic triangles, but no "telos of recovery." Instead, the film's conclusion returns Cecilia to the "heavy husband" Monk, the plot's antagonistic blocking figure, in direct violation of conventional new-comic practice. Allen's refusal to provide an upbeat, new-comic conclusion thus seems to mute substantially the film's celebration of its "bright idea."[7]

Further clarification of Allen's comic strategies in *Purple Rose* may be gained through a consideration of the film's "festive" aspects. As Frye has observed, Shakespeare's middle comedies of the 1590s draw heavily on the "green world" tradition of English folklore, and contain a "rhythmic movement from normal world to green world and back again" ("Argument" 68). While the normal, everyday world of Shakespearean comedy is often given over to tyranny, narrow legality, and inflexibility (as witnessed by the usurping duke's court in *As You Like It* and Shylock's Venice), the "green" world functions as a saturnalian holiday environment where a "metamorphosis" of real-world values occurs. Expanding upon Frye's analysis, C. L. Barber identifies the saturnalian pattern of Shakespearean comedy as a movement "through release to clarification" (4). Barber emphasizes the therapeutic, educational value of the pattern on the characters whose understandings are presumably broadened as a result of the "festive" experience. Festivity itself, Barber claims, comes to be understood "as a paradoxical human need, problem, and resource" (15).

Several parallels between *Purple Rose* and "festive" comedy are readily apparent. First of all, the film's fluctuation between the gritty reality of depression-era New Jersey and the world of cinematic make-believe functions as a more complex version of the "festive" movement from "everyday" to "holiday" and (usually) back again.[8] Allen further complicates the pattern by making it work both ways. While Cecilia from the film's opening sequence is so absorbed in the world of Hollywood fantasy and gossip that she cannot adequately perform her "everyday" chores as a waitress, Tom wants to get out of his confining screen role and into a romantic affair with Cecilia. As one of the studio executives notes, "the real ones want their lives fictional and the fictional ones want their lives real."

Further, the harsh nature of the film's "everyday" world, presided over by such grim figures as Monk and Cecilia's boss at the restaurant, provides a very close equivalent to the typically harsh, arbitrary "first" world of Shakespearean comedy. Not surprisingly, the only faintly festive locale within this world, aside from the Jewel theater, is the silent, empty amusement park where Tom resides during his sojourn in real life. By contrast, the "second" or holiday world of the film-within-the-film is one completely given over to carnivalesque frivolity, as wealthy socialites casually wing their way to Cairo in search of the exotic, returning in time to catch the evening floor show at the Copa. Even the boredom that motivates the

Cairo escapade underscores the Shakespearean implication that a world entirely given over to play may become unattractive and sterile. Possibilities for festive release seem especially strong when Tom re-enters the film-within with Cecilia, cancels the original script, and whisks Cecilia away for a night on the town. Responding to the welcome news that it is now every character for himself, Arturo, the Copa's maître d', breaks into a joyous impromptu dance number with the band.

Finally, Cecilia's status in *Purple Rose* is at least somewhat similar to that of many of Shakespeare's comic heroines. Her enslavement at the film's opening to her husband and her dismal job, as well as to the general malaise of the great depression, parallels the initial bondage of the Shakespearean heroine. Hermia and Portia are bound to their father's wills, Rosalind is restricted by the political usurpation of her father's court, and so on. As Shakespeare's young lovers seek out the festive release of the "green" world, so Cecilia finds her own form of temporary release through her daily visits to the Jewel. These visits, in turn, generate the more substantial though ultimately frustrated release of her adventures with Tom and Gil. And although Cecilia can control neither her own ultimate destiny nor that of any other characters, as Portia and Rosalind do, she does stand up courageously to Monk on several occasions, and achieves a minor triumph when she talks her married sister (Stephanie Farrow) out of quitting her waitress job in protest over Cecilia's dismissal. Perhaps there is even some magic associated with her unconscious role as the catalyst in Tom's fantastic breakthrough into real life.

Despite these parallels between *Purple Rose* and Shakespearean comedy, Allen's film does not deliver the "metamorphosis" of real-world values cited by Frye as the hallmark of the festive pattern. Such failure goes beyond Gil's self-centered victimization of Cecilia to a basic weakness of the festive medium itself, which is both charming and vapid. Once again, Frye's analysis of the duality of Shakespearean comedy serves to illuminate Allen's technique. According to Frye, Shakespeare endows both of his comic "worlds with equal imaginative power, brings them opposite one another, and makes each world seem unreal when seen by the light of the other." The overall effect, Frye argues, is "a detachment of the spirit born of this reciprocal reflection of two illusory realities" ("Argument" 72–73). At one point in *Purple Rose*, one of the silver-screen characters wonders why his world can't simply be redefined as the real world, and reality deemed a world of shadow and illusion. But the film as a whole does not endorse this position. Rather, Allen is constantly at pains to underscore the cruel disparity between escapist comedy and its gullible audience— this despite the fact that the film-within itself is both a tribute to and parody of the genre it represents. Essentially, the silver-screen environment contains no lasting value for its audience beyond that of temporary escape. Absorbed in great quantity, its effects may even prove harmful.

Remarkably, Allen manages to convey the radical shallowness of escapist comedy while simultaneously preserving audience identification with Cecilia, the ultimate fan of such comedy.

If *Purple Rose* does not transform the values of the everyday world it depicts, it at least allows for a very sophisticated cinematic debate between these values and those of escapist comedy. It is a debate which neither side can finally win. This standoff is perhaps best demonstrated in the precarious status of Tom, the one character who attempts physically to close the gap between the film's "real" and "reel" worlds. Cecilia already half-perceives the futility of Tom's quest when she confides her feelings about Tom to Gil: "I've met the most wonderful man. Of course, he's fictional—but you can't have everything."

At the film's conclusion, all the main characters return to their original places, with Gil, his career now safely back on track, the nominal victor.[9] Yet his face is not the last one we see. After a shot of a pensive, perhaps even guilt-ridden Gil on the airplane returning to Hollywood, the camera focuses on Cecilia as she once again enters the Jewel, and registers her change of expression from disappointment to renewed absorption as both she and we watch Fred Astaire and Ginger Rogers, the greatest purveyors of escapist film comedy, perform "Cheek to Cheek." In this final sequence, Allen seems to imply that although escapist cinema may offer us no substantial alternative to the rigors of everyday life, it can and should at times function as a therapeutic surrogate reality, especially for the Cecilias of this world. And although the concluding sequence may partially undercut the film's dominant premise on the essential disjunction between the dual realities that Shakespeare fuses into his "festive" pattern, it does so in a manner that makes objection quite beside the point.

We see, then, that Allen's generic strategies, though definitely related to inherited comic practice, tend to qualify if not undercut the patterns they invoke. The old-comic "bright idea" leads not to a full-scale Aristophanic celebration but rather yields to an ironic reversal of the stock new-comic resolution. And the "festive" elements, though ambiguous, even paradoxical manner. Blending modern irony and Chaplinesque pathos with his own wry sense of the incongruous, Allen delivers a film that reveals a family resemblance to several long-standing comic traditions, and yet departs markedly from those same traditions. Our final impression, consequently, is that of a gifted filmmaker shaping his own brand of comedy both out of and in reaction to comic tradition, just as his predecessors from Aristophanes on down have done.

Notes

1. *English Institute Essays, 1948*, ed. D. A. Robertson, Jr. (New York: Columbia UP, 1949) 48–73. Frye cites Dantean *commedia* as the fourth major comic type.

2. For an extended definition and treatment of Shakespeare's "festive" comedy see C. L. Barber, *Shakespeare's Festive Comedy* (Princeton: Princeton UP, 1959).

3. Richard Schieckel. "Now Playing at the Jewel," *Time*, 4 Mar. 1985: 78.

4. "Old and New Comedy." *Shakespeare Survey* 22 (1969) 3–4. On the Aristophanic comic pattern, see also Ann Barton, *Ben Johnson, Dramatist* (Cambridge: Cambridge UP, 1984) 113–114.

5. As several reviewers of *Purple Rose* have noted, Allen uses a similar premise in his short story, "The Kugelmass Episode" (*New Yorker*, 2 May 1977: 34–39), in which a college professor liberates Emma Bovary from the pages of Flaubert's novel and brings her to New York.

6. *Comic Transformations in Shakespeare* (New York: Methuen, 1980) 7. Pauline Kael criticizes Allen for this failure in her review of *Purple Rose* ("Charmer." *New Yorker*, 25 Mar. 1985: 104–108) According to Kael, Allen strains his "light, paradoxical story about escapism" by giving it a "morbid, unfunny subtext" and a "desolate, 'realistic' ending" (108).

7. Variations on the normal "festival" patterns may be found in *The Merchant of Venice*, which ends in the romantic world of Belmont, and in *Twelfth Night*, which, as Frye notes, appears to take place entirely in an "evergreen" world given over to perpetual carnival ("Argument" 68).

9. Stanley Kauffmann believes that the film's curricular pattern indicates a fundamental failure on Allen's part to develop his premise ("A Midsummer Night's Dream." *New Republic*, 1 Apr. 1985: 27). My own analysis attempts to show that Allen exhibits much more inventive skill in the film than Kauffmann gives him credit for.

Home, Hearth, and Hannah: Family in the Films of Woody Allen

WILLIAM BRIGHAM

"I think people should mate for life, like pigeons and Catholics," (Woody Allen, Manhattan).
"Family [is] the germ-cell of civilization" (Sigmund Freud, Civilization and its Discontents).

SPANNING A period of almost thirty years, from the waning of Hollywood's family melodramas, through the paradigmatic changes of the late 1960s and the 1970s, to the backlash of the 1980s, Woody Allen has produced an oeuvre as varied and important as any American filmmaker. The more than two dozen films he has written, directed, and—mostly—starred in are so unique that one seldom sees other filmmakers identified as being derivative of Allen (Nora Ephron and Rob Reiner's *When Harry Met Sally* (1989) is a recent exception). His work is stamped with such a personal and individual mark that he both enjoys (usually critically) and suffers (commercially) from a singular kind of categorization. Indeed, Allen's worldview has been criticized as severely limited to the intellectual life and penthouses of New York's Upper East Side and "that's not a place from which to make shrewdly gauged social observations. All you can see is pigeons and doormen" (Gopnik, 92). Notwithstanding the broad accuracy of this comment, Allen's films—just like the films of any American writer and director—provide telling representations of social institutions, roles, and norms. The family institution is one such example, and although at first the kind of family one thinks of in Allen's films is atypical, unstructured, even avant-garde, there is in fact considerable concurrence between Allen's view of what constitutes a family and the diversity extant in American society.

For Allen, the family institution seems an obvious and important one to include in most of his films. Certainly this can be traced to the centrality of the family institution in Western society, to Allen's reminiscences of his own upbringing and rejection of his biological family, or as Allen himself said (Lax, 180ff), the influence of his longtime companion Mia Farrow and the children they had together. But there are, no doubt, larger issues at work in Allen's musings and filmmaking. In an unusual pairing, Norman K. Denzin suggests that Allen and C. Wright Mills share the same strategy in examining

---

This essay was written specifically for this volume and is published here for the first time by permission of the author.

the postmodern era: "[Allen—like Mills] wants to examine the kinds of men, women and children this cultural moment has produced. He wants to examine how the modernist (and ancient) cultural myths concerning family, love, honor, sexuality, guilt, morality, greed, God, and meaning have worked their ways into contemporary life" (102). The complexity of many of Allen's films—*Interiors* (1978), *Manhattan* (1979), *Hannah and her Sisters* (1986), *September* (1987), *Another Woman* (1988), *Crimes and Misdemeanors* (1989), *Husbands and Wives* (1992)—some with two or three subplots of equal narrative focus and/or a phalanx of intertwining relationships, allows him to address in one film several of the myths Mills invokes. And his use of various filmic devices, such as flashback in *Annie Hall* (1977), *Another Woman*, *Interiors*, and *Crimes and Misdemeanors*; setting *Radio Days* (1987) in an earlier and presumably simpler era; or inserting clips from films of the classic era in *Play It Again Sam* (1972), *Annie Hall*, *Manhattan*, *Hannah and Her Sisters*, *Crimes and Misdemeanors*, and *Manhattan Murder Mystery* (1993), all give him the opportunity to call upon nostalgic and romanticized views of the human condition.

But these nostalgic detours are just that; temporary oases from a world from which Allen does not try to escape because he wants to understand it. "Allen's people, like Mills's people, are caught up in the problems of making sense of families which are collapsing, marriages which do not work, jobs which are unfulfilling, and careers which won't permit a merger of work with family life" (Denzin, 103). It is, Denzin says,"a deadly serious view of family . . . The world outside the family is as sick as the world inside the family, only in a different way. This is why Allen's males are always seeking a new family or woman. The one they've just left didn't work and the one they were born into doesn't work either" (Denzin, 103).

THE AMERICAN FAMILY

This family of the late-twentieth century that Allen is reflecting and presumably trying to understand is a result of converging cultural, technological, political, and economic forces as unique and impactful in their collectivity as any in history. Arguably the most important, and certainly the most elemental, of social institutions, the family in Western society has varied greatly over time in definition, form, and purpose. Yet contemporary pleas for a return to "traditional family values" presume a past characterized by continuity and solidity. Current forms of family relations, marriage and divorce, parenthood, and sexual values and behavior are often cited by political and religious conservatives as the unfortunate and undesirable result of social upheaval in the 1960s and 1970s. Yet as the following— written for the *Boston Quarterly Review* in *1859*—illustrates, the changes in and concerns about the family are long-standing: "The family, in its old sense, is disappearing from our land, and not only our free institutions are threatened but the very existence of our society is endangered" (quoted in Cherlin, 2). In fact family types and dynamics today are in many cases similar to earlier forms in both the nineteenth and twentieth centuries (Coontz; Cherlin 6–30), and the much acclaimed "extended family"—a nostalgic notion of three (or more) generations of a family happily coexisting in a rambling house—has always been "more of a utopian fantasy than an actuality" (Byars, 132; Collins, 411; Coontz), with the possible exception of its occurrence in the African American culture (Cherlin 107–14).

The reality of today's American family is that of single parenthood (Mednick); dual-worker households, including "second shift" workers (Hochschild), families constituting over 40% of the homeless (Shogren; The United States Conference of Mayors, 2; Kozol); continually high divorce *and* remarriage rates, resulting in the very common "stepfamily" (Collins 238–63; 444; Cherlin 6–30; 84–86; Smith); teenage parents (Jones et al.); "parachute kids" (those dropped into the United States for secondary school education by wealthy, primarily Taiwanese parents) (Hamilton); artificial insemination, in vitro fertilization, and surrogate mothers (Schenden); and a range of legal-moral quandaries, including same-sex marriages and parenting (Seligmann; Schenden; Collins, 469–73), custody of frozen embryos (cases in Tennessee and Australia), and, overarching all the foregoing, legal wrangling over just what constitutes a family. There has been, in short, a separation of the functions and roles that heretofore were firmly linked in at least the rhetoric of traditionalism: marriage, sex, procreation, and parenthood. The resulting diverse forms of relationships and support systems might all qualify as examples of what a family is or should be; to reach such a consensus, however, is not the agenda of this essay. As Randall Collins points out, "the stress we ought to place here is on the permanent *diversity* of types of families rather than on one form taking over entirely from the others" (Collins, 449).

All of this may beg the question of how *family* is to be defined and understood within the context of this discussion. For the purposes of examining depictions of the family in the films of Woody Allen, *family* shall be taken to mean any constellation of adults, or adults and children, who are continually reliant upon one another for emotional, social, financial, or other forms of support, regardless of the presence or absence of biological, legal, or traditional ties between and among them. Therefore, we can examine the large and almost borderless family of *Hannah and Her Sisters*, the same-sex relationship of *Manhattan*, the stilted nuclear family of *Alice*, or the many adult-adult relationships not sanctioned by marriage that populate virtually all of Allen's films. For it seems that Allen, in his search for an understanding of love, very easily transcends the traditional or stereotypical borders of family, marriage, and relationships.

Freud spoke of "fully sensual love" as opposed to "aim-inhibited love" to distinguish between, respectively, that of a couple drawn and held together via sex, and the affectionate relationship of parent and child. The former, he said, "comes into opposition to the interests of civilization," while in the latter case "civilization threatens love with substantial restrictions" (Freud, 48–50). Perhaps Allen, after Freud, wants to show the artificiality and restrictiveness of traditional relationships and families, as well as reflect the realities of the family in the modern era, and is therefore continually crossing over or cutting through their boundaries.[1]

Allen sometimes shows us what we ourselves are doing or, in areas of greater taboo, what we wish to do. It is readily observable that Allen has illustrated in many of his films the changing (as well as age-old) mores of sexuality, marriage, and family: artificial insemination in *Hannah*; same-sex couples in *Manhattan*, middle-aged men and their much younger trophy wives or girlfriends—*Manhattan*, *Hannah*, and *Husbands and Wives,* infidelity or extramarital affairs in *Crimes and Misdemeanors, Manhattan, Alice, Husbands and Wives,* and other films; separation and divorce in many films; teenage sexual precociousness in *Manhattan* and *Husbands and Wives*; and, as a reflection of his own life and that of others his age, in *Manhattan Murder Mystery*, the complacency and lifelessness that creeps into many long-standing relationships.

But it is the most richly textual of Allen's films, *Hannah and Her Sisters*, which offers the most explicit examination of contemporary families and relationships. Not only is the narrative and its parallel relationships interwoven through a triptych of the most traditional of family gatherings, the Thanksgiving dinner, but Hannah stands as no less than an incarnation of the institution of the family. She is the matriarch, indeed the only true parent, of the film: "Hannah, not her mother, occupies the center of this family and keeps it together. [Her] parents are decorative" (Girgus, 95). Hannah acts as mother to her children (who were conceived via artificial insemination with the help of her then-husband Mickey's friend); as mother (and wife) to her husband Elliot, as mother (and daughter) to her quarrelsome, infantile parents; and as mother (and sister) to her drug-taking sister Holly and her only somewhat more grounded sister Lee, who drinks too much. Toward the film's end, when Hannah (and others) are gaining clarification and direction in their lives, she says to her sister Holly, in the voice of a stereotypically unappreciated mother: "You're [Holly and everyone else] grateful but you resent me." At this moment she represents every mother (or father) who has believed and voiced this same thought: that after all they have done for their children—or *because* of what they have done, because of their grand capabilities—their children resent them. *Hannah and Her Sisters* is one of the finest contemporary filmic depictions of the family institution and its roles and norms, an institution long reflected in the popular cinema.

THE FAMILY IN FILM

Because of its universality and importance, the family has always been grist for the filmmaker's mill, whether as part of the background, as the context or underpinning for any type of narrative, or as the central focus, the very purpose of the film. But it was not until the 1950s that a specific set of generic conventions was employed in those films that subsequently became known as "family melodramas." Later, with the advent of critical (that is, Marxist, feminist, psychoanalytic, sociological) examination of films in the late 1960s and the 1970s, these family melodramas were viewed in a new light, as "a rich and ambiguous group of film[s] . . . that simultaneously championed and criticized the institution of the family and the gender roles it entails" (Byars, 133). Thomas Schatz suggests that "no other genre of films, not even the 'anti-westerns' of the same period, projected so complex and paradoxical a view of America, at once celebrating and severely questioning the basic values and attitudes of the mass audience" (Schatz, 223).

With their classic Hollywood resolution, the family melodramas of the 1950s (for example, *All That Heaven Allows* (1955), *Giant* (1956), *Written on the Wind* (1956), *Cat on a Hot Tin Roof* (1958), were ultimately celebratory of the "traditional" values and patriarchal family structure being invoked today by political and religious conservatives, but they also illustrated family conflicts and torments that have been a part of every historical era. In this way they served to momentarily undermine the capitalist, patriarchal dominance of post-World War II America, and to show how "women used their limited power to resist total male domination" (Byars 146).

Even the stars of these films made real-life contributions to the perpetuation of the stereotype of the nuclear family and domestic bliss. In the post-World War II era, organized efforts were undertaken by the Actors Guild to promote the otherwise domesticated lives of those whose names periodically popped up in the gossip columns. Speeches were "'given to civic groups around the country, emphasizing that the stars now embodied the rejuvenated family life unfolding in the suburbs'" (Lary May quoted in Coontz 27–28).

By the end of the 1960s and into the 1970s, a quite different family was being projected—and reflected—on movie screens. Driven by real as well as perceived changes in the American family, Hollywood updated the family melodrama with films like *Diary of a Mad Housewife* (1970), *A Woman under the Influence* (1974), *Alice Doesn't Live Here Anymore* (1975), *An Unmarried Woman* (1978), *Norma Rae* (1979), and others. These films did not rely upon the resolution of the classic period, which required the deus ex machina of a woman's temporary blindness (*Magnificent Obsession* (1954)) or a man's "mini-coma" (*All That Heaven Allows*), but instead ended more often than not by showing the female protagonist's independence and resiliency or, at least, the reality of a woman's life in the modern era.

The 1980s, a decade of backlash toward feminism (Faludi) and a return to macho (actually seriocomic) American posturing on the world stage (in Grenada, Panama, and—in the early 1990s—the orgiastic Gulf War), brought films that showed either the inevitable threat to the sanctity of marriage and family that feminism wrought (*Fatal Attraction* (1987), the Pygmalion effect of a man redefining or protecting a woman (*Pretty Woman* (1990); *Someone to Watch over Me* (1987), or the incompatibility of a career and personal happiness (*Baby Boom* (1987), *Working Girl* (1988)) (Faludi, 112ff.). In other cases, Hollywood merely eschewed the family for a renewed focus on the heretofore emasculated male (America) who fought to regain his central role in society and on the big screen. As Biskind and Ehrenreich (1980) put it, by the late 1970s "safe, tame domesticity faded as a social ideal, and its traditional antithesis—untamed machismo—came back from Vietnam with a castration complex" (Biskind and Ehrenreich, 201). Within a few years, Hollywood had discovered the box-office appeal of films like *First Blood*, *Missing in Action*, *Rambo: First Blood Part II*, *Rocky IV*, *Rambo III*, *Die Hard*, and *Die Hard II*. By 1992—the political year declared that of the woman—Hollywood was pitting women against one another in films like *Single White Female* and *The Hand That Rocks the Cradle*; the undomesticated, liberated woman, free from the bonds of the family, had become a dangerous psychotic (Connors). But in none of these forms did Hollywood respond to political conservatives and their "romantic nostalgia for the past [and] general effacement of the boundaries between the past and the present" (Denzin, 4). Conservatives would be further chagrined if it were suggested that the idiosyncratic Woody Allen might be one who shared their tendency to eliminate those boundaries of time, and who often called upon cinematic renderings of the past in order to initially suppress but ultimately understand, or at least accept, the present.

ALLEN'S CELLULOID FAMILY

Although Allen's cinematic world is usually limited to the confines of the borough of Manhattan, a reading list one might encounter in a Columbia University liberal arts program, and dinner either at Elaine's or from Chinese takeout, he nonetheless addresses issues of relationships and families that are universal in Western society, and most certainly in American culture:"He sees in family structures unresolved conflicts between fathers and sons (Judah and his father [*Crimes and Misdemeanors*]), mothers and daughters (*Hannah and Her Sisters*), mothers and sons (*Oedipus Wrecks*, 1989), sisters and sisters (*Hannah* again), brothers and brothers (Jack and Judah [*Crimes*]), brothers and sisters (Lester and Wendy [*Crimes*]). Family, Allen's (and society's) most primordial of social structures, is a site of inevitable conflict, tension, and dispute" (Denzin, 103). Additionally, Allen has focused on the common rifts and difficulties of husbands and wives in *Interiors, Manhattan, The Purple Rose of Cairo* (1985), *Hannah and Her Sisters, Radio Days, Another Woman, Crimes and Misdemeanors, Alice* (1991), *Husbands and Wives,* and *Manhattan Murder Mystery*. An examination of these relationships might begin with Allen's depiction of parents as a socializing force.

Allen's most common characterization—the existentially tortured man (or woman, as in *Another Woman* and *Alice*) struggling with some of the most overarching questions of humanity (God, death, sexuality)—often refers to the role of parents in the central character's inadequate or dysfunctional upbringing. Allen acknowledges the flaws in his own parents' raising of him and his sister: "Woody has often talked about his own parents constantly arguing when he was growing up" (Spignesi, 172); his parents' marriage, Allen says, was "a totally contentious relationship. They did everything except exchange gunfire" (Lax, 16). This anger often translated into corporal punishment of Allen, at least by his mother. While not uncommon in that era (1930s and 1940s), Allen's mother acknowledged that she spanked him: "I wasn't abusive, no. But I spanked you. . . . I hit you occasionally, yes," although Allen recalls that his mother "hit [him] every day when [he] was a child" (Lax, 19). Thus we should not be surprised when the parents of the autobiographical Little Joe in *Radio Days* use corporal punishment—most ordinarily an open-handed slap on the head or, in one instance, the father's belt on the rear end—as their primary socialization tool, they even object to the rabbi hitting their son because it is both their responsibility and, presumably, pleasure to do so themselves. Ike (*Manhattan*) responds to his young son's repeated demands for an expensive toy in a store window by slapping him on the head twice. In any event, Allen's parents' contentious marriage, a string of sometimes abusive or neglectful nannies (Lax, 15–16), and regular if not frequent corporal punishment resulted in Allen's not having a positive and solid familial support system during his early developmental years.[2]

On a more comic level, Allen says that he was "raised in a home where . . . the basic values were 'God and carpeting'" (Geist quoted in Spignesi, 40), and the religious beliefs and practices of parents in Allen's films are most commonly belittled. The character usually played by Allen will refer to the influence—either negative or benign, certainly not positive—of his parents' religious views, as in *Hannah*, when Mickey tells his parents of his plans to convert to Catholicism. His father is nonplussed and his mother flees to the bathroom screaming, "Of course there's a God, you idiot! You don't believe in God?":

Mickey: But if there's a God, then why-why is there so much evil in the world? Wha—Just on a simplistic level. Why-why were there Nazis?

Mother: Tell him, Max.

Father: How the hell do I know why there were Nazis? I don't know how the can opener works. (Allen, 1987, 133)

This sort of interchange between parents and their offspring in Allen's films is very common, and it illustrates so well Allen's penchant of mixing the very serious with the ridiculous. These parents in *Hannah* (as well as in *Radio Days*, *Annie Hall*, *Take the Money and Run* (1969), and *Oedipus Wrecks*) are both comic foils and representations of a type of socializing force, one that perhaps thwarts the psychosocial development of the protagonist.

Other references to religion and parents are found in *Manhattan*, as when Ike tells his friend Yale that he has quit his job and he will "probably have to give my parents less money. You know, this is gonna kill my father. He's gonna—he's not gonna be able to get as good a seat in the synagogue, you know. This year he's gonna be in the back, away from God, away from the action" (Allen 1982, 201). This mocking of his father's religious beliefs and practices illustrates Ike's disdain for an institution that his parents attempted to foist on him. In *Annie Hall*, Allen uses a split screen to juxtapose the calm and ordinary family of Annie with the cacophony of Alvy Singer's family dinner:

Mom Hall: How do you plan to spend the holidays, Mrs. Singer?

[Alvy's Mother: We fast.]

Dad Hall: Fast?

Alvy's Father: Yeah, no food. You know, we have to atone for our sins.

Mom Hall: What sins? I don't understand.

Alvy's Father: Tell you the truth, neither do we. (Allen 1982, 57)

The religious beliefs of an older generation are thus given short shrift in Allen's films. But these references are just a part of a larger view of family that can sometimes be rather negative.

References to family members are sometimes quite caustic, again exhibiting what Allen's characters see as the detrimental role parents and siblings have played in their lives. Hannah daydreams about her bickering, childlike parents: "They loved the idea of having us kids but raising us didn't interest them much" (Allen 1987a, 91). Mickey, also in *Hannah*, explains that he decided not to kill himself over the meaninglessness of life because first he would have to kill his parents, and then his aunt and uncle. These family members would suffer his loss so greatly that he both can't allow that suffering and he can't kill them. Thus, his family has thwarted him at every turn. In *Crimes and Misdemeanors*, Cliff says of his bombastic brother-in-law Lester, "I love him like a brother . . . David Greenglass" (whose testimony led to the execution of his sister, Ethel Rosenberg). In the opium dream sequence in *Alice*, the protagonist argues with her sister Dorothy about their upbringing; Dorothy proclaims that "[Dad] was a bore. Mom was a drunk." And in the biting yet ultimately poignant *Oedipus Wrecks*, Sheldon blurts out that he loves his mother, but wishes "she would disappear."

Several of these comments can be characterized as nothing more than one-liners, as evidence of Allen never fully divorcing himself from his origins as a gag writer and stand-up comic. Other jokes are references to very minor subplots or to merely tangential pieces of the larger narrative. At the same time one is struck by the fact that while virtually all of Allen's films focus on adult relationships, intellectual and sexual attraction, and love, the family—portrayed as a causative or socializing agent, arbiter, social anchor, or some other role—is also usually part of the fabric Allen weaves. Indeed, Allen's focus on various kinds of adult-adult (and, less frequently, adult-child) relationships and their inherent difficulties can be taken as largely representative of what it is to be a family today.

In *Crimes and Misdemeanors* the character of Professor Levy, who Cliff believes has captured one of the great truths of life, provides Allen's view regarding the impact of parents and siblings on development: "When we fall in love, it's a very strange paradox. The paradox consists of the fact that when we fall in love we are seeking to re-find all or some of the people to whom we were attached as children. On the other hand, we ask our beloved to correct all of the wrongs that these early parents or siblings inflicted on us."

There is a circularity to Allen's view of the family: It is an institution or set of social actors that inevitably imprints us in some negative fashion, but at the same time we seek out another family to help us alleviate the pain caused by the first family. But of all his depictions of family, it is in *Hannah and Her Sisters* that Allen focuses positively and affectionately on tradition and custom.

HANNAH AS ARCHETYPE

The domestic and the maternal prevail in *Hannah*: in the narrative, the protagonist, and in the other principal female characters. Holly and her friend April's entrepreneurial venture—the Stanislavski Catering Company—takes them no further than the kitchen and the serving tray, unless it can lead to a stable relationship with a marriageable male, and their rivalry over this man is certainly a sort of sibling or "sisterly" rivalry. Lee's romance with the much older Frederick is only a thinly disguised father-daughter relationship. When Lee cuts short one of Frederick's pedantic monologues, he says "I'm just trying to complete an education I started on you five years ago" (Allen 1987, 103). As one critic observed, "unlike some of Mr. Allen's previous heroines, these characters do not give up commitment in love to find fulfillment in art" (Dowd, 33).

As a counterpoint to the protagonist in *Alice*, who wants her independence and seeks to make a "meaningful" (that is, nondomestic) contribution to humankind, Hannah explicitly eschews such autonomy: "When I had the kids, I decided to stop working and just, you know, devote myself to having the family, and I've been very, very happy" (Allen 1987, 22). But she had recently returned to the stage as Nora in Ibsen's *A Doll's House* and now, having completed that role and sitting at the Thanksgiving table, says "So, now I got that out of my system and I can go back to the thing that makes me happiest" (Allen 1987, 22), and then takes her husband's hand and looks beatifically around the table. There is an obvious irony to this scene, as Hannah rejects not only a career in favor of her family, but specifically walks away from the role of Nora, the fictionalized woman struggling to break away from under the oppressive thumb of her husband and have a life of her own.

Hannah's willingness to do whatever it takes to hold her immediate and extended family together is seen as both an attribute and that which alienates her from family members. One is struck by her obsequious responses to Elliot's growing distance from her as his affair with Lee evolves, even though her strategy proves ultimately to be effective: "When Hannah . . . turns to him both tenderly and lovingly to help rather than berate him, she has begun to win her battle, a battle that some viewers probably would prefer to see her abandon for independence from both the family and men" (Girgus, 106).

It is left to a later Allen character, the protagonist in *Alice*, to flip the coin of maternity and to act upon her need for independence: "I'm the wife. You know, I, I take care of the children. I host the dinner parties. Arrange the social schedule. Try to look pretty so, so your friends can admire your taste. I've become one of those women who shop all day and gets pedicures. But I want to be. . . . There's more to me. . . . I want to do something with my life before it's too late." But comparisons between Hannah and Alice are misleading because Allen wants to depict two different types of families, in different socioeconomic groups, in these two films (although both, most notably the family in *Alice*, are living far above the means of the average family). But domesticity is still at the center of both films: In *Hannah* it is celebrated, in *Alice* temporarily rejected and permanently altered. The family is still foremost; it merely takes different forms and subscribes to somewhat different values.

The character of Hannah—as representation of the family institution—personifies, on the one hand, what Lasch refers to as "an island of security in the surrounding disorder" (Lasch 1979, 296), or a "haven in a heartless world" (Lasch 1977, 1), as evidenced by Elliot's thoughts upon his return to the marital bed after having sex with Hannah's sister: "And now I feel very good and cozy being here next to Hannah. There's something very lovely and real about Hannah. She gives me a very deep feeling of being a part of something" (Allen 1987a, 106). Hannah therefore offers and is the warmth and security of the family. But accompanying this security and the escape from disorder is the stifling nature and strictures of order. So Elliot, in the frustration over his dilemma of having to choose between Hannah or Lee, blurts out to Hannah:

> "You know, y-you have some very set plans of how your life should be structured. A-a house, uh, kids, certain schools, a h——, a home in Connecticut. I-it's all very . . . preconceived.
>
> Hannah: Yeah, but I . . . uh—I thought you needed that. When, when, when we met, you said your life was chaos.
>
> Elliot: I-I-I know, but there's got to be some give and take." (Allen 1987a, 119)

This last statement of Elliot's is all too typical of the self-centeredness of male characters in Allen's films. What Elliot means by "give and take" might be construed as him having the best of the two worlds in which he now lives—the domestic and the erotic; he wants to have both Hannah and Lee. In *Crimes and Misdemeanors*, when Judah's mistress Dolores threatens to reveal their affair to his wife, he pleads with her: "Think what you're doing to me!" The consequences of such a revelation for Judah's wife—and for Dolores, who stands to lose as well—seem lost on Judah. In *September*, after rejecting Lane, Peter says, "I already feel guilty enough because I did lead her on. . . . I just wasn't thinking about anyone else . . . just myself." It is the women in so many of Allen's films who seem to exhibit strength—maternal or otherwise—and we see this all too clearly in the trio of resolutions presented in *Hannah and Her Sisters*'s final sequence, the third Thanksgiving dinner; what is presented is a set of resolutions similar to those of the 1950s family melodramas, similarities rooted in the somewhat grand scope of both. For example, there are several lives, not just the protagonist's, with which we become concerned, and not "individual fates but the underlying moral process of the world" (Cawelti quoted in Modleski, 267). Allen is preoccupied with and overwhelmed by grand forces such as death, God, and sex, and also with socially constructed forces and "moral processes" like family and marriage. Cawelti, in examining the 1950s melodramas, saw them as "usually rather complicated in plot and character; instead of identifying with a single protagonist through his line of action, the melodrama typically makes us intersect imaginatively with many lives" (Cawelti quoted in Modleski, 267). But, again, this complexity of intersecting lives is always resolved at the end of the film melodrama, whether in the 1950s or in *Hannah*.

At the third and final family Thanksgiving gathering, we learn via a voice-over by Elliot that Lee has married the college professor she met upon her return to school; the education Frederick sought to continue has been usurped by a "real" teacher, one more "appropriate" to Lee's age: "Oh, Lee, you are something," Elliot muses. "You look very beautiful. Marriage agrees with you" (Allen 1987a, 176). Lee has achieved the ideal of guilt-free love and marriage, albeit to someone who will continue to serve as much of a mentor to her as Frederick (or Elliot) did. Then, "the movie cuts to Hannah, leaning contentedly against a doorway into the living room and listening to the off screen Evan play the piano. Elliot, holding his drink, walks over to her. They look at each other for a beat; Elliot then hugs Hannah, pulling her towards him. She leans her head on his shoulder, fingering his jacket lapel. They look off screen together, happily, intimately, at the off screen guests [while Evan and Norma play and sing "Isn't It Romantic"]" (Allen 1987a, 178).

The family has been reunited and the marriage revitalized, primarily because of Hannah's strength and perseverance, which overwhelmed Elliot's inability to make some manner of definitive move. In a session with his psychoanalyst, Elliot confessed "I-I can't seem to take action. I'm-I'm like, uh, Hamlet unable to kill his uncle. I want Lee, but I can't harm Hannah" (Allen 1987a, 143). Additionally it is the determination of Lee to change her life that leads her to finally push Elliot away: "Ah, it's over! Elliot, I mean it. It's over!" (Allen 1987a, 153).

The third sister—in the film's final scene—achieves resolution of her lifelong wandering and lack of direction. As she primps in front of a hallway mirror, Hannah's ex-husband Mickey walks up and we learn that he and Holly are now married:

> Mickey: "You know, . . . I-I used to always have Thanksgiving with Hannah . . . and I never thought that I could love anybody else. And here it is, years later and I'm married to you and completely in love with you . . . It'd make a great story. . . . A guy marries one sister . . . doesn't work out . . . many years later . . . he winds up married to the other sister." (Allen 1987a, 180)

The character of Mickey has been marginalized throughout the film, even in flashbacks, when he is married to Hannah. His infertility is cause for obvious strife between them, and results in the eventual (genetic) pairing of Hannah and Norman, Mickey's close friend, when Norman consents to helping them with artificial insemination. Thus, even as Hannah's husband, he was outside this family biologically; their eventual divorce and his lack of attention to their sons only further marginalizes him. An earlier attempt to reenter the family by dating Holly is disastrous, but when he runs into her in a record store years later they hit it off, and it is the beginning of Mickey's "rebirth" as a member of Hannah's family.

The final images of the film are of Holly and Mickey after Mickey has recounted the unusual history of his involvement in the family:

Mickey: "I don't know how you're gonna top that."

Holly: "Mickey?"

Mickey: "Mmm, what?"

Holly: "I'm pregnant." (Allen 1987a, 181)

So a "miracle baby" is the final deus ex machina that seals the family circle shut; marriage, domestication, and maternity, all supported by true and meaningful love—are the hallmarks of Allen's and society's ideal or traditional family.

In examining the seminal family films, the melodramas of the 1950s, Byars identifies three prerequisites for the resolution of those films: "The female-oriented melodrama cannot end with its female protagonist continuing a life independent and alone. . . . The solution may be obtained only through the action of a female character, generally the protagonist, and is achieved only through a fantastic narrative rupture" (Byars, 148). Like the protagonists of these earlier films, Hannah and each of her sisters are essentially alone throughout much of the film: Hannah, although reassured by Elliot, knows that a gulf has opened between them and that she is rejected and resented by other family members; Lee knows that to forge her own identity she must leave Frederick, but not for Elliot, and thus she is in some netherworld; and Holly, who, although she may have found her calling in writing plays, must deal with her inability to sustain, or even initiate, a relationship. While each is hopeful, they all realize that their lives are incomplete without a man and, in each case, they take the action necessary to fill that void. Hannah is resolute in keeping her husband and her family together; Lee searches for intellectual grounding and finds, surreptitiously, emotional satisfaction; Holly—through her skills as a writer— attracts Mickey the writer. And while no "fantastic narrative rupture" is necessary in the first two cases, it is the miracle baby of Holly and Mickey that finally fulfills Byar's formula for melodramatic resolution.

POST-*HANNAH* FAMILIES

The resolution necessary in the 1950s films—the desire to perpetuate the ideal of a nuclear family rooted in domesticity—is exactly that which religious and political conservatives call for today. That one could find this theme recurring in the films of Woody Allen seems, at first blush, to be somewhat incongruous. Yet an examination of the films that follow *Hannah and Her Sisters* indicates that Allen now tends toward a more typical resolution, specifically focusing on maintaining traditional family and relationship structures. *Oedipus Wrecks*, *Crimes and Misdemeanors*, *Alice*, *Husbands and Wives*, and *Manhattan Murder Mystery* offer varying examples of this type of resolution.

In *Oedipus Wrecks*, Sheldon (Allen) is berated by his nettlesome mother and told not to marry the single-parent shiksa he brings home for mom's approval: "Where do you come with a blonde with three children? What are you, an astronaut?!" Then, after struggling with the comic consequences of successfully wishing for his mother's disappearance, and after being left by the blonde Lisa, Sheldon meets and falls in love with "a girl just like the girl who married dear old (departed) dad." Treva, an erstwhile psychic, tells Sheldon upon meeting him, just as his mother always tells him, that "you look so thin. Are you eating enough?" The mother, upon seeing this younger mirror image of herself, is reunited with her son and Sheldon is doubly protected from the cruel world by these two maternal figures. Considering the stated Freudian basis of this tale, Allen proposes that the family provides models for our future mates, as he more explicitly illustrates in his next film, *Crimes and Misdemeanors*, where Professor Levy proclaims that "we are seeking to re-find all or some of the people to whom we were attached as children."

While somewhat more complex, and rather less complete, the resolution of *Crimes and Misdemeanors* is another post-*Hannah* example of Allen's growing tendency to provide closure to the several conflicts his more serious films contain. Judah's affair is, of course, abruptly and gruesomely ended by the death of his mistress, a murder that he ordered. Yet through the aid of a narrative rupture—a transient is charged with the crime—Judah suffers no legal consequences and he and his wife plumb new depths in their relationship. However, the moral burden he will always carry detracts from the manner of domestic resolution offered by *Hannah*.

In a rather typical intertwined scenario, the character of Halley in *Crimes*, whose husband slept with her best friend in their own bed, is pursued by Cliff—whose marriage is a sham—but she is won by the pompous Lester, the brother of Cliff's soon-to-be ex-wife (who announces with glee that she has "met someone"). It is only Cliff and his divorced sister—whose disastrous dating history haunts her—who fail to gain mates; they are family to one another in their individual solitude. Resolution is not complete, but the familial connection between the two "losers" suggests a common inability to sustain relationships; as products of the same family, they deserve each other and their loneliness.

While the denouement common to the 1950s melodramas required the eventual pairing of the female and male protagonists, usually through the aggressive action of the woman, the modern era allows for a resolution that still provides the female with the opportunity for such action, but toward a different end. In *Alice*, a woman realizing that the cocoon of New York elite society has cut her off from the reality and suffering of so many other people, leaves her husband to work with Mother Teresa in India. Upon returning to New York, she sets up household with her children and lives the simple and spartan life of so many other single parents (yet in contradiction to many real-life situations, with considerable alimony and child support). To the dismay of her former socialite friends, "she spends all her spare time with her children!" The pairing here is not female with necessary male, but single mother with children; absent is the filter of nannies, limo drivers, and cooks—a real (modern) family.

In *Husbands and Wives*, the focus is on middle-age angst and the resulting marital discord; children are largely absent now, grown and at college. Allen seems here to be showing his age a bit and also acknowledging the problems faced by middle-aged women. Sally, whose husband has left her for a younger woman, says "You're great until you start to show your age and then they want a new model." Gabe suggests that his college students aren't interested in him: "They don't want an old man"; his wife Judy replies, "I think an old man does better than an old woman." But ultimately the comfort and security of old relationships is what seems to predominate in *Husbands and Wives*, as evidenced by the reconciliation and attitude of Sally and her husband Jack: "Love is not about passion and romance necessarily. It's also about companionship. It's like a buffer against loneliness." Although Gabe has a flirtatious fling with a very young and precocious student of his ("Why do I hear $50,000 of psychoanalysis dialing 911?"), he knows that to pursue an affair would be foolhardy for him and a dead-end detour for her. Setting aside the recent real-life lapse in judgment by Allen, his maturity is reflected in this filmic decision, especially when compared to the final sequence of *Manhattan* thirteen years earlier, in which Ike literally races across town to stop his very young former lover Tracy from leaving town. In that instance, as she rebuffs him, it is the youngster who is the mature one, telling him "You have to have a little faith in people." Although on his own by the end of *Husbands and Wives*, Gabe still seems to appreciate the benefits of marriage and the family, he just finds it very difficult to hold it all together. In discussing his novel with the adoring college student Rain, she says, "Are our choices really between chronic dissatisfaction and suburban drudgery?" To which Gabe responds, "No, but you know that's how I'm distorting it to show how hard it is to be married." The key seems to be that traditional conceptions of relationships and families don't have to prevail; as Gabe continues

"You can't force yourself to conform to some abstract vision of love or marriage. Every situation is different."

And in his most recent film, *Manhattan Murder Mystery*, Allen continues to examine the problems of middle-aged life as he presents a couple who have grown apart at that time in their lives when their son has gone off to college and they are forced to deal with exactly what their now-abridged family is all about. The wife seeks adventure by investigating the mysterious death of a neighbor and she is joined in her escapades by a male friend who is attracted to her. The husband is also pursued by a sultry writer, and the two couples dance around, in their conversations only, the edges of affairs, but never embark on them. By film's end the husband and wife join investigative forces, a team in crime and, once again, matrimony. Their marriage is revitalized by the adventure, the wife's suitor is dispatched, and the family is stabilized. This film provides the most benign or mundane of family/relationship representations: A long-married couple with a grown child; harmless flirtations with friends or associates; and the final realization that if both partners commit to it, the marriage can be saved. It might seem that such a tidy resolution and "traditional" message fit into the oeuvre of Douglas Sirk more logically than that of Woody Allen, yet the pattern established by most of the post-*Hannah* films suggests that this has become the filmic agenda of the latter.

THE FAMILY HOME

The emotional structure and dynamics of the filmic family can often be located in the physicality and ambience of the family home, in which the film's characters act out their relational dramas. In *Interiors*, *Hannah and Her Sisters*, and *September*, Allen presents three families and their homes that differ from one another only slightly more than they are alike.

Interiors, Allen's first film after the seminal *Annie Hall*, served to rupture his relationship with many critics and with portions of his audience. Allen's paean to the much-revered Ingmar Bergman was as somber and spare as *Annie Hall* was engaging and chock full of one-liners and sight gags. Its representation of a family in almost total disarray at the film's outset was not unburdened in the least by its dystopian finale. This aspect of the film is one of its greater departures from the uplifting resolution of *Hannah and Her Sisters*, and is its greatest similarity to *September*. *Interiors* features, as does *Hannah* and *September*, females in the central roles; with the exception of one who is a close friend, all are related as siblings, mothers, or daughters.

The common thread is the character who is the ineffectual or dysfunctional mother of the senior generation: the emotionally distraught and suicidal Eve (the mother of all) in *Interiors*, the alcoholic and flirtatious

Norma in *Hannah*, and the hard-drinking, peripatetic, and loquacious Diane in *September*. Eve is surrounded and, usually, supported by a trio of daughters; similarly, Norma and her three daughters (including the mother of the lot—Hannah) form another dysfunctional nest. Diane, the painfully insecure and unfulfilled former movie star, is always estranged—emotionally and geographically—from her only child and daughter Lane, who must rely upon the support of her best friend Stephanie for mothering. These three- and four-fold configurations are the core of each of these films.

The narrative of each film realizes its imagery partially through the physical surroundings of the home; more specifically, the physical structures mirror the family structures. Although we are exposed to conflict and dysfunction in *Hannah*, there is an underlying warmth and closeness that results in part from the press of large numbers of family and friends milling about in Hannah's apartment at each of the three Thanksgiving dinners. In addition, the homey clutter of the apartment evokes a feeling of comfort amidst not only old friends and family members, but memorabilia, favorite books and objects d'art, and other artifacts of the family. Even the sweaters Elliot and Hannah wear at Thanksgiving evoke a feeling of warmth and solidity; in the final sequence of the film, Hannah reaches up and gently strokes the edges of Elliot's sweater as they cuddle in the door frame of their living room. Contrastingly, the spare, cold, and rigid loft that Lee and Frederick share is a clear representation of a relationship that cannot survive.

The *September* Vermont house in which the entire film takes place is an interesting contrast to Hannah's apartment. Although bathed throughout in golden hues, this home is devoid of a feeling of togetherness and instead is full of foreboding; what should be warm colors feel quite cold when they reflect the dynamics of this narrative. While the conflicts and separations of *Hannah and Her Sisters* initially suggest a splintering of the family and a diminution of importance of the family's gathering spot, Hannah's apartment, the Thanksgiving dinners always pull us—and the family—back home. But in *September*, when members of the family leave, they do not return: Howard—accepting the rejection of Lane—leaves without a good-bye, and returns only to stand literally in the background; Diane bids a dramatic farewell to her daughter, Lane, leaving us with the suspicion that neither of them anticipates a reunion soon; Stephanie will return to her husband and children, ending her temporary participation in this other world; Peter, failing to complete his novel or to sufficiently seduce Stephanie, goes back to New York to mull over his life. Lane is alone with the memories of Peter's rejection, her mother's denial of the ever-growing chasm between them, and the house—which her mother wanted to wrest from Lane's control. Diane's refusal to admit that the tentative family ties have most certainly been severed is reflected in her ironic plea to Lane: "This is the family house. How can you sell this place?!" The surviving family is Lane, alone in the family home; a home of warm, inviting colors but of cold and lonely ambience.

Interiors, of course, presents the ultimate example of such a barren ambience. The structural interiors of the family home and Eve's apartment are spartan and superficially aesthetic, and are arranged and constantly rearranged in a forced and artificial way. Correspondingly, the psychic interiors of the family members are virtually devoid of emotionality, are dressed with the thinnest layers of civility toward one another, and are arranged in relation to one another in the same forced and artificial manner, as each parent pushes Renata toward Joey, or uses their children as go-betweens in their splintered relationship. It is as if they are rearranging a vase on the living room mantle.

The film opens with Arthur, the father, realizing in retrospect that the world created for her family by his dutiful wife was a facade: "It was all so perfect, so ordered. Looking back of course, it was rigid. . . . I will say . . . it was like an ice palace" (Allen 1982, 114–15). Eve, an interior designer, is constantly remodeling and rearranging the interiors of homes, including her children's and her own, as if interior decorating was a means of rearranging the psychic or emotional interiors of the homes' occupants. It was an easy but facile way of bringing order and beauty out of chaos and drabness, although Eve's style as a designer proves no more beneficial or successful than her style as a wife, mother, or human being.

Interiors is a film remarkably devoid of color: Every character is wrapped in whites, light beiges or grays, or black; each wall, lamp, and vase is white, beige or the lightest of pastels. There is a clear absence of color in the physical surroundings and in the personalities and relationships of the family members. One scene captures quite well the colorless family and its home: Arthur's proclamation that he is leaving his wife is made at the breakfast table in the emotionless manner we imagine he employs daily as a Manhattan attorney. Eve's response, while ultimately emotional, is as muted as the pale dressing gown she wears at that moment. Renata and Joey, adults at the time, sit motionless and mute until Eve blurts out to Joey, "Will you please not breathe so hard" (Allen 1982, 123). The mostly absent third daughter, TV actress Flynn, while possessing somewhat more pizzazz than other family members, nonetheless appears to outsiders as clearly being a member of this family. Renata's husband Frederick remarks that Flynn is "a perfect example of . . . form without any content" (Allen 1982, 126). He might be speaking of the emotionality of the entire family as well as the physical structures in which they live.

Interestingly, Allen more often than not has family members looking *away* from their home, gazing out windows at the beach and ocean or at the Manhattan skyline unable, it seems, to see anything inside their home (that is, inside themselves) or afraid to face what is there. Their home is not what the architect David in *Hannah and Her Sisters* referred to as "vital structures," or what April, in response, called "organic." There is no such sense of life, little or none of the healthy and necessary interdependence of the components of an organism; these homes and this family are as much a facade as any movie set. In one of the film's final scenes, Joey at last talks with Eve in honest terms and gives voice to that which we have already seen: "I think you're, uh . . . really too perfect . . . to live in this world. I mean, all the beautifully furnished rooms, carefully designed interiors . . . everything so controlled. There wasn't any room for—uh eh, any real feelings. None" (Allen 1982, 172). Even Eve's earlier suicide attempt is enacted in this unemotional and controlled way; she methodically puts black tape on door jambs and window cracks in preparation for turning on the gas. When she is finished, the camera pulls back and we see that there actually is an aesthetic quality and symmetry to the newly applied black borders on the stark white interior of her apartment. As Eve eases herself down on a very stylish divan we witness a perversely tasteful suicide attempt; again, form without content.

The dreariness of *Interiors* takes on a new hue with the arrival of Arthur's lady friend, Pearl, who gives the lie to her name by dressing only in the most shocking of reds and oranges. Her wardrobe and her personality clash with both the physical and the emotional interiors of the family, all culminating in her drunken solo dance at her's and Arthur's wedding party, during which she shatters one of Eve's vases. Pearl brings the outside world with her into this family in a way that the other outsiders—Frederick and Mike, Joey's companion—have not. She announces shortly before the wedding that staying at the family's beach home "means redoing so much of the house . . . [because] it's . . . kind of pale" (Allen 1982, 162). But even Pearl cannot overcome the dark force that drives this family. Finally accepting Arthur's rejection and her replacement by Pearl, Eve is successful in taking her own life; the film ends with her funeral service, and we see everyone in the family—including Pearl—draped in black. Pearl's vivacity (and her wardrobe) have been stifled by Eve's operating, as it were, from the grave. One imagines this family continuing to rearrange and remodel its interiors in an attempt to find just the right configuration. Eve's influence, like any mother's, will most certainly continue to dominate the lives of all the characters, and they will succeed only in maintaining the most appropriate and aesthetically pleasing, yet superficial, emotional and structural interiors.

MOTHERS AND DAUGHTERS

Interiors, *Hannah and Her Sisters*, and *September* overlap one another in many ways. Allen's biographer wrote that "if a horse player were to describe *September*, he would say it is by *Hannah* out of *Interiors*" (Lax,

352), and Allen acknowledges that "all were meant to be serious pieces that examine family relationships. . . . *September* is less cerebral and much, much warmer than *Interiors* but not as warm and familial as *Hannah*" (Lax, 355). The direct and obvious connection of these three films is not just their interiors, but also—in *Interiors* and *Hannah and Her Sisters*—the trio of sisters and their relationship to their mother. The strongest character of each quartet is the eldest sister—Hannah and Renata—both of whom care for and support a mother who is either alcoholic or suicidal. Sibling rivalry or conflict exists between the eldest and the middle sister—Hannah and Holly, Renata and Joey—while the youngest sisters, Lee and Flynn, are usually presented as the most physically attractive of each trio.

Hannah's maternal proclivities are matched, within the confines of a different narrative, by Renata (the mother of a young girl), who is called upon by both her mother and father to help Joey find her way in the world, and upon whom Flynn looks as an exemplar of a "serious" artist, just as Hannah was used as the role model for Holly and Lee to emulate. Additionally, Renata is the one sister who continues to provide her mother with (false) hope of a reconciliation with Arthur, while Joey wants to press the truth upon her mother—just as Joey's counterpart in *Hannah*, Holly, does with her play about the family, which includes "the character of the mother . . . just a boozy old flirt with a filthy mouth" (Allen 1987a, 154).

The outsiders to each family also share certain characteristics and behavior with one another. Both families suffer the wrath of an angry artist named Frederick; a writer in *Interiors* and a painter in *Hannah*. These namesakes are opposites in terms of their relationships with their female partners, however, with Renata's Frederick feeling inferior to her and Lee's lover lording his superior knowledge and talent over her; in any event, neither couple is well-suited. Just as Elliot pursues and temporarily wins Lee's affections, Frederick—in a drunken funk—attempts to rape Flynn; the difference in style and substance between the two speaks volumes about the difference between *Hannah and Her Sisters* and *Interiors*.

The conflict between the eldest and the middle sister is evidenced in *Hannah* at the ill-fated luncheon attended by all three sisters. As Allen's camera continually circles the table, disorienting the audience to match the confusion, conflict, and restlessness of the trio, Holly announces that she wants to take several months—literally at the expense of Hannah—to try her hand at writing. In her ever-maternal voice, Hannah suggests how Holly might spend the time "more productively. . . . A person doesn't just say one day, 'Okay, now-now I'm finished as an actress. Now I'm a writer'" (Allen 1987a, 139). This same maternally critical attitude is seen in Renata when she and Frederick look over some of Joey's photographs: "Poor Joey. She has all the anguish and, uh, anxiety, the artistic personality, without any of the talent. And, naturally, I'm put in the position of having to encourage her. . . . She should just marry Michael, and stop her obsessive worrying about being so damn creative!" (Allen 1982, 142). Marriage and domesticity are the realization of what, traditionally or stereotypically, any mother (or mother figure) wants for her daughter; artistic creativity is not a realistic or pragmatic goal for Hannah's or Renata's sister. And while Holly *is* successful in her artistic endeavors, she is happiest and most fulfilled with the miracle baby, a denouement that Joey rejects. Upon learning of her pregnancy, Mike says, "You know, we could have a kid. It wouldn't be the end of the world," to which Joey responds, "For you maybe. For me it'd be the end of the world" (Allen 1982, 144). This story line—from the birth of a baby being the end of the world in *Interiors* to it serving as the poignant and romantic end of the film in *Hannah*—is quite a leap for Allen. And this plot of course best captures the difference in these films, in these families: One entails a premonition of, focus on, and even hope for, death; the other is full of life-affirming love, maternity, family, and domesticity.

Notwithstanding the protestations of political and religious conservatives and neoconservatives, the family as an institution is in no danger of perishing, although its functions and form will no doubt continue to evolve, or respond, to sociocultural or economic forces. Woody Allen's filmic image of the family, if his past several films are evidence, will continue to reflect these changes, even if tangentially, but nonetheless will be rooted in the traditions of marriage and domesticity. Allen has shown in *Hannah and Her Sisters* and the films following it that there is a concurrence between his view of family and the growing diversity of this institution in American culture. Indeed, his views may be more in line with what conservatives see as the paradigmatic formation of the 1950s nuclear family, largely a fiction in itself, while at the same time Allen reflects contemporary culture realistically. Allen's reliance on romanticized and nostalgic views of the past, both in his flashbacks and his use of clips from the films of the 1930s and 1940s, illustrates the era and the traditions in which he is grounded—notwithstanding his life among the intellectual elites of New York and his own aforementioned family debacle. But these sentimental looks back are only temporary, for Allen brings himself and his audience to contemporary realizations of family conflicts and dynamics. It is in *Hannah and Her Sisters* that he does this best, and it is here that he shows his traditional hand by resolving those conflicts in a way reminiscent of a much earlier time in Hollywood. There is in *Hannah* a maturity of attitude, or at least a recognition by Allen of the power and—sometimes—appropriateness of tradition. This maturity becomes something different in *Husbands and Wives* and *Manhattan Murder Mystery*—perhaps an acceptance of years advancing too quickly—but it does continue in the vein of traditionalism so common to his work.

Notes

1. Such theoretical or academic notions are, of course, confounded by the real-life mishaps of Allen. His romantic and sexual liaison with the adopted daughter of his longtime lover Mia Farrow seems to give life to these Freudian considerations. I am quite intentionally limiting the discussion here to Allen's cinematic behavior and renderings while acknowledging the inseparability of his personal and professional worlds.

2. The extent to which this background contributed to his filmic images of family—in any form—might seem obvious but is best left to more psychological considerations of Allen.

Works Cited

Allen, Woody. *Hannah and Her Sisters*. New York: Vintage Books, 1987a.

—. *Three Films of Woody Allen*. New York: Vintage Books, 1987b.

Four Films of Woody Allen. New York: Random House, 1982.

Biskind, Peter, and Barbara Ehrenreich. "Machismo and Hollywood's Working Class." *Socialist Review* 50–51 (May-June 1980). Reprinted in *American Media and Mass Culture: Left Perspectives*. Edited by Donald Lazere. Berkeley: University of California Press, 1987. 201–15.

Byars, Jackie. *All That Hollywood Allows: Re-reading Gender in 1950s Melodrama*. Chapel Hill: University of North Carolina Press, 1991.

Cherlin, Andrew. *Marriage, Divorce, Remarriage* Rev. ed. Cambridge: Harvard University Press, 1992.

Collins, Randall. *Sociology of Marriage and the Family: Gender, Love and Property*. Chicago: Nelson-Hall, 1985.

Connors, Joanna. "Bashing: Films Play Women as She-devils." *San Diego Union Tribune*, 3 October 1992; C3.

Coontz, Stephanie. *The Way We Never Were: American Families and the Nostalgia Trap*. New York: Basic Books, 1992.

Denzin, Norman K. *Images of Postmodern Society: Social Theory and Contemporary Cinema*. London: Sage, 1991.

Dowd, Maureen. "The Five Women of 'Hannah and Her Sisters.'" *New York Times*, 2 February 1986: sec. 2.

Faludi, Susan. *Backlash: The Undeclared War against American Women*. New York: Crown, 1991.

Freud, Sigmund. *Civilization and Its Discontents*. Translated by James Strachey. New York: W.W. Norton, 1961. Translation of *Das Unbehagen in Der Kultur*, 1930.

Geist, William. "The *Rolling Stone* Interview: Woody Allen." *Rolling Stone*, 9 April 1987. Reprinted in *The Woody Allen Companion*, edited by. Stephen J. Spignesi, 39–55. Kansas City: Andrews and McNeel, 1992.

Girgus, Sam B. *The Films of Woody Allen*. Cambridge: Cambridge University Press, 1993.

Gopnik, Adam. "The Outsider." *New Yorker*, 25 October 1993; 86–93.

Hamilton, Denise. "A House, Cash—and No Parents." *Los Angeles Times*, 24 June 1993; sec. A.

Hochschild, Arlie, with Anne Machung. "The Second Shift: Working Parents and the Revolution at Home." In *Family in Transition: Rethinking Marriage, Sexuality, Child Rearing, and Family Organization*, edited by Arlene S. Skolnick and Jerome H. Skolnick, 431–38. 7th ed. New York: Harper Collins, 1992.

Jones, Elise F., et al. "Teenage Pregnancy in Developed Countries." In *Crisis in American Institutions*, edited by Jerome H. Skolnick and Elliott Currie, 277–94. 8th ed. New York: Harper Collins, 1991.

Kozol, Jonathan. *Rachel and Her Children: Homeless Families in America*. New York: Fawcett Columbine, 1988.

Lasch, Christopher. *Haven in a Heartless World: The Family Besieged*. New York: Basic Books, 1977.

—. *The Culture of Narcissism: American Life in An Age of Diminishing Expectations*. New York: Warner Books, 1979.

Lax, Eric. *Woody Allen: A Biography*. New York: Alfred A. Knopf, 1991.

May. Lary. "Movie Star Politics." In *The Way We Never Were: American Families and the Nostalgia Trap*. New York: Basic Books, 1992.

Mednick, Martha T. "Single Mothers: A Review and Critique of Current Research." In *Family in Transition: Rethinking Marriage, Sexuality, Child Rearing, and Family Organization*, edited by Arlene S. Skolnick and Jerome H. Skolnick, 363–78. 7th ed. New York: Harper Collins, 1992.

Modleski, Tania. "The Search for Tomorrow in Today's Soap Operas." In *American Media and Mass Culture: Left Perspectives*, edited by Donald Lazere, 266–78. Berkeley: University of California Press, 1987. 266–278.

Schatz, Thomas. *Hollywood Genres: Formulas, Filmmaking, and the Studio System*. New York: Random House, 1981.

Schenden, Laurie K. "Wins and Losses." *Los Angeles Times*, 22 September 1993; E1–2.

Seligmann, Jean. "Variations on a Theme." In *Family in Transition: Rethinking Marriage, Sexuality, Child Rearing, and Family Organization*, edited by Arlene S. Skolnick and Jerome H. Skolnick, 518–23. 7th ed. New York: Harper Collins, 1992.

Shogren, Elizabeth. "Families Total 43% of Homeless, Survey Reports." *Los Angeles Times*, 22 December 1993; Sec. A.

Skolnick, Jerome H., and Elliott Currie, eds. *Crisis in American Institutions*. 8th ed. New York: Harper Collins, 1991.

Skolnick, Arlene S., and Jerome H. Skolnick, eds. *Family in Transition: Rethinking Marriage, Sexuality, Child Rearing, and Family Organization*. 7th ed. New York: Harper Collins, 1992.

Smith, Lynn. "Building a Family in Steps." *Los Angeles Times*, 6 October 1993; sec. E.

Spignesi, Stephen J. *The Woody Allen Companion*. Kansas City: Andrews and McNeel, 1992.

United States Conference of Mayors, The. *The 1990 United States Mayors Report on Homelessness*. Washington, D.C.: The United States Conference of Mayors, 1990.

Frame Breaking and Code Breaking in Woody Allen's Relationship Films

TERRY L. ALLISON AND RENÉE R. CURRY

WOODY ALLEN has been making films for thirty years. In that time he has gained a reputation with some critics for consistently providing strong and central roles for women. Critics such as Sam B. Girgus find the roles for women genuinely crafted with independence and integrity. By association with these roles and by the representation of himself as a "feminine" male, Allen has been heralded by Girgus as a filmmaker "espousing major change" (Girgus, 9), presumably between the sexes. Richard Feldstein, however, finds no friend to women in the films of Woody Allen; rather, he notes that Allen's women become "specular icons in a circuit of desire" (Feldstein, 69). Further study of Allen's negative/positive representations of women become rather moot when viewed as part of his larger agenda, which is to play in the field of late-twentieth-century relationships between men and men; women and men; and women and women. Specifically, Woody Allen toys with "breaking the frame" (Hedges, xiii-xvi) of cinematic screen space for men and for women while he also breaks codes of prescribed gender behavior.

The risks that Allen takes by situating relationship narrative as the primary focus of his work invite a variety of theoretical interpretations guided by feminist, cultural studies, and gender studies analyses. These interpretations include reading Allen as usurper of "masquerade" (Irigaray, 220; Doane, 82; Kuhn, 257); Allen as participant in "looked-at-ness" (Cohan, 205); Allen as user of "feminine screen space" in order to extend his own artistic persona (Hedges, 88); Allen as adherent to communion/agency theories of gender roles (Bakan in Spence and Heimlich, 16; LaFollete, 61); Allen as reviser of masculinity and stardom (May and Striwerda, xii-xv); and, Allen as "trafficker" in women (Sedgwick, 3, Rubin, 180–83). While exploring each of these arguments as they relate to Allen's films proves revealing, we argue that all of these readings point toward variations of Allen as code-breaker. Therefore, our analysis will engage many of the theoretical interpretations mentioned in this introduction, with a concentration on Hedges's work on screen space, May and Striwerda's work on masculinity, and Sedgwick's work on trafficking in women.

This essay was written specifically for this volume and is published here for the first time by permission of the authors.

Woody Allen explores the terrain of relationship risk taking in order to extol the importance of risk and change. Exactly what is at stake in any particular relationship often remains unspoken, but Allen suggests that issues of male bonding, more satisfying male-female relationships, maintenance of a secure masculinity, and a demythologizing of the female sisterhood constitute worthwhile pursuits. To examine risk and relationship in Woody Allen's films, we will explore *Manhattan* (1979), *Hannah and Her Sisters* (1986), and *Manhattan Murder Mystery* (1993). These films will permit us to examine Allen's work during both his peak period and the current phase of his filmmaking.

After much experimentation with cinematic depictions of relationships in films, Allen reached a period of artistic success with such films as *Manhattan* and *Hannah and Her Sisters* from his middle period, and then continued such exploration in *Manhattan Murder Mystery*. In *Manhattan* Allen both playfully and dangerously explores marriage, divorce, lesbianism, fatherhood, male bonding, and the love of an older man for a child/woman. In particular, he interrogates the existence of screen space typically allotted to women; the narrative issue of masculinity; and the psychological issue of communion and agency. Also, he traffics in women by situating three different types of women with whom to have relationships: the lesbian, the intellectual heterosexual woman, and the child/woman. Eve Sedgwick cites Gayle Rubin's work when she describes the trafficking relationship between patriarchy, heterosexuality, masculinity, and women: "Based on readings and critiques of Levi-Strauss and Engels, in addition to Freud and Lacan, Gayle Rubin has argued in an influential essay that patriarchal heterosexuality can best be discussed in terms of one or another form of traffic in women: it is the use of women as exchangeable, perhaps symbolic, property for the primary purpose of cementing the bonds of men with men" (Sedgwick, 26).

In *Manhattan*, Isaac (Woody Allen) has been divorced by Jill (Meryl Streep) because she has met a "more masterful" woman. Jill writes a book about hers and Isaac's marriage, from which Isaac's male friend, Yale, later quotes a passage. In this passage, Jill explains her preference for lesbian lovemaking: "Making love to this deeper, more masterful female, made me realize what an empty experience, what a bizarre charade sex with my husband was." Allen excerpts this quote in the film to multilayered effect: to depict lesbians as hostile to men, to depict lesbian sex as more fulfilling than heterosexual lovemaking, to further Isaac's vulnerability, to lessen his sexual prowess in public, and to express Yale's interest in Isaac's sexual reputation. With this scene Allen reveals his interest in the terrain and in the complicated codes of relationships for late-twentieth-century males.

A piece of this terrain, Allen suggests, is the male seen as inadequate when juxtaposed against the lesbian as a choice for a late-twentieth-century lover. Woody Allen's handling of this relationship works both through narrative discourse as well as at the level of screen space and the position-ing of the female character. According to Inez Hedges,

> Because film is a visual medium, space is an important area of cinematic expressiveness. This includes not only the two-dimensional "screen space" that gives a film its particular look, but also the three-dimensional "diegetic space." Diegetic space can be mediated through a character, through the point-of-view shot which is clearly attributable to the character's act of look-ing. . . . The use of point-of-view shots lends importance to the character thus highlighted, whose perception becomes a link between the spectator and the story. The failure in film to mediate information about the diegetic space through women characters leads to the serious consequence of rein-forcing a social fact of life: the cutting off of a woman from the full explo-ration of space. (Hedges, 70)

Although Jill's words, as mediated by Yale, are present in this scene, Jill's character is not. The point-of-view that interprets the lesbian word is male. A heterosexual male reader reads the words to a heterosexual male and a heterosexual female listener. By designing this multilayered, multinarrated, and multi-interpretive scene, Allen makes clear his determination to play in the field of screen space and its relationship to gender positioning.

By having Yale narrate Jill's narration in her book, Allen also displays the masculine urge to resound the female word in his own voice. The mas-culine must reclaim the authoritative position of voicing because he can-not afford to let the female have say. Likewise, when it comes to screen space, Allen's character, Isaac, struggles to reclaim the screen space once dedicated to him as Jill's husband in this film. He should be standing at her side (or rather, she should be standing at his), but Jill's lesbian lover has filled that space. Therefore, though he claims he did so accidentally, Isaac attempts to kill Jill's lesbian partner. Allen does not suggest killing, even symbolically, the masculine in order for Isaac to become the feminine male; instead, he wants only to kill the other woman to gain access to the woman he wants. Isaac ultimately aims to reinstate masculinity, and if he cannot do that with a particular woman—Jill, in this case—he will reenact his agency repeatedly by moving from woman to woman until he feels comfortably masculine. This episode suggests Allen's willingness to display the fragility of masculinity and to interrogate its desire to secure both a place in his protagonist's desired woman's heart as well as a significant space on the screen.

Hedges reminds us that the women in these films become, to some extent, mere vehicles for the expression of a male artistic persona: "In films made by men, the strategy of presenting the world as an extension of a female personality is often used as a metaphor for the filmmaker's artis-tic persona. Ingmar Bergman and Woody Allen both exemplify this prac-tice; in *Persona* and *Interiors* they are simultaneously exploring some of the problems of the artistic mind through female characters and making statements about femininity. In both films, however, women are shown in very traditional terms" (Hedges, 90). The lesbian woman in this film affords Allen the opportunity to explore concerns, or perhaps fears, about the stereotypically perceived effeminate artist.

The woman Isaac accidentally tries to kill has taken his place as parent, transmitting her artistic skills to his son, Willy. Isaac believes that these artistic skills may threaten his son's incipient masculinity and heterosexuality when he asks Jill (as if his son could engage in only these two choices): "Does he play basketball, does he wear dresses?" Despite Allen's own status as artist and his playing a writer in this film, Isaac portrays the role of father not as transmitter of ideas, culture, or artistry, but of traditional masculine values, such as sports, competition, and seduction of women. Allen's on-screen characters throughout his films usually define their fatherhood roles through sports. Dressed in athletic clothing, Isaac first arrives to take Willy to play basketball. Isaac later plays with Willy in the Divorced Father-Son All Stars, a baseball league. Allen chooses to film Shea Stadium as one of the opening shots of *Manhattan*, and near the film's closing, as Isaac lists the things that make life worth living, the name of Willie Mays immediately springs to his lips. Sports have defined the arenas of masculinity and femininity in the twentieth century, separating the boys from the girls, the men from the women (Pronger 17). Allen's on-screen characters often declare their masculinity through their sports activities and spectatorship.

In *Manhattan* Isaac also initiates his son into the world of heterosexual romance. Though Willy is quite young, many years away from puberty, Isaac points out to him two tall, beautiful women as father and son are shepherded into a restaurant, Elaine's. Isaac inappropriately suggests to Willy that he should have made a play for the women, and that he blew his opportunity, since one of the women in particular, the "brunette," would have gone for Willy. Isaac wants to ensure that since he has been ousted from the male role in Jill's household, Willy will fulfill in his stead the burden of masculinity. To counter the effects of Willy's female-run household, Isaac develops strategies so that his son will engage in what he views as "proper" relationships both with men, through sports, and with women, through seduction.

Allen's characters do not take on a new nurturing fatherhood (which May and Striwerda promote) as an alternative to traditional fatherhood models, nor does he develop other possible ways of fathering. Furthermore, the ultimate demands of the masculine leave him without a male friend. Throughout most of *Manhattan*, Isaac and Yale explore their friendship and their other relationships. Allen presents the men as real friends who carry on real conversations and share feelings. While the two men play racquetball, thus enacting the unintimate "parallel play" typical of intramale relationships (Striwerda and May, 97), they do not merely engage in superficial bonding; instead, they talk about their relationships with women. From one perspective, their talk seems steeped in seriousness; every discussion is fraught with angst about their wives, lovers, and careers, and even Yale's fear of becoming a father. Allen's men talk about things men do not usually discuss; they participate in communion.

However, as usual for Allen, this new, vulnerable masculinity masks an underlying competition for women. The racquetball game serves more as exercise and pleasure than competitive sport, but their conversation during it, their working out of relationships, amounts to Yale turning over Mary, his extramarital affair, to Isaac, while Isaac voices a desire to give up Tracy, his present lover, so that he can take on Mary. This scene allows Allen to play in and with the stereotypes about male machismo. It also further allows him to demonstrate how trafficking in women works. As Sedgwick points out when discussing the work of René Girard, "In any erotic rivalry, the bond that links the two rivals is as intense and potent as the bond that links either of the rivals to the beloved . . . . For instance, Girard finds many examples in which the choice of the beloved is determined in the first place, not by the qualities of the beloved, but by the beloved's already being the choice of the person who has been chosen as a rival" (Sedgwick, 21). Though both Yale and his wife, Emily, had previously encouraged Isaac to stick with the seventeen-year-old Tracy, as soon as Yale finds himself encumbered with Mary, Isaac quite willingly demotes Tracy and promotes Mary. This male conversation may not involve backslapping or lewd comments; nevertheless, under the guise of real relationships and shared feelings, the men have asserted their right to traffic in women, to trade them around when necessary.

Ironically too, Isaac quits his job as writer for a television program in order to write fiction—thereby questioning the role of male as potential financial provider and caretaker of dependent women and children. Thus, for the last half of the film, he remains without tangible "work"—he has produced four chapters of a book, but art traditionally constitutes an effeminate type of work. We see him instead frequenting art galleries with Tracy and science exhibits with Mary.

When with these women, Isaac's antics and fears betray his competition for occupying the screen space typically allotted to women in film. In one scene with Mary (Diane Keaton), he runs through the rain with her in Central Park. She holds a newspaper over her head, and he keeps grabbing at it to protect his head, a nonmasculine antic. Masculine codes of behavior construct the expectation that the male, Isaac, keep the female, Mary, from getting wet. However, Allen, as director wanting to break the codes of such limiting and polarizing behaviors, makes Isaac care more about keeping himself dry than about the female he is supposed to be protecting. It is this breaking of the code that makes the audience laugh.

Isaac also has to have Tracy spend the first night in his new apartment because he admits his fear of staying alone in new places, again breaking a stereotypical relationship code about who needs protection from being alone. Allen shows these simple behavior modifications as signifying the new male apparent in Isaac: he has shed any chivalric sense of protecting women, and in its stead has instituted the impression that women can protect men. On the surface the film flaunts just such a code-breaking ideology—in fact, Allen's entire body of work purports that relationships, rather than the typically male-directed epic action of classic Hollywood cinema, serve as the most elevated subject matter. Work, politics, and the world exist as secondary issues at best. We argue that by centralizing relationships, Allen, in the guise of the characters he designs for himself, and in his screen management of these central male characters, suggests that femininity and masculinity, however we choose to define these terms, cannot be polarized.

Near the end of *Manhattan*, Isaac, "betrayed" by Mary and Yale, realizes that he must have the love of a younger woman because it is more pure. In fact he has romanticized the purity of Tracy's love because, although Tracy professes to love him, she proves the least purely romantic of any of the film's characters. He conveniently forgets her supposition about love: "Well, I don't know, maybe people weren't meant to have one deep relationship. Maybe we're meant to have, you know, a series of relationships of different lengths. I mean, that kind of thing's gone out of date." Isaac's denial of her burgeoning beliefs about love negates Tracy as an independent thinking woman in order to preserve his image of her as one capable of love by his definition.

Once the revelation about his desire for Tracy becomes clear, he turns into the man of action, the agent activating this love. He runs through the streets of Manhattan toward Tracy in order to rekindle this communion. By so doing, he suggests that definitions of communion as feminine and agency as masculine prove interchangeable when male desire becomes activated. Communion becomes the most important thing to him. But the preservation of the relationship did not take priority months before when Tracy wanted it to; the relationship only takes precedence now, when Isaac learns Tracy is leaving the country, because Isaac will be left alone with a damaged ego. At the end of this film, Isaac becomes the purely masculine agent.

Girgus views the creation of Tracy as a "truly original character, a young woman who becomes a blending of romanticized feminine adoration, vulnerable innocence, and unselfish sophistication" (Girgus, 64). Nothing seems truly original about Tracy; she seems rather the same young, innocent representation of male adoration whose independence and sophistication have been ignored in order for the older man to love her like a child. Girgus admits that "her [Tracy's] love, as he [Isaac] realizes at the end, comes closest to being the true one for him. However, it is true only in a thoroughly idealistic and narcissistic sense" (Girgus, 65). This idealism, however, never leaves Isaac. He acts out the supposed vulnerable position, pleading with Tracy not to go, suggesting to her that in six months' time she will become corrupted and forget about him. Importantly, however, he undercuts this pleading by never suggesting that he go along with her to London. He will not accompany, nor follow, a woman into her life even though his work as a writer is portable, and even though he lives in an apartment he avows to hate. He does articulate that relationships require sudden changes, but he assumes that they are her changes to make. He will not, or can not, escape/leave the familiar masculine encoding that entitles him to go where he wants, when he wants, and with whom he chooses. Allen enacts the characteristics he deems expected by the construct of the code-breaking male, but ultimately, when the role conflicts with his self-concept as a masculine agent, he either sheds that attribute typically deemed feminine or refuses, as in the case of not offering to accompany Tracy, to participate in the ultimate demands of genuine code breaking.

In *Manhattan* Isaac and Yale lose their friendship through their competition over Mary. Though Isaac initially engaged in some potentially compromising intimacies with Mary (before Yale handed her over to him), when Yale reclaims Mary, Isaac feels betrayed. "Yeah, well I saw her first!" Yale retorts when Isaac accuses him of taking advantage of his trust. Isaac's telling query in response to Yale, "What are you, six years old?," demonstrates how the two men ultimately based their friendship not on adult intimacy but on childish competition for women whom neither can own. Their sharing and feeling conversations serve as weak supplementation to profoundly male competitive urges to traffick in women. The men's actions betray the purported intimacy of their conversation; the talk was all talk.

By the time of *Hannah and Her Sisters*, Allen has given up on the representation of significant male friendships. In this film, Allen ostensibly turns his camera to relationships among women. In particular, he again explores the terrain of risk taking in relationships, and he also more intricately plays with encoded screen space; narrative exploration of masculinity and competition; and, the terrain of love triangles and trafficking in women. As artist, Allen gives birth to a plethora of women characters, but he cannot allow them to develop. He seemingly wants to create a world of women and to invigorate cinematic space with female action, but these women once again exist as mere backdrop for male action. The point-of-view shot keeps these women as "looked-at" figures, rather than as explored characters. According to Inez Hedges, women are conventionally positioned in the three-dimensional, diegetic space in a manner that makes them seem more passive than the male characters. In the first place, most point-of-view shots are authorized by the look of male characters. Secondly, women characters are less likely to initiate action. This means that they function like two-dimensional figures, similar to the landscapes against which they are photographed" (Hedges, 88).

The characters of Hannah (Mia Farrow), Lee (Barbara Hershey), and Holly (Dianne Wiest) represent a circle, an ovum of sisterhood, a daringly impenetrable bond that is enticing to the male characters, much like the egg chemically attracts and appeals to the sperm, an interest of Allen's since the early days of *Everything You Always Wanted to Know about Sex* (1972).

We first receive information about this circle of women through the voice-over of Hannah's husband, Elliot (Michael Caine). As he studies Hannah's sister, Lee, and tells us how much he loves Lee, the camera examines her from his point of view. Hannah interrupts his reverie with a touch on the arm: "Elliot, Elliot, sweetheart, have you tried these?" "These" refers to the delicacies that her other sister, Holly, has prepared for Thanksgiving, but in the context of Elliot's reveries, Hannah's question ironically comes off as a question about whether he has "tried" her sisters. Elliot replies that her sister, Holly, is a terrific cook. He calls to Holly, who, as she walks down the hall toward him, again we see from his point of view, "Why don't you open a restaurant?" Thus all the sisters have been introduced to us via Elliot. They have been rounded up and identified by a man. He has watched one, one has touched him, and he has addressed another. The sisters exist by virtue of Elliot's recognition of them and by their recognition of him. He is the agent of their cinematic communion. The camera does not cluster them together as a central unit, but rather as a set of individuals not too distant from the same man. After these introductions, Holly tells Hannah that she needs to speak to her alone. Elliot calls out as they walk away, "I'm her husband, she tells me everything." He covets inclusion in their sisterhood and demonstrates a threatened man at the film's first portrayal of the women going off together.

The Woody Allen character, Mickey, roaming around on the periphery of this film, also covets inclusion in this sisterhood. In a flashback, the film reveals that Allen had once been married to Hannah but had left the marriage and the space he occupied in her life because, due to his infertility, the couple decided to become impregnated with his friend's sperm. Mickey thought he would be able to handle the oddity of the situation, but the film leads us to believe that he could no longer share screen space/life with Hannah once other sperm had infiltrated his domain. Once again, screen space, defined in this case as Hannah's body, is something he wants to occupy both figuratively and literally, but only as a means of control.

When Mickey's marriage to Hannah fell apart, he dated Holly once, thereby trying to stay connected with the sisters, but the date proved disastrous. Time goes by, however, and he comes to see Holly in a different light. In fact, while Mickey has remained the same, Holly has changed her personality to become more suitable for him. They fall in love, which allows Mickey back into Hannah's house. In fact, we see him at the end of the film comfortably resituated there, giving thanks at Thanksgiving dinner for the new central space next to Holly that he now occupies on the screen.

Allen cannot permit the film simply to be about sisters. It becomes a film about men trying to infiltrate a group of sisters. As in other films, Allen eventually recaptures the virility and masculinity of his on-screen character. Allen culminates the film by having Mickey's purported sterility turn into fertility. Though he failed to impregnate one sister, Hannah, he succeeds with another, Holly. Allen threatens Mickey's masculinity, but restores it when the right woman comes along.

The terrain of masculinity and its accompanying issues of competition and fatherhood becomes apparent when the other, more virile, male donor of the sperm ousts Mickey from his role as head of household. The friend, Norman (Tony Roberts), like a similar friend, Rob, played by the same actor in *Annie Hall*, has moved to Hollywood and achieved higher career status and wealth, leaving Mickey behind to struggle with artistic success. Norman appears only briefly in the film, to place Mickey within a competitive career framework and on an imaginary Kinscy scale, towards the less competitive, more artistic, more feminine end.

Mickey also fails as a father. Allen depicts one fatherly interaction between him and his twin boys: Mickey brings the boys baseball mitts for their birthday, though they are too young to appreciate them. This gift of the gloves highlights that even when his male protagonists' children, always boys in the films, can barely stand or walk, Allen sees the role of father as one in which the father gives the sons gifts that bring them into the realm of the masculine. Allen could not have chosen a more obvious iconology for transmitting the masculine (Clements). In a very brief moment in the film, Allen reveals how easily he repudiates the space of the code-breaking male.

In this same visit to the kids, Mickey reveals his lingering distress about the divorce by referring both to Elliot and to himself as losers. He comments on Elliot to Hannah: "I like him cause he's a loser. He's awkward, clumsy, like me. I always like an underconfident person. You've always had great taste in husbands." In this discourse, he not only names himself a loser, but he claims to like himself that way, and furthermore, he ushers himself once again into Hannah's inner circle by allowing that he and Elliot merely duplicate each other.

This desire to occupy the domestic screen space, to reframe the story of sisters into male-female couples, evidences an obsession not with wanting to share that domesticity or to simply live there, but rather to make it exclusive and to try to break up the ring around the sisters. Elliot wants to separate Lee from Hannah and Hannah from her sisters, and Mickey wants to separate Holly from Hannah by making her less dependent. Each of the men in the film wants one woman or more to himself, and he does not want the women to have any other attachments. Mickey wanted Hannah exclusively; the entry of his friend's sperm ruined this sole arrangement. Elliot wants both women, Lee and Hannah, but he does not want either of them to have each other. In a vicious discussion with Hannah at the second Thanksgiving, he informs her that no one knows how to love her, not him nor any of her sisters. He wants her to feel isolated from her loved ones. Frederick (Lee's lover, played by Max Von Sydow) shamelessly articulates both his need for Lee alone and his contempt for all other people. These men cannot conceive of women as separate from their need to love or be loved by them.

The fact that one of the triangles in the film consists of three women, three sisters, attests to Allen's willingness to play with the whole concept of relationship triangles and the resultant messiness and incestuousness surrounding relationships. He suggests that some men fear a sisterhood, a group of women who can potentially bond with one another, and he revels in demonstrating that these bonds of sisterhood are sunderable. A particularly memorable scene that explores this triangle—of course, it's designed as circle in the film so as to mock women's supposed ways of being—is the scene in which the three sisters dine together, seemingly only with one another.

The camera in this scene makes its impish presence so obvious that it becomes an intrusive reporter of the scene and virtually interrupts any potential intimacy among the sisters, as well as that between the audience and the characters. Although Allen's character, Mickey, has no place at the lunch table with the women, Allen the director certainly makes his presence behind the camera known to the characters and to the audience. The camera circles around and around the women at a dizzying pace. It makes the women's inner circle seem nauseating, dim-sighted, and hostile. After quite a few rotations, Lee announces that she is dizzy. She presumes the dizziness ensues from all the talk, but the camera halts suddenly as if it and its plot have been uncovered.

We argue that Lee herself becomes self-reflexive about the treatment the camera deals the women (not an isolated occurrence in Allen's films: in *Purple Rose of Cairo* [1985], cinema characters commonly reflect upon their roles in the film). Once Lee draws attention to the camera's dizzying take, the camera stops, but so too does the scene. Allen thus allows his women characters to demonstrate seeming insight into and power over the ways in which perception by external mechanisms—such as cameras or patriarchal manipulations—distorts women's relationships with each other. However, he undercuts any sense of directorial sensitivity to the treatment of women's intimate space by cutting away from both the substantive confrontation in the scene—that between Holly and Hannah—and the confrontation between Lee and the camera work.

The only screen space in which Allen takes an interest is that into which he can insert himself artistically. He has no desire nor intention to record a straightforward story about Hannah and her sisters. Woody Allen prefers to portray a dizzying, circuitous story about everything but the intimacy of the sisters. This story chronicles Mickey's reentry into Hannah's family, and it exposes Elliot's affair, which threatens to divide further the sisters. Hannah and her sisters provide mere blurry filler for the men's stories. Lax tells us that neither Farrow nor Allen could ever understand Hannah (Lax, 292). One would think that the namesake character of the film might be worth comprehending, especially by its creator and its interpreter.

At the end of the story, Allen finally makes his entrance back into Hannah's house and interjects himself into the desired domestic space. We see him approach Holly's face in the mirror. Then he occupies that space with her; they kiss and symbolically become one in the mirror. From their dialogue we discover that they have married, thus two also have legally become one in the frame of the mirror—the camera frames them in the same space. He then tells Holly, who has become a writer, to write a story about how a man marries one sister and then marries another. Ironically, this story has just been told to us on the screen under the guise of something called *Hannah and Her Sisters*.

In *Manhattan Murder Mystery* Allen explores the risk-taking terrain in relationships that offers new definitions of relationship bargaining, new masculine agency, and a continuance of play with screen space. This film opens with Larry (Allen) and Carol (Keaton) attending a hockey game at Madison Square Garden. Carol has agreed to come to the game, though visibly bored and annoyed, in exchange for Larry's attending all of a Wagner performance at the Metropolitan Opera. From the outset of the film Allen establishes a dichotomy between the realm of the masculine and the feminine. Where Allen could have chosen basketball, another sport played at Madison Square Garden, he chooses hockey, one of the few sports that until very recently remained the exclusive domain of the male athlete. Hockey, along with football and boxing, qualifies as among the most masculine sports primarily because it relies on aggression and violence: "Athletic competence is actually a secondary feature of hockey, especially in the NHL—the real appeal lies in its significance as a 'man's game.' The masculine aesthetic of hockey becomes almost sacramental through its violence and bloodshed" (Pronger, 22). Opera and musicality sit at the opposite extreme to hockey, and are associated not simply with the feminine, but with the effeminate gay as well (Brett, 11). Journalists and writers of fiction also posit opera as an opposite to sport, particularly violent sport (Silverman, 23; Maupin, 81). Heterosexual men can display tears, anger, and excitement at sports events; gay men can do so at opera performances.

While Carol sits miserably through the entire hockey game, thus fulfilling her end of the bargain, Larry will not sit through the entire opera performance. Allen uses his Jewish heritage, in conflict with the Nazi embrace of Wagner's music, to excuse himself from the Wagner opera, when actually he is fleeing his association with the feminized space of the operatic art. Allen may pay lip service to and may verbally stage a performance as the feminine male, willing to trade places with his wife, but he will not allow himself physically to occupy screen space typically allotted to women by sitting through the entire performance. He must escape his association with the feminine or gay male aesthetic before the performance overwhelms him.

Allen uses position switching throughout the film to suggest possible sharing of gender roles and to play with redefining concepts of agency and communion. In *Manhattan Murder Mystery* a simple role reversal, which has the objective of showing Allen to be an egalitarian film director, portrays the male protagonists, Larry (Allen) and Ted (Alan Alda), as uninterested in a murder mystery. Larry especially wants to maintain a status quo existence within a safe domestic sphere. We hear from his wife, Carol, that he used to be more fun, more interested in the outside world. Read in terms of the psychological definition of masculinity, Larry used to be more masculine, he used to have more agency in the world, he used to like action and mysteries. The audience is supposed to enjoy Larry's whining pleas for stability, but Carol's dialogue, which implies that a dull marriage is headed toward a particularly sour conclusion, keeps the audience from viewing the domestic character as the stable, pleasing one.

Larry now fully occupies domestic screen space, a cinematic positioning typically afforded to women alone. Hedges claims that women characters who step outside of the confines of typically prescribed cinematic space frequently end up ensconced in domestic space, but that they have struggled to redefine this space, "the traditional locus of the housewife." Hedges finds it "exciting to imagine a film in which the woman character would move outside the home, performatively creating her space as she moved through the narrative" (Hedges, 103). Absurdly, Allen toys with just such a new arrangement, only he adds a twist. His character, Larry, tries to redefine domestic space, while Carol moves outside the house into the performative space of the murder mystery sleuth. Housebound and happy enough, Larry wants to keep to himself and wants his wife to join him as a partner in a lifelong nuclear family of two (now that their son has left for college).

In this film, Carol prefers to be the woman of action and would prefer her husband to be the man of action. Larry has become the man of complaints: he nags, he whines, he pulls at her clothes. The film chronicles his attempt to disengage from the feminine space, which has caused him to become undesirable to women. His attempts include trying to boss her around and demand that she cease investigating the murder, but they do not work. He has lost his masculine viability. The women, Carol and Marcia (Anjelica Huston), a client of Larry's, whom Larry finds sexually appealing, are interested in the mystery emerging from the neighboring apartment; thus, they break the frame of typical screen space and activity allotted to women (Hedges, 88).

Ted becomes interested in the mystery only because he wants Carol's attention, and Larry becomes interested in the mystery when he wants Marcia's attention. A role reversal ensues as the men feign interest in the mystery in order to get the women's attention.

At first glance, this movie has all the potential of finally redefining screen space and breaking the frame of stereotypical movement for men and women characters in film, thereby creating a new type of male while at the same time affording women the opportunity to feast their intelligence and their imaginations on the solving of a mystery. In the end, however, a male redemption scene occurs, with Allen as rescuer. Once again the director suggests that something about masculinity forces a rescue of women—women do not really know the world well enough to penetrate the arena of mystery. The traditional route is an easy one for Allen to take; even Hedges admits that a new type of film would be difficult to make: "it would necessitate the construction of a new relation between the subject and her environment literally at every step" (Hedges, 103). In Allen's film, the women foul up and have to be rescued, and once Larry rescues Carol he becomes much more sexually interesting in her eyes. The marriage is reinvigorated because he takes on the role of a man. Passivity changes its robes for the male agency and security that wins out in the end.

Allen suggests some further role reversal within the marriage of Larry and Carol. Larry plays both wife and mother at various times in the film. Though Carol cooks, fulfilling a typically feminine role, she seeks to turn her cooking into a professional skill by starting her own restaurant. Though Larry works as an editor at a publishing house, he also cooks within his own home. Once, when Carol is out with Ted, who is helping her improve her wine-buying skills, the film audience views Larry preparing the couple's evening meal even after he has worked a full day. Larry's place in the kitchen merits comment from neither character, suggesting that he belongs there equally with Carol. When the couple's college-age son visits for his birthday, Larry does not fulfill the sports-educating role of the earlier father figures in Allen's films. Instead, while Carol examines a potential restaurant site, Larry takes their son to Brooks Brothers to buy him a cashmere sweater. Not only does Larry fulfill this typical mothering role, he discusses the purchase in detail with his preoccupied wife, placing Larry in the feminine and Carol in the masculine positions.

Gender roles and relationships reign in this film—jobs and ambition are demoted in meaning. But the essence of this film is that of danger. A murder has occurred here, and the murder in the apartment next door stands in for the death of new roles for women. Carol's desire to breathe some newness into the relationship is equated with playing with murder. Though the lead female characters in *Manhattan Murder Mystery* become the most astute investigators of the mystery, Allen will not allow them agency to resolve it. Carol becomes paralyzed by jealousy and becomes a kidnap victim of the murderer. She can only play this victim role because Allen, in the midst of the plot to trap the murderer, sends Carol home to change her clothing. Though in the next stage of the plot Carol should be standing side by side with Larry, Allen disposes of her so that Larry can perform the role of rescuer. Ted, the other male lead, furthers the plot by acting as somewhat reluctant seducer of Helen, the young lover of the murderer, Mr. House. Ted gains his agency through seduction.

While Carol sits struggling to free herself of the ropes from which only Larry can liberate her, Marcia has no further role in the capture of the murderer. Though instrumental in the entrapment of the murderer, Marcia disappears at the end, becoming distinctly absent when Larry goes to find the murderer of his neighbor and the kidnapper of his wife. Larry must meet Mr. House and, in exchange for the kidnapped Carol and black-mail money, he must produce the body of Mrs. House, which the investigation team claims to have. When Mr. House forces Larry at gunpoint to reveal the body in the trunk, Larry reveals nothing but a mannequin. Though Allen has Marcia teach Larry the importance of the poker bluff in an earlier scene, when Larry must bluff successfully, Allen does not produce Marcia to assist him. The plot almost screams for Marcia to come springing from the trunk to surprise and disarm Mr. House. Instead, in a final fake moment in the film, Larry somehow escapes Mr. House, running through his gunfire, and rescues Carol. In order to recapture the masculine, Allen gives to Larry the agency that both Carol and Marcia should share.

In Allen's films, the acts of breaking the frame and breaking twentieth century relationship codes provide humorous attempts, but genuine attempts nonetheless, to explore the problems with and the potential for creating new male and female characters for the screen who would engage in action that could potentially defy patriarchal limiting structures. However, the real challenge to the patriarchal structure would be the nonredemptive, nondemanding male, the one in *Manhattan* who might have gone with Tracy to London when she asked him, the one in *Hannah and Her Sisters* who might have stayed in a marriage unendowed by his fertility, or the one in *Manhattan Murder Mystery* who might have stepped aside while Carol and Marcia solved the mystery. Allen has arrived at the point of being able to interrogate narrative and cinematic framing of gender, but, at the end of his relationship films, he ultimately does not offer to revise or to recreate this coding into a new practice. He restores the frames that he breaks, only to break and restore them again in his cycle of relationship films.

Works Cited

Brett, Philip. "Musicality, Essentialism and the Closet." In *Queering the Pitch: The New Gay and Lesbian Musicology*, edited by Philip Brett, Elizabeth Wood, and Gary C. Thomas, 9–26. New York: Routledge, 1994.

Cohan, Steven. "Masquerading as the American Male in the Fifties: *Picnic*, William Holden and the Spectacle of Masculinity in Hollywood Films." In *Male Trouble*, edited by Constance Penley and Sharon Wills, 203–32. Minneapolis: University of Minnesota, 1993.

Doane, Mary Ann. "Film and the Masquerade: Theorising the Female Spectator." *Screen* 23 (1982): 74–87.

Feldstein, Richard. "Displaced Feminine Representation in Woody Allen's Cinema." In *Discontented Discourses: Feminism/Textual Intervention /Psychoanalysis*, edited by Marleen S. Barr and Richard Feldstein, 69–86. Urbana: University of Illinois, 1989.

Girgus, Sam B. *The Films of Woody Allen*. New York: Cambridge University Press, 1993.

Hedges, Inez. *Breaking the Frame: Film Language and the Experience of Limits*. Bloomington: Indiana University Press, 1991.

Irigaray, Luce. *The Sex Which Is Not One*. Ithaca: Cornell University Press, 1985.

Kuhn, Annette. *The Power of the Image: Essays on Representation and Sexuality*. London: Routledge and Kegan Paul, 1985.

LaFollete, Hugh. "Real Men." In *Rethinking Masculinity: Philosophical Explorations in Light of Feminism*, edited by Larry May and Robert A. Strikwerda, 59–74. Lanham, Maryland: Rowman and Littlefield, 1992.

Lax, Eric. *Woody Allen: A Biography*. New York: Vintage Books, 1991.

Maupin, Armistead. *Babycakes*. New York: Harper Collins, 1984.

May, Larry, and Robert A Striwerda. "Fatherhood and Nurturance." In *Rethinking Masculinity: Philosophical Explorations in Light of Feminism*, edited by Larry May and Robert A. Striwerda, 75–92. Lanham, Maryland: Rowman and Littlefield, 1992.

Pronger, David. *The Arena of Masculinity: Sports, Homosexuality, and the Meaning of Sex*. New York: St. Martins, 1990.

Rubin, Gayle. "The Traffic in Women: Notes Toward a Political Economy of Sex." In *Toward and Anthropology of Women*, edited by Rayna Reiter, 157–210. New York: Monthly Review Press, 1975.

Sedgwick, Eve Kosofsky. *Between Men: English Literature and Male Homosocial Desire*. New York: Columbia University Press, 1985.

Silverman, Jeff. "Getting over It: How Does a Straight Guy Get beyond

Homophobia? A Gay Football Player Gives Him Some Answers." *Los Angeles Times Magazine*, 30 January 1994, 22+.

Spence, Janet T., and Robert L. Heimlich. *Masculinity and Femininity: Their Psychological Dimensions, Correlates and Antecedents*. Austin: University of Texas Press, 1978.

Strikwerda, Robert A., and Larry May. "Male Friendship and Intimacy." In *Rethinking Masculinity: Philosophical Explorations in Light of Feminism*, edited by Larry May and Robert A. Strikwerda, 95–110. Lanham, Maryland: Rowman and Littlefield, 1992.

Woody Allen: American Prose Humorist

MARC S. REISCH

WOODY ALLEN has written plays, film scripts and essays. He is the most successful comic writer and actor today. Unlike many other comedians, he does not restrict his humor within the confines of one discipline. He is as successful in the movies as he is in his humorous essays and plays. Humorists like Ring Lardner and Thurber wrote plays but not movies. Robert Benchley wrote some film scripts and starred in a few shorts,[1] but he never had the success in movies Woody Allen has today, nor did Benchley write plays. Though he did write successfully for the radio, Benchley never had the tremendous success Allen has had in the media.

This versatile comedian sums up his life in a few concise words in his book *Getting Even*.[2] "Woody Allen was born on December 1, 1935, in Brooklyn. He attended Midwood High School and was ejected from both New York University and City College in his freshman year. Turning to professional writing in 1952, he wrote for many television comedians, such as Herb Shriner and Sid Caesar. In 1964 he decided to become a comedian himself. In addition to his numerous night club and television performances, Mr. Allen has made three record albums of live concert appearances."

Since 1964 he has written two plays, *Don't Drink the Water* (1967) and *Play It Again Sam* (1969). He starred in the movie version of *Play It Again Sam*, 1972, and wrote, directed and starred in *Take the Money and Run*, 1975, *Bananas*, 1971, *Sleeper*, 1973, *Everything You Wanted to Know About Sex but were Afraid to Ask*, 1974, *Love and Death*, 1975, *Annie Hall*, 1977, *Interiors*, 1978, and *Manhattan*, 1979. In 1967 Allen supplied the comical English dialogue for a Japanese detective film. He called the film *What's Up Tiger Lily*. His essays have appeared in the *New Yorker*, *Playboy*, *Evergreen Review*, *Chicago Daily News*, *New Republic* and *New York Times*. He collected the essays appearing in these magazines and newspapers and added some new material in his two books, *Getting Even*, 1972, and *Without Feathers*, 1976.[3]

Allen's essays take their inspiration from scholarship, current books and movies. Unlike Thurber, Benchley and White, Allen ignores family humor for the most part and makes only occasional reference to marriage. No small children appear in any of his essays. His treatment of experience is not easy to pinpoint. Reviewing Woody Allen for the *New Leader* Isa Kapp

Reprinted by permission from the *Journal of Popular Culture*, vol. 17, no. 3 (Winter 1983): 68–74.

writes in exasperation, "perhaps first-class humorists like Mark Twain, Robert Benchley, Peter de Vries and on a lower rung, Nicholas and May and Mort Sahl, have all had a greater capacity than Woody Allen to be serious. Their starting points have been exact perceptions of reality, of something intrinsically laughable not about man's creations but about man himself. Allen, pondering dance, drama, literary criticism, educational curricula, pursuing art rather than life, is often awkwardly suspended between the devils of comedy and the deep unnavigable sea of culture."[4]

If reality is as Isa Kapp would have it—"something intrinsically laughable . . . about man himself"—wouldn't that "something" and that "particular reality" be apparent only when the humorist points it out? But Mr. Kapp holds fast to a concept of "reality" that is as out of date as the Stanley Steamer. He perceives an observable reality. But Woody Allen delights in "man's creations," as Kapp himself notes. Allen interests himself in how man perceives himself, and his subject matter offers a chance to deal with man and his perception of life.

Most likely Kapp has a taste for an older, earlier humor which deals with a reality that is outside man and about man. Walter Blair pinpoints the difference. He writes that the modern humorists "take little stock in Josh Billings' old fashioned claim that 'you have got to be wize before you can be wity.' Their point seems to be that nobody is wise and nobody can be."[5] But Walter Blair has characterized all of modern humor, whereas the point is that Woody Allen has leaped a little further into the abyss of nihilism. Josh Billings found his reality in the palpable, the observable. Allen relies on the notion that in fact the mind is capable of infinite buffoonery and so wisdom is just ridiculous. After all, the mind must act on observable reality before perception. Allen makes laughter out of the very process of mind sifting an observable reality. He is therefore capable of some outlandish remarks: "The lion and the calf shall lie down together, but the calf won't get much sleep."[6] "The universe is merely a fleeting idea in God's mind—a pretty uncomfortable idea if you've just made a down payment on a house." "Eternal nothingness is O.K. if you're dressed for it."[7]

Allen's nihilism consists in the denial of all given truth. He assumes an absurd reasoning. One thing is as meaningless or meaningful as another. Richard Boyd Hauck points out in A Cheerful Nihilism that the "absurd view is realistic, it depends partly if not wholly on the assumption that any value can be judged arbitrarily when seen from a point outside the framework which produced the value in the first place."[8] In other words, the humorist's success is in his peculiar perception. In "The Schmeed Memoirs,"[9] Allen produces a memoir about Adolf Hitler which Hitler's barber has written. In a "Twenties Memoir"[10] a contemporary of Gertrude Stein's circle in Paris remembers that notable group of expatriots and the frequency with which Gertrude Stein broke Ernest Hemingway's nose.

These two essays and many like them illustrate noticeable shifts in point of view. If Albert Speer had written "The Schmeed Memoirs" nobody would laugh. Similarly if Malcolm Cowley had written the "Twenties Memoir" nobody would scream with delight.

Writing for the *Saturday Evening Post*, David Brudnoy accounts for Allen's shift in point of view. He remarks that Allen is "Dada, he is his own Yiddische mamma, he is every underachiever who ever grew up to over compensate."[11] Allen's work is Dada. He is a latter day disciple of Tristan Tzara. In terms of a contemporary discussion of humor, Allen's mode of perception is through "absurd creation." Richard Boyd Hauck defines "absurd creation" to mean that "creation itself is absurd and that the process is one in which a creator creates absurdity."[12]

Allen is an existential humorist. In the 1970s he is Camus, but with a sense of humor. All Allen's essays and literary plays are exercises in absurd creation. For example, the narrator of "My Philosophy"[13] attempts to adjust the relationship between some abstract "first principle" and a "teleological concept of being which Schopenhaur called . . . 'will' but his physician diagnosed as . . . hay fever." Allen plays jokes on "absurd creation" in the same way Tristan Tzara played jokes on Dada. He assigns a meaning to "will"—a "first principle"—but then gives the "will" all the power of biological irritation.

Like the cracker barrel philosophers, Allen makes shrewd analyses of the world around him, but unlike them he dramatizes his observations. Russell Baker comments humorously in his "Sunday Observer" column in the New York *Times Magazine*. He writes about Allen's movies: "Woody Allen has some of Chaplin's power to make us feel superior by playing the loser. He makes us laugh by being more miserable in almost every respect than the most miserable specimen of humanity in his audience. We sit laughing in contentment with our own superiority while he fails tests of manhood which the meekest of us could pass without exertion. Then he betrays us. He gets the girl. . . . When America's leading schlemiel sends you out feeling like a schlemiel, that, friend, is having schlemielhood ground into your soul."[14] Allen does not make the movie viewer or reader feel superior as Mr. Baker contends, though Allen's characters are always clever and finally triumphant. In the movie *Take the Money and Run*, Virgil Starkwell wins the heart of a beautiful laundress. In his essay "Mr. Big,"[15] a pretty professor of physics at Bryn Mawr kills God. In a burlesque of Mary Astor and Humphrey Bogart in the *Maltese Falcon*, the physics professor throws herself at the main protagonist's feet:

> "Kaiser," she said, suddenly trembling, "You won't turn me in?"
> "Oh, yes, baby. When the Supreme Being gets knocked off, somebody's got to take the rap."
> "Oh, Kaiser, we could get away together. Just the two of us. We could forget about philosophy. Settle down and maybe get into semantics."

In "Mr. Big" Kaiser is a cool collected detective, but Allen makes him humorously human. After all, at the beginning of this little drama he listens to his client's case while he opens a "deck of Luckies and a pack of gum" and has one of each. Kaiser can cooly shuck off the beautiful girl. He knows that others will land in his lap. In *Take the Money and Run*, Virgil Starkwell, happily locked away, has an attractive wife who visits him in jail. Allen's characters all seem to say, "You are a schlemiel like me, but even you can succeed—in a way."

What this amounts to is a revolution in the concept of the "Little Man." Russell Baker criticizes Allen's use of the older formula of Little Man comedy. The comic character is an idiot. He makes mistakes the observer never would and he is finally unable to carry through his intentions and uphold his dignity. Allen's characters carry through their intentions though they cannot uphold their dignity. His characters make stupid mistakes, but then can anyone say they have never stubbed their toe or asked stupid questions? His characters are sympathetic and assume the observer will identify with them. Far from having schlemielhood ground into his face, the observer can take comfort in the knowledge that even a schlemiel can have a moment of glory.

Here is a sense of dislocation from the norm, an absurd sense. Anything is possible when a person is allowed the freedom to fantasize. Allen's absurd creations make liberation from the self possible. It is a liberation that allows a transcendence over the limitations of an observable reality. Common sense, or horse sense, can have no place in a system where as Walter Blair notes "no ideas are very sound."[16]

Where the absurd sense is transcendent as it is in Allen's work, identity is a constant problem. Allen's persona never assumes one character name such as Simon Suggs, Petroleum V. Nasby or Mr. Dooley. His narrators rarely name themselves. They are various book reviewers, critics, scholars and authors. When names do appear, Allen uses them for the life of the essay or play and then drops them. The problem of identity is another facet of absurd creation. He creates people who populate a particular essay in order to realize the fantasy. Even the subjects as opposed to the narrators of the essay are not immune to a peculiar metamorphosis. Just as "will" constantly changes its meaning in the essay entitled "My Philosophy," people as subjects of an essay change their identities. Allen's essay "But Soft . . . Real Soft"[17] is a case in point:

> I have just read . . . that the real author of Shakespeare's works was Christopher Marlowe. The book makes a very convincing case, and when I got through reading it I was not sure if Shakespeare was Marlowe or Marlowe was Shakespeare or what. I know this, I would not have cashed checks for either one of them—and I like their work.

When reading Allen's essays, the reader must understand he might have to deal with an essay in which the author is capable of insisting you "understand you are dealing with a man who knocked off *Finnegans Wake* on the roller coaster at Coney Island, penetrating the abstruse Joycean arcana with ease, despite enough violent lurching to shake loose [his] silver fillings."[18] Like Thurber's Walter Mitty, Allen's narrator practices any number of poses. But unlike Walter Mitty, Allen's narrator never wakes up to find his delusions shattered by a very real and domineering reality in the form of a merciless woman. Walter Mitty only tries to create the reality that suits him. Allen's persona constantly suits himself, and as soon as something intrudes on one fantasy he constructs another.

But despite the fact that Allen's persona triumphs over reality, he is a Little Man nonetheless, "dwarfed" as Morris Yates points out "by the monsters of industry, science, business and government."[19] In regard to "ideas and values [he is] uncertain."[20] He is most frequently a small and frail human being like Charlie Chaplin's famous tramp.

The term "Little Man" defines Allen's characters only insofar as the Little Man is an observable and physical reality. When Allen's characters are off in roller coasters penetrating the abstruse Joycean arcana of *Finnegans Wake* they are absurd men; they are Little Man when they receive a blow from a pillow "that could stun a plow horse."[21] Whenever Allen's characters become aware of themselves physically and when they experience physical discomfort they are Little Men.

On the whole, Allen's characters reject the intellectual sentiments Yates finds in the Little Men. Whereas the Little Man respects a "golden mean, everyday common sense, personal integrity, monogamous marriage, a stable family, [and] a measure of personal and political freedom,"[22] Allen's characters need respect no one sentiment over another; they have no moral sense of value. His world is absurd. In "The Schmeed Memoirs,"[23] Hitler's barber Schmeed writes: "As I told the tribunal at Nurenberg, I did not know that Hitler was a Nazi. The truth was that for years I thought he worked for the phone company. When I finally did find out what a monster he was, it was too late to do anything, as I had made a down payment on some furniture." Allen's characters simply lay waste to any "positive" sentiments the Little Man might have. His characters reject "positive" sentiments and sentimentality. His one and only value is self preservation and the gratification of bodily needs: "Thought: Why does man kill? He kills for food. And not only food: frequently there must be a beverage."[24]

But like other Little Men, Allen's characters are lonely and unable to communicate. Their wild imaginations are frequently beyond the reach of any "normal" human being. The protagonist in "A Little Louder, Please"[25] tries to catch the attention of a gorgeous woman in a bar. For "fifteen minutes [his] 'pass the relish' had been the central theme of [their] conversation." Finally he tries another line:

> "I understand egg futures are up," I ventured finally feigning the insouciance of a man who merged corporations as a sideline. Unaware that her stevedore boyfriend had entered, with Laurel and Hardy timing, and was standing right behind me, I gave her a lean hungry look and can remember cracking wise about Kraft-Ebing just before losing consciousness. The next thing I recall was running down the street to avoid the ire of what appeared to be a Sicilian cousin's club bent on avenging the girl's honor.

Allen's character is not lonely just because he is cowardly and avoids violent encounters. Someone may physically dominate him, but he will always try again when the physical threat is no longer present. Not many "normal" people can appreciate the protagonist's inspired absurdity. Though when he does receive a physical jolt, he drops the pose and immediately opts for self-preservation. Underneath that attempt at a smooth exterior lies an unconscious awareness of personal deficiency.

His unconscious sense of personal inadequacy allows Allen's persona to be sympathetic with the modern philosopher's identity problems. In "My Philosophy"[26] the narrator states:

> I remember my reaction to a typical luminous observation of Kierkegaard's: "Such a relation which relates itself to its own self (that is to say, a self) must have constituted itself or have been constituted by another." The concept brought tears to my eyes. My word, I thought, to be that clever! (I'm a man who has trouble writing two meaningful sentences on "My Day at the Zoo.") True, the passage was totally incomprehensible to me, but what of it as long as Kierkegaard was having fun?

Since so much of Allen's work has appeared in the *New Yorker*, a brief comparison with his predecessors there is worthwhile. Allen continues the Little Man tradition but simultaneously parodies it. When E. B. White, Thurber, S. J. Perelman and Benchley assume a middle brow attitude, Allen assumes a high brow attitude. The earlier generation of humor writers for the *New Yorker* subscribe to the original aims of that magazine. A prospectus of the *New Yorker* declares, "it will hate bunk. . . . It's integrity will be above suspicion."[27] Allen's characters make bunk a virtue and entirely sidestep the question of integrity. By consistently assuming a high brow attitude, but still remaining a Little Man beset by the ways of the world, Allen's characters parody the *New Yorker* writers who had wanted to clear away the excess baggage that bunk brings in its wake.

Allen achieves his humor by serving up art and life, and simultaneously creating a most absurd framework for the reception. The personae frequently assume an intellectual pose. They are schlemiels who are unable to communicate; they are fraught with self-doubt, but they triumph through absurd creation:

And how can I believe in God when just last week I got my tongue caught in the roller of an electric typewriter? I am plagued by doubts. What if everything is an illusion and nothing exists? In that case I definitely overpaid for my carpet. If only God would give me some clear sign! Like making a large deposit in my name in a Swiss bank.[28]

When he experiences self-doubt or physical discomfort, Allen's personae are Little Men beset by the world. But when they "over-compensate" and exercise their faculty for "absurd creation," the personae are not Little Men; they are triumphant. For this reason Allen uses the "reductio ad absurdum" to better effect than any of his predecessors. In "Spring Bulletin"[29] he defines the absurd: "The absurd: Why existence is often considered silly, particularly by men who wear brown and white shoes." (Allen wears brown and white shoes on the cover of *Getting Even*. He also wears brown and white shoes in the movies *Bananas*, *Take the Money and Run* and *Sleeper*.) He even reduces the absurd to absurdity and so is a modern Dadaist.

But even though Allen's personae think and act in the most absurd way, what convictions prompt the author to write? David Brudnoy reviews *Without Feathers* and draws a conclusion from the book's motto: "If as Emily Dickinson wrote, 'hope is the thing with feathers,' our quintessential nebbish asks: what is the thing without feathers? . . . the common denominator of Woody Allen's wit is hopelessness, the thing without feathers."[30] But in fact Allen's persona insists "How wrong Emily Dickinson was! Hope is not the 'thing with feathers.' The thing with feathers has turned out to be my nephew. I must take him to a specialist in Zurich."[31] Allen the writer *is* the specialist from Zurich. Behind his apparently aimless absurdity is a concern with what he sees as an aimless and absurd universe. "The thing with feathers" is a psychological case. Allen's personae are things with feathers: forlorn beings in an absurd universe.

While Allen entitled his first collection of essays *Getting Even*, his second collection has progressed beyond the effort to "get even" with the imbecilities of the world. The world may seem apparently hopeless, but Allen's neurotic personae keep trying to make sense. They do "make" sense when they get the girl. But more frequently they do not make sense. Finally the direction of Allen's humor is to create sense where there is no sense and to find hope where there was none.

Notes

1. Benchley wrote and starred in *The Treasurer's Report* (1930) and *How to Sleep* (1935).

2. Woody Allen, *Getting Even* (New York: 1972).

3. Woody Allen, *Without Feathers* (New York: 1972). The essays and plays in Allen's two books appear originally in the following magazines: *Without Feathers*, "Selections from the Allen Notebooks," *New Yorker*, XLIX, Nov. 5, 1973; "Examining Psychic Phenomena" *New*

Yorker, XLVIII, Oct. 7, 1972; "A Guide to some of the Lesser Ballets," *New Yorker*, XLVIII, Oct. 28, 1972; "The Scrolls," *New Republic*, CLXXI, Aug. 31, 1974); Lovborg's Women Considered," *New Yorker*, L, Oct. 28 1974; "The Whore of Mensa," *New Yorker*, L, Dec. 16, 1974; "Death(A Play)," first appears in *Without Feathers*; "The Early Essays," *New Yorker*, XLIX, Jan. 20, 1973; "A Brief, Yet Helpful, Guide to Civil Disobedience," *Playboy*, XIX, 12, Dec. 1972); "The Irish Genius," *New Republic*, CLXXI, Feb. 22, 1975; "God (A Play)," first appears in *Without Feathers*; "Fabulous Tales and Mythical Beasts," *New Republic*, CLXXI, Nov. 30, 1974; "But Soft . . . Real Soft," first appears in *Without Feathers*; "If the Impressionists had been Dentists," first appears in *Without Feathers*; "No Kadish for Weinstein," *New Yorker*, LI, March 3, 1975; "Fine Times: An Oral Memoir," *New Yorker*, LI, March 17, 1975. *Getting Even*: "The Metterling List," *New Yorker*, XLV, May 10, 1969; "A Look at Organized Crime," *New Yorker*, XLIV, August 15, 1970; "The Schmeed Memoirs," *New Yorker*, LXVII, April 17, 1971; "My Philosophy," *New Yorker*, XLIV, Dec. 27, 1969; "Yes, But Can the Steam Engine do This?" *New Yorker*, XLI, Oct. 8, 1968; "Death Knocks," *New Yorker*, XLIV, July 27, 1966; "Spring Bulletin," *New Yorker*, XLIII, April 29, 1970; "The Gossage-Varbedian Papers," *New Yorker*, XLI, Jan. 22, 1966; "Noted from the Overfed," *New Yorker*, XLIV, March 16, 1968; "A Twenties Memory," first appears as "How I became a Comedian," *Panorama, Chicago Daily News*; "Count Dracula," first appears in *Getting Even*; "A Little Louder, Please," *New Yorker*, XLI, May 28, 1966; "Conversations with Helmholtz," first appears in *Getting Even*; "Viva Vargas," *Evergreen Review*; "The Discovery and Use of the Fake Ink Blot," *Playboy*, XIII, 8, Aug. 1966; "Mr. Big," first appears in *Getting Even*.

Eleven essays and one literary play are not included in his two volumes, because they either appear too late for inclusion in the last volume or Allen did not wish to include them. They are: "Shindai," *Playboy*, XVI, 2, Feb. 1969; "Snow White," *Playboy*, XVI, 12 (Dec. 1969); "Reminiscences: Places and People," *New Yorker*, LI (Dec. 29, 1975); "By Destiny Denied," *New Yorker*, LII (Feb. 23, 1976); "At the Cremation: Remembering Needleman," *New Republic*, CLXXV (July 24, 1976); "Confessions of a Burglar," *New Yorker*, LII (Oct. 18, 1976); "The Kuglemass Episode," *New Yorker*, LIII (May 2, 1977): "The Lunatic's Tale," *New Republic*, CLXXIII (June 13, 1977); "The UFO Menace," *New Yorker*, LIII (June 13, 1977); "The Condemned," *New Yorker*, LIII (Nov. 7, 1977); "Fabrizio's: Criticism and Responses," *New Yorker*, XLV (Feb. 5, 1979). The literary play is "Query," *New Republic*, CLXXV (Sept. 18, 1976). This study will not consider these four pieces: "The Girls of Casino Royale," *Playboy*, XIV, 2 (Feb. 1967); "My Family Album," *Playboy*, XIV, 11 (Nov. 1967); "I'll Put your name in Lights," *Playboy*, XVIII, 7 (July 1971); "Everything You Always Wanted to Know About Sex . . . You'll find in my New Movie," *Playboy*, XIX, 9 (Sept. 1972). The first and last are publicity stunts, while the other two are gags.

4. Isa Kapp, "A Cowering Man of Sensibility," *New Leaders*, LVIII, 11 (May 26, 1975.

5. Walter Blair, *Horse Sense in American Humor* (Chicago: Univ. of Chicago Press, 1942), p. 296.

6. Allen, "The Scrolls," *Without Feathers*.

7. Allen, "My Philosophy," *Getting Even*.

8. Richard Boyd Hauck, *A Cheerful Nihilism* (Bloomington: Indiana Univ. Press, 1974), p. 6.

9. Allen, *Getting Even*.

10. *Ibid.*

11. David Brudnoy, "Without Feathers," *Saturday Evening Post*, CCXLVII, 9 (Dec. 1975), p. 67.

12. Hauck, *A Cheerful Nihilism*, p. 5.

13. Allen, *Getting Even*.

14. Russell Baker, "Sunday Observer: Betrayed," *New York Times Magazine* (August 24, 1975).

15. Allen, *Getting Even*.

16. Blair, *Horse Sense in American Humor*, p. 293.

17. Allen, *Without Feathers*.
18. Allen, "A Little Louder, Please," *Getting Even*.
19. Norris Yates, *The American Humorist: Conscience of the Twentieth Century* (Ames: Iowa State Univ. Press, 1964), p. 356.
20. *Ibid.*
21. Allen, "Shindai," *Playboy*, XVI, 2 (Feb. 1969).
22. Yates, *The American Humorist*, p. 13.
23. Allen, *Getting Even*.
24. Allen, "Selections from the Allen Notebooks," *Without Feathers*.
25. Allen, *Getting Even*.
26. Allen, *Without Feathers*.
27. Quoted in Yates, *The American Humorist*, p. 227
28. Allen, "Selections from the Allen Notebooks," *Without Feathers*.
29. Allen, *Getting Even*.
30. Brudnoy, "Without Feathers," p. 67.
31. Allen, "Selections from the Allen Notebooks," *Without Feathers*.

Love and Death and Food: Woody Allen's Comic Use of Gastronomy

RONALD D. LEBLANC

O N THE basis of its title alone, *Love and Death* (1975) seems designed largely as a tribute to some of the lasting achievements of nine-teenth- and twentieth-century Russian culture. Indeed, Woody Allen in this film spoofs (warmly and gently) many of the giants of classical Russian literature, music, and cinema to whom he was indebted for inspiration, ideas, and techniques as a writer and filmmaker. The movie, as a result, contains numerous allusions to Russian artists ranging from Dostoevski and Tolstoy to Eisenstein and Prokofiev. The score for *Love and Death*, for example, includes selections from Prokofiev's composition for Eisenstein's *Alexander Nevsky* (1938) as well as from his *Lieutenant Kizhe Suite* (1934) and *Love for Three Oranges* (1921);[1] cinematic allusions, meanwhile, are made to Eisenstein's *Potemkin* (1925) and to Bondarchuk's *War and Peace* (1968). The central target of Allen's parody, however, is the nine-teenth-century Russian novel and specifically the "loose and baggy mon-sters" of Tolstoy and Dostoevsky. Set in tsarist Russia during the time of the Napoleonic wars and centered upon a bespectacled hero who plans to murder the French emperor, *Love and Death* prompts immediate associa-tions, of course, with Tolstoy's classic *War and Peace* (1869).[2] There are distinctively Dostoevskian echoes, on the other hand, in the film's theme of a man sentenced to death and then reprieved at the last moment (*The Idiot*, 1868), in the trio of brothers who make up the Grushenko family (*The Brothers Karamazov*, 1880), and in the moral dilemma that con-fronts the hero when, à la Raskolnikov, he contemplates the act of murder (*Crime and Punishment*, 1866).[3] This Dostoevsky connection is humor-ously laid bare in Allen's film during the jail-cell conversation between Grushenko and his father on the eve of Boris's execution, when names from the titles and heroes of Dostoevsky's works are called forth in a comic litany of literary reference.[4]

If the film's artistic and philosophic ambitions are to pay homage to the two towering figures of nineteenth-century Russian literature, Dostoevsky and Tolstoy, then the bathos at work in *Love and Death*—a bathos that repeatedly deflates and reduces the film's serious, elevated ideas—calls to mind yet another great nineteenth-century Russian writer: Nikolai Gogol.

Reprinted by permission from *Literature/Film Quarterly*, vol. 17, no. 1 (1989): 18–26. Copyright © 1989 by *Literature/Film Quarterly*, Salisbury State University.

It is entirely possible that during his younger years, when he took to reading various Russian, Scandinavian, and German authors, Allen became acquainted with the works of Russia's greatest comic writer.[5] The question of direct influence aside, an affinity with Gogol suggests itself in the way that Allen captures the absurdity of human life and the anxieties of modern man, casting them both in a grotesquely comic light. Like Gogol, Allen possesses the gift for humorously deflating the pretensions of his fictional characters—be those pretensions social, political, sexual, or philosophical. One device, common to both Gogol and Allen, for bringing about this comic deflation is the use of food imagery. In Gogol's works, as many critics have noted, the demands of the stomach are invariably made prominent and predominate over those of the heart or head. A central concern of nearly all his fictional characters, especially in the early Ukrainian tales, is how well—and how often—they will be able to satisfy their appetite for food and drink. Indeed, an entire book, Alexander Obolensky's *Food-Notes on Gogol* (1972), has been written on this very subject.[6] Woody Allen, for his part, has written a gastronomic version of *Notes from the Underground* in his short sketch "Notes from the Overfed," a work that derived, in the author's words, from "reading Dostoevsky and the new *Weight Watchers* magazine on the same plane trip."[7] Allen has been quoted as saying that he finds all food "funny" and at one point actually considered calling his Russian film either *Love, Food and Death* or *Love, Death and Food*.[8] Gastronomy, therefore, was obviously meant to figure quite prominently in the comic design of this film.

Woody Allen's comic use of gastronomy is, of course, hardly unprecedented. In western literature, food and drink have traditionally served as symbols of life and sensuality, and robust, earthy humorists—from Rabelais and Cervantes to Fielding and Sterne—fully exploited the comic possibilities that presented themselves whenever their heroes sat down at table to satisfy their hunger, that most basic and primitive of human instincts. In his study of Rabelais and the medieval popular-festive tradition, Mikhail Bakhtin has outlined how in carnivalized literature—with its atmosphere of license, gaiety, and liberating laughter—eating served to reflect the sense of freedom, collectivity, and abundance that was experienced in the "inverted" world of popular folk culture. The banquet imagery in *Gargantua et Pentagruel* (1532) thus conveys the democratic spirit that is unleashed during carnival festivities, when the laws, prohibitions, and restrictions that dominate everyday life within official culture are temporarily suspended and men are suddenly made equal.[9] With the rise of the modern realist novel, however, food imagery in literature came more and more to acquire a decidedly mimetic function, providing a metonymic device for satirizing contemporary bourgeois life. Literary realists in nineteenth-century France, for instance, regularly exploited fictional meals as psychological and sociological synecdoches through which to criticize the personalities of their characters as well as to condemn the values of the society in which they lived.[10] Gustave Flaubert (whom Victor Brombert accuses of suffering from an "alimentary obsession") used extensive gastronomic and gustatory imagery in *Madame Bovary* (1857) as a way to expose the shallowness and bankruptcy of the heroine's bourgeois way of life.[11] "Bovarysme," as reflected in the daily eating rhythm at Emma's household, suggested the very monotony, triviality, and vapidness of middle-class existence.

With comic writers, such as Molière and Gogol, however, the enjoyment of food is used not only to condemn the banality of bourgeois philistines (à la Flaubert), but also to continue to celebrate in Rabelaisian fashion the pure physical joy of life and its primitive sensual pleasures. A similar aim seems to inspire Woody Allen, for one of the primary roles that food imagery plays in his films is to remind us—amidst all the lofty philosophical speculation engendered by abstractions such as "love" and "death," "war" and "peace," "crime" and "punishment"—of immediate physical sensations and instinctual urges. The act of eating, by returning us to our bodies, helps to affirm the *élan vital* of human life. This reminder is especially relevant for anxiety-ridden modern man, of course, since these two aspects of his being—the psychological and the physiological, the cerebral and the instinctual—have become divorced from each other. Indeed, one of the most important lessons that Boris Grushenko comes to learn by the end of *Love and Death* is that man is hopelessly split between mind and body. "The mind embraces all the nobler aspirations—like poetry and philosophy," the hero explains. "But—the body has all the fun!" That corporeal "fun," as Allen makes abundantly clear throughout his film, is to be had in satisfying appetites both sexual and gastronomical.

When Sonja, assuming the pose of a Dostoevskian infernal woman (like Nastasìa Filippovna in *The Idiot*), intones in an early scene of the movie that she could well be considered "half-saint and half-whore," Boris, who champions the life of the instincts throughout *Love and Death*, comments sagely, "Here's hoping I get the half that eats."[12] The implication here is clear, of course, that Grushenko is also hoping he will get the half that enjoys engaging in sex. Divided between the aspirations of the intellect and the urges of the body, Boris Grushenko—as another paradigm of the basic Woody Allen cinematic persona—is a seemingly sex-starved individual whose libidinal desires, he would have us believe, are never adequately satisfied.[13] Although Boris is attracted to cousin Sonja largely because she is able to engage in deep philosophic discourse with him, what he is really yearning for throughout the movie is sexual gratification. *Love and Death*, as a result, comes to constitute what Foster Hirsch calls a "schlemiel comedy"—"a mingling of sex and philosophy, as a search for sex shares the stage with the quest for the meaning of life."[14] And in this film the search for sex predominates because Allen, as Maurice Yacowar notes, consistently "subordinates philosophy to the appetites and sens-es."[15] Like sex, eating is for Allen an activity which debunks the sterile and futile philosophizing of intellectuals and reaffirms instead life's essential vitality by satisfying one of man's most basic appetites. Not surprisingly, food and sex are often linked together in his films, a connection perhaps most graphically illustrated in *Bananas* (1971) where the director pays tribute to the famous scene of erotic dining in Tony Richardson's film ver-sion of *Tom Jones*.[16]

In *Love and Death*, this connection between food and sex is made clear in the scene where Sonja, convinced that Boris will die on the following day as a result of his duel with Count Anton Lebedkov, agrees at last to have sex with the hero. When she suggests that they go upstairs to make love together, Boris says, "Nice idea! I'll bring the soy sauce." Similarly, an invitation to tea by the beautiful, inviting, and promiscuous Countess Aleksandrovna is interpreted by Boris as an opportunity to "run a quick check" of her errogenous zones. Later, after Boris and the Countess have succeeded in consummating their lovers' tryst, the shot of their post-coital satisfaction is accompanied by the same balalaika music that had been played earlier in the film at the Grushenko party scene, where people were shown merrily eating, drinking, and dancing. The Freudian connec-tion between bed and board is also established in the Boris-Sonja relation-ship, especially during the early stages of their married life together, when the hero is desperately seeking to win his bride's heart. The conjugal ten-sion the couple feels is made palpable in scenes that alternate in locus between the bedroom ("Don't—not here!," Sonja objects when Boris starts to caress her in bed) and the kitchen (Sonja shatters the wine glass in her hand and sweeps the dishes off the table onto the floor). Indeed, when Boris finally does succeed in winning Sonja over and gaining her love and affection, that change in their marital relations is presented not in bed but at table, where we see the couple not only enjoying Sonja's first soufflé (so heavy that it breaks the table in two) and her dishes made out of snow ("Oh, sleet—my favorite!"), but also holding hands and talking of having children together.

This linking of the sexual with the gastronomical sharply distinguishes Allen's use of food imagery from that of Gogol, whose characters, in a so-called "retreat from love," reflect their creator's own aversion to sex and generally regress from genital to oral modes of libidinal satisfaction.[17] "Food, and not love," Obolensky writes with regard to Gogol, "is the usual motivation in his stories."[18] With Woody Allen, on the other hand, food and sex go together naturally as objects of desire; his characters seek the "half" that both eats and fornicates. Thus Allen's fascination with eating, as Douglas Brode points out, results in a tendency to use food as a symbol for sex rather than as its substitute.[19]

In any event, food——whether it be the geometrically correct blintzes of Grushenko's mother, the cookies fed to the village idiot Berdykov, the herring and wine sauce secreted upstairs by the fish merchant Voskovec, or the bowls of snow food prepared by Sonja (the "frigid" bride)—serves as a source of pleasure in *Love and Death*, gratifying the senses and providing a strong affirmation of life in the face of all the destruction caused by war, violence, and death. This life-affirming role of food is humorously noted in the death-bed scene where Voskovec has no sooner passed away than his widow is encouraged to forego bereavement and continue with the process of living. "The dead pass on and life is for the living," the bedside doctor tells Sonja. "I guess you're right," she responds. "Where do you want to eat?" This exchange reveals that for the characters in *Love and Death*, eating and living are nearly synonymous activities. And the food that most strongly symbolizes life in this movie is wheat. Thus when Boris visits Sonja on the eve of his duel and contemplates his near-certain death at the hands of the noted duellist, he rhapsodizes comically about the "staff of life":

> To die . . . before the harvest. The crops, the grains, fields of rippling wheat. All there is in life is wheat. . . . Oh, wheat. Lots of wheat. Fields of wheat. A tremendous amount of wheat. . . . Yellow wheat. Red wheat. Wheat with feathers. Cream of wheat.

Later, after Boris's death, as the twice-widowed Sonja tries to convince herself that life must go on, she and Natasha strike a Bergmanesque pose (cf. *Persona*, 1966) and utter repeatedly the word "wheat." "Wheat," Boris interrupts. "I'm dead; they're talking about wheat." Hours earlier, as Boris sat in a prison cell awaiting execution for his attempted murder of Napoleon, his dread of impending death had been somewhat allayed by the sight of a cart filled with delicious French pastries ("Of course, it was a French jail, so the food was not bad").

This motif——eating as synecdoche of living——is comically inverted, however, when the Russian army reaches the front and witnesses a scene of widespread devastation in which the bodies of numerous dead soldiers are strewn across a smoke-filled battlefield. "Boy, this . . . this army cooking will get you every time," Boris remarks to his comrades. Allen plays here on the comic dichotomy between what food ought to be (an object not only of pleasure but also of sustenance, a source of life) and what, in the army, it really is: namely, something so poorly prepared that it makes ill and even kills those who eat it.[20] Similarly, when Boris returns to Sonja in a posthumous visit following his execution and tries to describe for her what death is like, he tells her that it resembles the food at a familiar restaurant ("You know the chicken at Tresky's restaurant? It's worse!").

War, like death, is likewise often juxtaposed to eating in *Love and Death*, as Allen uses food, the symbol of life-affirmation, as a device for comically deflating military pretensions. Napoleon's invasion of Austria is attributed to a shortage of cognac ("Is he out of Corvoisier?"), while the Battle of Austerlitz is reduced to a game of American football, complete with cheerleaders exhorting their team on and vendors peddling red-hots (blinis) and beer to the Russian troops. Later, during the Napoleonic invasion of 1812, the destructive war that has been raging for the last seven years in Europe is reduced to a ridiculous culinary contest between the leaders of the two most powerful armies in the world. The battle is over which dish will be developed first: the pastry named after Napoleon or boeuf Wellington? Conversely, when Boris, an avowed pacifist (and "militant coward"), objects to joining in the fight to stop Napoleon, those of his countrymen who advocate war try to change his mind by arguing that the French army poses a threat to the two things the hero holds most dear: women and food. "What are you going to do when the French soldiers rape your sister?" Boris is asked when he refuses to enlist. Later, during basic training, when Boris again questions the wisdom of going to war to stop Napoleon, the aftermath of French rule in Russia is described in gastronomical terms:

> Imagine your loved ones conquered by Napoleon and forced to live under French rule. Do you want them to eat that rich food and those heavy sauces? Do you want them to have soufflé every meal and croissant?

The joke here, of course, is not only that the quality of life under foreign occupation should be measured in terms of diet (rather than, say, political liberties and individual rights), but also that the soldiers would prefer bland Russian food to tasty French cuisine. A similar absurdity is sounded when Boris, who urges that Russian crops be destroyed in advance of the French troops, notes that "it's tough to light borscht."

Whereas Allen uses food (like sex) as an affirmation of life and a source of enjoyment in the face of the destruction threatened by war, the dread caused by fear of death, and the abstraction from life inherent in philosophical speculation, he at the same time recognizes that eating is a paradigm not only of pleasure but also of power. Although in *Love and Death* to eat signifies primarily to taste (*goûter*) there are nevertheless instances in the film when to eat means to destroy and devour (*manger*).[21] Food, in other words, can serve as a means of domination as well as a source of enjoyment. We have already seen intimations of this in Allen's juxtaposition of food and eating to war and death: army food kills, death is worse than the chicken at Tresky's restaurant, under French rule Russians will be forced to live on a diet of Gallic cuisine. The most memorable instance of eating as power and domination, however, occurs early in the film when Boris and his cousin Sonja present competing perceptions of nature. To Sonja's teleological view of nature (and particularly her Liebnitzean idea that this is "the best of all possible worlds"), Boris provides a sufficiently cynical, Voltairian response, positing instead a Darwinian universe of natural selection:

> To me nature is the . . . you know . . . I don't know . . . spiders and bugs and . . . and . . . and big fish eating little fish and . . . and . . . and . . . plants eating, uh, plants, and animals eating animals. It's like an enormous restaurant. That's the way I see it.

The restaurant, a civilized place normally associated with elegant dining, where eating is a pleasurable activity (*goûter*), is here comically transformed into a primitive jungle of cannibalistic beasts where, in accord with the law of survival of the fittest, to eat is to dominate, to destroy, and to devour (*manger*).[22]

The metaphor of nature as an enormous restaurant, although used comically here, manages nonetheless to make a serious statement about the dog-eat-dog world in which we live.[23] Man must exist with the fear of being devoured by forces larger than himself and, ultimately, by death itself, which is portrayed in Allen's film, appropriately enough, as a "grim reaper" who is ready to harvest human lives. If young Boris Grushenko's strange and vivid dream of waiters stepping out of coffins to dance a Viennese waltz served as sufficient warning to him that he "would not grow up to be an ordinary man," it also prepares the viewer to see a connection between food and death—between dancing waiters in the "enormous restaurant" of life and Boris traipsing with the grim reaper in a dance of death in the film's finale.

It seems ironic that food and drink, which are used throughout *Love and Death* mainly as a way to affirm life in the face of war, death and the sterility of intellectual speculation, should also be used in this and other Allen films as effective metaphors for posing ultimate questions about man, life, and the universe. In *Annie Hall* (1977), for instance, Alvy Singer's opening comedy monologue includes a food joke that encapsulates a stark view of the human condition:

> There's an old joke. Uh, two elderly women are at a Catskills mountain resort, and one of them says: "Boy, the food at this place is really terrible." The other one says, "Yeah, I know, and such . . . small portions." Well, that's how I feel about life. Full of loneliness and misery and suffering and unhappiness, and it's all over much too quickly.[24]

In *Love and Death*, as Boris and Sonja debate the moral ramifications involved in assassinating Napoleon, Kant's categorical imperative is alluded to in a food joke that once again resorts to the restaurant metaphor:

> Boris: Sonja, Sonja, I've been thinking about this. It's murder. What if everybody acted like this? It'd be a world full of murderers. You know what that would do to property values?

Sonja: I know. And if everybody went to the same restaurant on the same evening and ordered blintzes, there'd be chaos. But they don't.

"I'm talking about murder," Boris deadpans, "she's talking about blintzes." Although Sonja's analogy here attempts to deflate her husband's moral qualms, the actual effect is to lend Kant's imperative greater concreteness and thus to communicate it more effectively. In both instances, therefore, Allen uses food jokes not just for laughs, but also for serious commentary about life.

This serio-comic element in Allen's films once again brings to mind the example of Gogol, whose major contribution to Russian literature, critics have contended over the years, consisted in his ability to mix serious social critique with amusing representations of characters, settings, and events. His satiric comedies—with their grotesque exaggerations, absurd illogicalities, and comic distortions—prompted in their audience "laughter through tears." Like Gogol, Woody Allen seeks in his film to convey a serious message about the human condition, while at the same time poking fun not only at the message itself but also at some of the artistic vehicles traditionally used to convey it. As a parody of the Russian philosophic novel and the Hollywood film epic, *Love and Death* thus combines serious metaphysical concern with rich comic form. The artistic result is, as Benayoun puts it, "a farce based on ideas," where the ideas themselves are not necessarily debunked and discredited.[25] In keeping with the serio-comic designs of Allen's Russian film, gastronomy plays a double role as both a deflator of philosophic pretensions and a conveyor of ultimate questions. Eating in *Love and Death* may be said to serve as a remedy for—as well as a reminder of—the modern malady of alienation, the propensity toward chronic depression that Allen elsewhere labels "Ozymandias Melancholia" (cf. *Stardust Memories*, 1980). As paradigm of pleasure (*goûter*) as well as power (*manger*), food here affirms the physical joy of human existence at the same time as it reminds us of life's inherent cruelty, injustice, contingency, and meaninglessness.

Gastronomy, however, provides Allen—as it did Gogol—with an appropriate metaphor not only for human life, but also for artistic creation itself. Gogol, whose passion for Ukrainian cuisine and Italian pasta is well documented, often spoke of the writer as a "chef" and of the literary work as a "dish" served up to the reader. Thus when overly eager Russian readers clamored for the appearance of Part Two of his masterpiece, Gogol responded that "*Dead Souls* are not like bliny, which can be prepared in an instant."[26] And in his essay, "A Few Words about Pushkin" ("Neskol'ko slov o Pushkine," 1835), Gogol observed that in order to understand and appreciate the great Russian poet,

one must be to a certain extent a sybarite, who has long since had his fill of coarse and heavy foods and who now eats no more than a thimble full of game fowl and savors such a dish, one whose taste seems utterly indefinable, strange and totally unpleasant to a person accustomed to swallowing the concoctions of a peasant cook.[27]

Woody Allen likewise resorts to gastronomic metaphors to explain his art, especially when expressing his desire to be recognized as a serious film-maker rather than merely another cinematic funny man. "Drama is like a plate of meat and potatoes," he notes in an interview in *Newsweek*. "Comedy is rather the dessert, a bit like meringue."[28] Funny films, he observes elsewhere, are "like eating ice cream all the time," and many of his own comic pieces in the *New Yorker* he has dismissed as "sheer dessert."[29] *Love and Death*, in this context, offers its audience a complete meal: both the main course and the dessert, both the "meat and potatoes" and the "meringue." By blending serious philosophic concerns and artistic intentions together with broad physical comedy, witty verbal humor, and clever literary/cinematic parody, Woody Allen has concocted here a verita-ble smorgasbord—a funny film that seeks to satisfy the viewer's hunger for humor as well as his appetite for substantial intellectual and aesthetic nourishment. Like so many of Allen's films, *Love and Death* provides us with what one critic calls "chicken soup for the soul."[30]

Notes

1. The score for the film was intended to be made up entirely of music by Igor Stravinsky, claims Ralph Rosenblum who served as film editor for *Love and Death*. "I listened to a lot of Stravinsky," writes Rosenblum, "and found he's too overpowering for the film. He was like a tidal wave, drowning every part of the picture he came in contact with. As an alternative, I introduced Woody to three compositions by Sergei Prokofieff." See Ralph Rosenblum and Robert Karen, *When the Shooting Stops* (New York: The Viking Press, 1979), p. 270.

2. Most reviewers of *Love and Death* regarded Allen's film primarily as a parody of Tolstoy's novel. Geoff Brown, for instance, called it a "demented version of *War and Peace*." See *Monthly Film Bulletin*, 42, No. 502 (1975), 241. Michael Deskey, meanwhile, referred to *Love and Death* as a "cockeyed, minor *War and Peace*." See *Films in Review*, 26 (August/September 1975), 435. Finally Judith Crist, in a review entitled "War & Punishment, Crime & Peace—Or Something Along those Lines," called Allen's new film "a perfect pastiche of *War and Peace*." See *New York*, 8 (1975), 66.

3. Robert Benayoun, in his book *The Films of Woody Allen*, trans. Alexander Walker (New York: Harmony Books, 1985), regards the hero Boris as a Raskolnikov in the army (p. 42). See also Benayoun's review of *Love and Death*, entitled, appropriately enough, "Raskolnikov au régiment (*Amour et guerre*)" in *Positif*, 175 (1975), 56–58.

4. Father: Remember that nice boy next door, Raskolnikov?
   Boris: Ya.
   Father: He killed two ladies.
   Boris: No! What a Nasty Story!
   Father: Bobok told it to me. He heard it from one of the Karamazov Brothers.
   Boris: He must have been Possessed.
   Father: Well, he was a Raw Youth.

Boris: A Raw Youth? He was an Idiot!
Father: And he acted Insulted and Injured!
Boris: I hear he was a Gambler.
Father: You know——he could be your Double.
Boris: Really? How novel!

5. According to biographers, Allen in the late 1950s (after unsuccessful undergraduate stints at New York University and City College) hired a tutor to guide him through some of the world's great literature. Allen mentions Gogol's masterpiece, "The Overcoat" ("Shinel'," 1842), in his short story "A Little Louder, Please." See *Getting Even* (New York: Random House, 1971), pp. 105–106. The severed nose of the leader in *Sleeper* (1973), it seems to me, might well allude to Gogol's comic grotesque tale, "The Nose" (1836).

6. Alexander Obolensky, *Food-Notes on Gogol* (Winnipeg, Canada: Trident Press, 1972). See also Natalia M. Kolb-Seletski, "Gastronomy, Gogol, and His Fiction," *Slavic Review*, 29, No. 1 (1970), 35–57, Jan Kott, "The Eating of *The Government Inspector*," *Theatre Quarterly*, 5, No. 17 (1975), 21–29, and Ronald D. LeBlanc, "Satisfying Khlestakov's Appetite: The Semiotics of Eating in *The Inspector General*," *Slavic Review*, 47, No. 3 (1988), 168–199.

7. *Getting Even*, p. 81. Another Allen story from this collection that involves a food motif is "Yes, But Can the Steam Engine Do This?," which chronicles the invention of the sandwich by the Earl of Sandwich (pp. 35–40). In another anthology, *Side Effects* (New York: Random House, 1980), Allen includes such gastronomic pieces as: "The Diet" (pp. 63–69), which reduces Kafka's *The Trial* to a tale of dieting; "A Giant Step for Mankind" (pp. 91–98), which traces the development of the Heimlich maneuver as a result of scientific research; and "Fabrizio's: Criticism and Response" (pp. 123–129), which travesties the restaurant review, using it as a platform for literary, cinematic, and political criticism.

8. "Food is funny in itself. It makes me laugh," Allen confessed in an interview with Robert Benayoun. "I even thought of calling my Russian film *Love, Food and Death* or *Love, Death and Food*! I had a scene cut, which I shot in Paris, where Diane Keaton and I are on the way to assassinate Napoleon and stop at the home of a Jewish couple, at Yom Kippur, and eat a full dinner, only our plates have no food on them. It was very funny, but not usable." See *The Films of Woody Allen*, p. 162.

9. Bakhtin delineates his theory of carnivalization in both *The Problems of Dostoevsky's Poetics*, trans. Caryl Emerson (Minneapolis: University of Minnesota Press, 1984) pp. 101–180, and *Rabelais and His World*, trans. Hélène Iswolsky (Cambridge, Ma: M.I.T. Press, 1968). Richard Berrong presents a critique of Bakhtin's theory of carnivalization in his recent book, *Rabelais and Bakhtin: Popular Culture in "Gargantua and Pentagruel"* (Lincoln and London: University of Nebraska Press, 1986). For a study of Rabelais's use of gastronomy, see Michel Jeanneret, "'Mon patrie est une citrouille': thèmes alimentaires dans Rabelais, et Folengo," in *Littérature et gastronomie* (Papers on French Seventeenth-Century Literature, Biblio 17), ed. Ronald W. Tobin (Paris-Tübingen-Seattle: Papers on French Seventeenth-Century Literature, 1985), pp. 113–148. See also Jeanneret's recent book, *Des mets et des mots: banquets et propos de table à la renaissance* (Paris: Corti, 1987).

10. See, for example, James Brown, *Fictional Meals and Their Function in the French Novel, 1789–1848* (Toronto: University of Toronto Press, 1984).

11. Victor Brombert, *The Novels of Flaubert. A Study of Themes and Techniques* (Princeton: Princeton University Press, 1966), pp. 49–51. For studies that examine the use of gastronomy in Flaubert's novel, see Lilian R. Furst, "The Role of Food in *Madame Bovary*," *Orbis Litterarum* 34 (1979), 53–65, and James Brown, "A Note on Kitchens in *Madame Bovary*," *USF Language Quarterly*, 17. Nos. 1–2 (1978), 55–56. Allen himself uses Flaubert's novel (or at least its heroine) in his story, "The Kugelmass Episode." See *Side Effects*, pp. 41–45. Jonathan Culler discusses this story in "The Uses of Bovary," *Diacritics*, 11, No. 3 (1981), 74–81.

12. As Kevin Smith (a former student) once pointed out to me, Sonja's line may well

refer not only to the heroines of Dostoevsky but also to the lyric persona of Anna Akhmatova, the twentieth-century Russian poetess whose verse was harshly condemned in 1946 by Andrei Zhdanov (Stalin's watchdog over the arts) as "the poetry of a half-crazy gentlelady who tosses between the bedroom and the chapel." "Half-nun and half-harlot or rather both nun and harlot," Zhdanov wrote of Akhmatova, "her harlotry is mingled with prayer." Quoted in Edward J. Brown, *Russian Literature Since the Revolution* (New York: Collier, 1963), p. 227

13. See, for example, Ross Wetzsteon, "Woody Allen: Schlemiel as Sex Maniac," *Ms.*, 6, No. 5 (November 1977), 14–15.

14. Foster Hirsch, *Love, Sex, Death and the Meaning of Life: Woody Allen's Comedy* (New York: McGraw-Hill, 1981), p. 134.

15. Maurice Yacowar, *Loser Take All: The Comic Art of Woody Allen* (New York: Frederick Ungar, 1979), p. 168. "In *Sleeper* most of Woody's jokes are about bodies; in *Love and Death* he kids the mind," notes Hirsch. "This is a comedy about intellectual affectation: big words and abstract concepts keep getting in the way of Boris and his sometime girl friend Sonja, who reluctantly becomes his wife. The two of them fall into pseudo-intellectual discourse when what they would really rather do is fall into bed." See *Love, Sex, Death, and the Meaning of Life*, p. 76.

16. Hartmut Kiltz has devoted an entire book to the theme of erotic dining in nineteenth-century European literature. See his *Das erotische Mahl: Szenen aus dem "chambre separee" des neunzehnten Jahrhundert* (Frankfurt: Syndikat, 1983). James Brown explores the connection between food and fornication in the nineteenth-century French novel in his book, *Fictional Meals and Their Function in the French Novel*. See especially pp. 12–14, 42–43, 50–51.

17. Hugh McLean,"Gogol's Retreat from Love: Toward an Interpretation of *Mirgorod*," *American Contributions to the Fourth International Congress of Slavicists* (The Hague: Mouton, 1958), pp. 225–244. For treatment of Gogol's aversion to sex, see Simon Karlinsky, *The Sexual Labyrinth of Nikolai Gogol* (Cambridge, Ma.: Harvard University Press, 1976), Daniel Rancourt-Laferriere, *Out From Under Gogol's Overcoat: A Psychoanalytical Study* (Ann Arbor: Ardis, 1982), and Tommaso Landolfi's short story, "Gogol's Wife," in his *Gogol's Wife and Other Stories*, trans. Raymond Rosenthal et al. (New York: New Directions, 1961), pp. 1–16.

18. Obolensky, *Food-Notes on Gogol*, p. 6.

19. Douglas Brode, *Woody Allen: His Films and Career* (Secaucus, N.J.: Citadel Press, 1987), p. 45.

20. Army cooking had been satirized earlier in the film when Boris, who is told to clean the latrine as well as the mess hall, asks how he will be able to tell the difference between the two.

21. For the distinction between *goûter* (or eating as pleasure) and *manger* (or eating as power and violence), I am indebted to Ronald W. Tobin. See his article, "Les mets et les mots: gastronomie et sémiotique dans *L'ë cole des femmes*," *Semiotica*, 51 (1984), 133–145.

22. Another comic inversion of the restaurant—at a more graphic level and in reverse order (that is, from the primitive jungle to the civilized world) occurs in *Bananas* (1971), during the hilarious scene where Fielding Mellish orders sandwiches and cold slaw for his band of South American revolutionaries at a local jungle "deli."

23. Douglas Brode (wrongly, I think) subsumes nearly all of the food imagery in Allen's films under this "enormous restaurant" metaphor, arguing that "hunger"—emotional and psychological as well as physical—is largely what motivates the behavior of Allen's characters from the early *Don't Drink the Water* (1969) to the more recent *Purple Rose of Cairo* (1985). See *Woody Allen: His Films and Career*, pp. 81, 89–92, 110–111, 123, 138–140, 155–156, 178, 235–239, 247–249.

24. See the screenplay for *Annie Hall* in *Four Films of Woody Allen* (London: Faber and Faber, 1983), p. 4. Another food joke with broad existential implications occurs at the end of *Annie Hall*, when Alvy Singer says: "I-I thought of that old joke, you know, this-this-this guy

goes to a psychiatrist and says, 'Doc, uh, my brother's crazy. He thinks he's a chicken.' And, uh, the doctor says, 'Well, why don't you turn him in?' And the guy says, 'I would, but I need the eggs.' Well, I guess that's pretty much how I feel about relationships. You know, they're totally irrational and crazy and absurd and . . . but uh, I guess we keep goin' through it because, uh, most of us need the eggs." See *Four Films of Woody Allen*, p. 105.

25. Benayoun, *The Films of Woody Allen*, p. 42. This combination of the farcical and the intellectual leads, in Benayoun's opinion, to a "satirical meditation on the thought processes themselves," to "a comedy of procrastination," which suggests a parallel, he maintains, not with Gogol but with Chekhov.

26. See the letter to S. T. Aksakov of March 6, 1847 in the fourteen-volume complete collection of Gogol's works, *Polnoe sobranie sochinenii* (Moscow-Leningrad: Akademiia nauk, 1940–1952), XII, 187. The translation here is mine.

27. Gogol, *Polnoe sobranie sochinenii*, VIII, 54.

28. Quoted in Benayoun, *The Films of Woody Allen*, p. 41. In an interview with *Esquire* magazine, Woody Allen used a similar gastronomic metaphor to characterize his work. "A comedy, for me, has the quality of being a little dessert, a diversion," he said. "The real meat and potatoes are serious films." Quoted in Douglas Brode, *Woody Allen: His Films and Career*, p. 34.

29. See Benayoun, *The Films of Woody Allen*, p. 161, and Eric Lax, *On Being Funny: Woody Allen and Comedy* (New York: Charterhouse, 1975), p. 224.

30. Frank Pierson, as quoted in Douglas Brode, *Woody Allen: His Films and Career*, p. 18.

A Portrait of the Artist as a Neurotic:
Studies in Interior Distancing in the Films of
Woody Allen

RONALD S. LIBRACH

I was not bored, as I had feared I might be; rather, I found myself fascinat-
ed by the alacrity with which these great minds unflinchingly attacked
morality, art, ethics, life, and death.

—*Woody Allen, "My Philosophy"*

I

WOODY ALLEN'S singularity as an important filmmaker results largely
from his unique approach to philosophical problems. The *New
Yorker* pieces, for example, are frequently devoted to reducing classic
philosophic profundities to nonsensical, jargon-ridden aphorisms. Allen
knows well enough that even the greatest of philosophical systems are
basically elaborate, self-willed rationalizations for the philosopher's temperament or mood and he himself is honest enough to remind us that his
own philosophical overview derives in large part from a sincere and therapeutic analysis of his own psychological problems—namely, the fact that
he tends to whine too much.

Alvy Singer, Allen's persona in *Annie Hall*, for instance, is an incessant
whiner, and *Annie Hall* itself is Allen's most successful attempt to construct a syllogism that will justify the philosophy of whining. In the film,
both Allen and Diane Keaton play themselves with only the most transparent fictional pretense, revealing a new dimension to the career that Allen
has made of devoting most of his creative energy to talking about himself.
Annie Hall examines and extols this whining comic persona, and the film
seems to have come at a time when Allen realized that the best way to
examine his own life was to find out why his audience has always found it
so funny. As the film's title suggests, Diane Keaton is the aspect of his life
on which Allen chose to focus his examination: he seems to have reasoned
in *Annie Hall* that, since his audience found his relationship with Keaton

Reprinted by permission of the author from *The Missouri Review*, vol. 9, no. 2 (1986):
165–184. Copyright © 1993 by Ronald S. Librach.

so improbable, he could get the maximum comic effect out of that improbability by playing it with maximum transparency.

Annie Hall, certainly Allen's most perfectly realized film at the time, was followed by his announcement that he intended to test his maturity as an artist by embarking upon a "serious dramatic" film—"not middle serious . . . , not bittersweet, but very heavy stuff, really heavy. . . . [In] *The Seventh Seal* that constant, unrelieved gloom, the intensity of feeling, the religious solemnity, are very pleasurable to me—it's hypnotic."[1] The result was *Interiors*, the story of three sisters (the Chekhovian analogy is not unintentional), their father, whose middle-age, upper middle-class *angst* serves as the film's catalyst, and their mother, a neurotic interior decorator. On the surface, *Interiors* seems to be a perfectly realized example of what Woody Allen means by "very heavy stuff." Most of his critics, however, found its seriousness to be as oppressive as they found *Annie Hall's* brisk but thoughtful comedy to be fresh and exhilarating.

But the recollection of any number of scenes from previous Woody Allen films (say, the cinema foyer scene in *Annie Hall*, in which Woody produces Marshall McLuhan to foil a pompous loudmouth) should remind us that nobody who bristles at intellectual pomposity the way Woody Allen does is likely to succumb to it. Indeed, there are moments in *Interiors* when one feels vaguely uneasy about dismissing it as an exercise in pretentious intellectualism. What I hope to do is explain the source of these conflicting critical responses in Allen's unique conception of the film.

First of all, let's outline the syllogism that governs Woody Allen's "philosophical" view of things; we will find, I think, that *Interiors* plays a clever variation on the terms of that syllogism. Although it's not quite accurate to characterize the film as "parody," this variation certainly has ironic implications which are not only profoundly sensible but often splendidly funny.

II

Although the most obvious thing about the typical Woody Allen persona in *Interiors* is its conspicuous absence, the film is nevertheless concerned with the theme of the persona. In fact, it is precisely the absence of his persona in *Interiors* which allows Allen to explore, with considerable ingenuity, a promising new dimension to a favorite theme.

The nutty but carefully detailed, essentially realistic world of *Annie Hall* has given way in *Interiors* to a starker and more scrupulously stylized world. Nevertheless, both of these fictional worlds are conceived as fantasies, concoctions of an imagination which has, up until *Interiors*, always felt compelled to account for its irregular view of the world by placing itself in the middle of that world—that is, by displacing itself in a persona which it finds dramatically agreeable and which makes the audience more comfortable with the looking-glass world on the screen. The audience can actually see the fabulator move about in this world, even if he, too, is often imperiled by its absurdities.[2]

In this sense, Woody Allen has always been as much an "expressionistic" dramatist as Ingmar Bergman, to whom *Interiors* makes numerous visual allusions, some paid in homage, others ironic. In effect, both directors explore the principle of composition which Strindberg adumbrates in his preface to the *Dream Play*—the principle of allowing the play's action to express, directly and without mediation or excuse, the vagaries of the main character's dreams or imaginings: "On a flimsy foundation of actual happenings," explains Strindberg, "imagination spins and weaves in new patterns: an intermingling of remembrances, experiences, whims, fancies, ideas, fantastic absurdities and improvisations, and original inventions of the mind."[3] Interestingly, Allen's description of the screenplay for *Annie Hall* echoes both Strindberg's principle and his terminology: *Annie Hall* says Allen, was conceived as "a stream of consciousness showing one individual's state of mind, in which conversations and events constantly trigger dreams, fantasies and recollections."

That Ingmar Bergman has spent his entire career practicing Strindbergian principles is virtually self-evident. But to force a specific correlation between the psychodramas of August Strindberg and those of Woody Allen, even the vicarious one filtered through Allen's professed admiration for Bergman, would soon lead to silly and useless overstatement. At the same time, however, both Allen's films and his writings express his belief that he thinks a little like Ingmar Bergman, although he himself often contributes to the whimsical aspect of this notion, as in the playlet *Death Knocks*, in which the hero plays gin rummy with Death. What we must admit, I think, is that Strindberg's program for a drama of "fantastic absurdities and improvisations" sounds as much like the description of a Woody Allen movie as it does such Bergman films as *The Face* and *Cries and Whispers*. More importantly, *Interiors* should testify not only to Allen's astute recognition of the kinship between Bergman's thinking and his own, but also to his purely comic ingenuity, which incorporates much the same dramatic idea as that which informs Bergman's practice: namely, the structural (and often symbolic) relationships among (1) the mind of the fabulator, (2) character of his persona, and (3) the fanciful world which, between them, fabulator and persona conjure up.

A Woody Allen film, for example, will conjure up one of two different worlds. On the one hand, *Bananas*, *Sleeper*, and *Love and Death* are, respectively, parodic, futuristic, and historical fantasies, and they foreshadow, ironically enough, the wholly self-contained fantasy world *Interiors*. On the other hand, *Play It Again, Sam* and, to a lesser extent, *Take the Money and Run* prefigure Allen's experiment in both *Annie Hall* and *Manhattan*—the transformation of the "real" world into the kind of absurdist world which the typical Allen protagonist always envisions and whines about. Except for *Interiors*, however, all of these films have two things in common. First, each serves as a stage for the persona of the individual whose mind concocted it. Without the dramatic presence of this persona, the worlds of these films would be senseless and indecipherable.

The second common denominator in these films is that believability depends entirely upon Woody Allen's *performance*. Ironically, it is harder to make believable this latter category of films. Just as important as expressionism's emphasis on dreamlike structure is its insistence that the mind responsible for the world of the play be cast upon the stage in the middle of it, a befuddled dreamer among his own dreams. Allen insists upon this principle at the end of *Annie Hall*. As Alvy, he appears at the rehearsal of a play that he has written—a precise inverse reflection of *Annie Hall* itself, with someone else playing Alvy's part in a story that turns out happily. Woody/Alvy talks to us for a moment about the relationship between his roles in both dramas. What we learn from this monologue is that Woody's own performance embraces the dual role of fabulator *as* performer. He is both a functioning imagination and a figment of it. In scenes like this one, he reminds us that his personality is not only the topic of the film but its medium as well.

To a large extent, the autobiographical *Annie Hall* is a small-scale allegory of Allen's own growth. Allen acknowledges that his concept of what's "funny" altered significantly when he made the transition from gag-writer to nightclub performer: "I'd started out thinking I could be funny if my material was funny," he has explained, "but I began finding out that you have to be a performer." Allen's thoughts about his ability as a performer were turning away from an interest in *what* he did on the screen and towards an interest in *who* was doing it—that is, towards a realization that both story-value and gags could improve in consistency and intelligence only if anchored in *character*. When Allen said of *Sleeper* that he intended its scenes to be funny "because I [will] make them funny," what he had in mind, I think, was not so much some transition from verbal to physical humor, but rather a growing recognition of his potential development as a comic persona in the tradition of Chaplin and Keaton.[4]

III

If Woody Allen's comedy matures fully in *Annie Hall*, the film's success depends largely upon Allen's ability to integrate the biography and behavior of its central character with the autobiographical ingredients that go into fashioning his own performance. By means of this integration, Woody Allen seems to be announcing in *Annie Hall* that, after twenty-one years on an analyst's couch, he has finally "found" himself. Along with the Diane Keaton relationship, the most important autobiographical ingredient in

Annie Hall is its treatment of Allen's development from gag-writer into the quintessential embodiment of his own humor. In an important sense, Allen has enlisted his audience in striking his psychological balance through the simultaneous delivery of the joke and the development of the persona: the audience watches his persona as it fantasizes and, at the same time, copes with a world of his own making. Like whining, performance is therapy.

Like Allen's own, Alvy Singer's reticence to make the transition from writer to writer/performer is basically neurotic. The transition itself is part of the therapy that Woody Allen has prescribed for himself, but he also knows that the *compulsive need* to strike some kind of balance with the world which one shares with others is, at bottom, another manifestation of neuroticism. The central intelligence in a Woody Allen film is always unabashedly neurotic, but that neuroticism always reflects a certain tension. On the one hand, there is the intensely private relationship between Allen and his persona—a privacy which he protects jealously even when, as in *Annie Hall*, it leads to peevishness and eventual isolation; on the other hand, there is the Allen persona's perpetual need to establish relationships—both with women and with his audience. This tension can never be wholly resolved, because most of the characters that populate the world in which Allen wants to take part also represent those aspects of the real world which have alienated him in the first place.

Neuroticism, however, serves Allen both as fancy's apologist and as its chief means of expression. During his twenty-one-year stint on the analyst's couch (reduced, out of some curious sense of proportion, to fifteen years in *Annie Hall*), Woody Allen has developed and refined what can only be characterized as the full-fledged *theme* of neuroticism. In Allen's hands, neuroticism becomes both an irrefutable, philosophically respectable worldview and a principle of character psychology and dramatic composition.

The neurotic's worldview pulls in two opposite but equally fruitful directions. It expands into a philosophically and psychologically feasible hypothesis, but it also reduces to a sophistic, perversely rationalized syllogism—the type that Beckett and Borges, for example, like to examine in order to pursue whimsical permutations and corollaries. A Woody Allen film is devoted to dramatizing one central premise: namely, that if each person exists harmoniously with others only in a world which answers to his private fantasies, then there is no perspective from which to measure *anyone's* disjunction from "reality" or success of one's relations with others. Hence the web of tenuous personal relationships which, especially in *Manhattan* and *A Midsummer Night's Sex Comedy*, constitutes the social fabric of the life of the typical Allen protagonist.

The chief usefulness of this syllogism is that it exposes a certain fallacy: namely, the conventional notion that the appearance of this exteriorized world, accompanied by the dreamer's belief that he has successfully displaced himself in it, constitutes "aesthetic distance." If the neurotic believes strongly enough in the success of his self-displacement and in the objectivity of this exteriorized world, then he may also succumb to the equally false notion that dramatic art can give truthful expression to—and thus purge—painful interior states of mind. For Woody Allen, these fallacies tend to be perpetuated by artists who have not had the benefit of his obsession—and experience—with neuroticism.

In this sense, *Interiors* clarifies the final irony which governs Woody Allen's concept of dramatic composition. For Allen, the persona is at once a delusive and therapeutic fabulation: it is inevitably the agent of a "distancing" which is inherently spurious, and its absence, as in *Interiors*, makes possible not some illusion of objectivity, but rather a more accurate rendering of the relationship between an imaginative world and its source in a particular imagination. Such a relationship, despite its transparency as fiction, nevertheless performs a psychologically more truthful, and therefore more humanistic, function than"serious" drama of a "naturalistic" bent.

IV

Woody Allen's comic world may be infinitely rich in its inventions and complexities, but it is also bound to be hermetic, its ironies reflecting upon and illuminating its own conceits rather than "real" shared human experiences. This remains true, I think, up through *Annie Hall*; it is a problem to which Allen attends conscientiously in *Manhattan*, *Sex Comedy*, and *Broadway Danny Rose*. Up until this point in his career, the humanism of his films is vouchsafed primarily by their honest attention to the quality of the individual imagination, however neurotic. The syllogism from which he constructs his imaginative world is thus necessarily a sophistic argument—a fact which we can perhaps clarify as we compare Woody Allen's governing syllogism to one of Borges' favorite sophistries: his parable about Shakespeare, who left London and returned to Stratford because "He had to be some one."

Borges' legend has it that, upon his death, Shakespeare complained to God, "I . . . want to be one and myself." "Neither am I anyone," replied God; "I have dreamt the world as you have dreamt your work . . . , and among the forms in my dream are you, who like myself are many and one." Shakespeare's character portraits, according to Borges, are personae which he assumes so that others will substantiate his reality: he calls an audience into existence "so that others would not discover his condition as no one." The persona thus accounts for the audience and is real; but since the reality of Shakespeare himself depends upon the dreams of a profoundly problematical dreamer, no one can testify to his reality. In short, Borges creates a Shakespeare who dramatizes his epistemological dilemma for himself in every scene that he writes and enacts.[5]

Woody Allen's strategy with regard to his audience is much the same as the one which Borges attributes to Shakespeare the fabulator/actor. As the gesture whereby the persona comes into existence, performance is necessary for Allen. It allows the persona to exist on the same ontological level as all the other people who populate his imaginary world. What *Annie Hall* makes clear, however, is the fact that those people are mirror reflections of the people in Woody Allen's audience—of people in the *real* world. Alvy Singer performs his comedy in the midst of real-life circumstances: there is virtually no mediation whatsoever between the real-life experiences in which Alvy finds his material and the opportunities he takes to perform it. Alvy is funny in a gradeschool classroom, in the kitchen, at the tennis club, in bed, at parties, bars, health food restaurants, and perhaps most importantly, in the streets of New York, where passers-by are living proof that the real world actually conforms to the image of the world which Alvy Singer is always whining about.

When he stops one couple, for example, to find out why they don't have the kinds of problems he has, the man replies blithely that it's because he hasn't a brain in his head and is thoroughly shallow; "And so am I," chirps in the girlfriend. It's not simply the inspired silliness of the lines that makes the vignette so funny; the comic effect also results from the fact that they are spoken in a context—the streets of New York—which is as real and as familiar as *our* world, but which is transformed instantaneously into the perfect image of Woody Allen's unique and irregular universe. They're also spoken by people who seem at first to be just like *us* but who suddenly utter the magic words which whisk them away into the looking-glass world that Woody Allen has waiting for them.

Exposed to scenes like this, we cannot help but assume that Woody Allen is absolutely right and that his whining has been justified.

But as we have seen, Allen is, by his own admission, growing more sober, and in these moments, he also manages to remind us of the possibility that his reasoning is indeed pure sophistry. Does Woody Allen's peculiar sensibility privilege him to expose the world in its *genuine* absurdity, or does it condemn him to see it eternally in absurd and often grotesque images of his own fabulation? The answer, of course, lies somewhere between these two possibilities: pompous loudmouths *do* spout McLuhan in theater queues, but the one in *Annie Hall* is a character in a tale told by a neurotic who's undergone years of psychoanalysis, and we may have to remind ourselves that this particular loudmouth may well signify nothing.

To remind ourselves of this paradox is to remind ourselves that the subject of a Woody Allen film is always the comic imagination itself. That imagination enters into and works its effect upon our world only when

Woody Allen commits it to performance, and that is why we—frequently impersonated by people like our couple from New York— have to be a part of every Woody Allen film, just as we were part of his nightclub routine. Like many nightclub comedians, Allen adopted the strategy of direct address, but the evening's topic was fairly unique especially in the intimacy of its treatment—for instance, "I think I will review for you some of the outstanding features of my private life and put them in perspective, and then we'll have a brief question-and-answer period and evaluate them." What follows is a series of outtakes from the autobiography of a neurotic undergoing what he emphasizes to be "strict Freudian analysis." Our narrator is unabashedly neurotic but the routine works because *we* gradually become just as interested in *his* neurotic misadventures as *he* is, and the more insanely neurotic they are, the more interested *we* become. We thus enter into Woody Allen's world, and, judged from the inside, his cynical and absurd view of things starts to become plausible again; the syllogism seems a little less sophistic.

We can now conclude our description of the way this syllogism governs the conception of *Annie Hall*. Woody Allen has lived the life which seemed so improbable when he imparted it to Alvy Singer in the film: he has made the transition from anonymous gag-writer to writer/performer, and he has gained the most beautiful live-in lover that any short, red-headed, neurotic Jewish comedian could reasonably hope for—exactly the kind of woman about whom his nightclub jokes so often fantasized—and he has extolled that relationship on the screen, where we have found it both as improbable and as comic as he figured we would. According to the syllogism, then, Woody Allen has indeed been right all along in his interpretation both of his life and of our place in it. It stands to reason, too, that he has also been right in his interpretation of the world and that his whining has been justified. Allen's reasoning, of course, is still sophistic. Its value comes from the fact that it is designed to interpret the way that the comic imagination works—not necessarily "reality" itself. Inevitably, it is also a self-serving view of things, but Allen has an operative metaphor to cover this contingency—namely, jokes which celebrate a kind of metaphorical masturbation whereby the monologist derives pleasure from his own comic persona. Complimented for his sexual prowess in *Love and Death*, Woody's Boris allows that "I practice a lot when I'm alone." Or, as Alvy Singer tells Annie Hall: "Don't knock masturbation—it's sex with someone I love."

V

We may now look more closely at *Interiors*, which, like most Woody Allen films, is a dream play peopled with typical Allen neurotics. The difference, however, is that, in *Interiors*, Allen simply documents his characters' lives and their world. He does not displace them in that whimsical world which would have been necessary if he were going to objectify his own persona. Many critics were suspicious when Allen, who has always thought of dramatic sobriety as standing in one-to-one correspondence with pretentiousness, announced that *Interiors* was to be a "serious dramatic" film, but I think that we may now say that Allen was prompted to label *Interiors* as he did because he realized what kind of film it would have to be if it were not to depend upon the displacement of his own persona. To eliminate the performance of his own persona is to reject both its characteristically whimsical world and its audience. The result in *Interiors* is a perfectly hermetic world which belongs to the people who inhabit it and which rises to heights of Allenesque humor only whenever their pretensions to seriousness become sufficiently transparent to reveal the ironic presence of their creator.

The inherent irony of this posture allows Allen to deal more fully with his two key themes. The world of the characters in *Interiors* is, first, a straight-faced mirror-image of the looking-glass reality of *Annie Hall*— that is, of the world which appears whenever the world must be made to conform to the image which the Allen persona has of it."[6] Second, the radically expressionistic nature of the drama of *Interiors* allows Allen to resolve the problem which, to his mind, arises from the fallacious notion that an objectified drama can truthfully express an interior one and, by permitting the neurotic to strike a balance with the audience that shares "real" world with him, alleviate his neuroticism.

Interiors divides fairly evenly into two parts. The first half introduces us to a wealthy, sixtyish lawyer (E. G. Marshall) who decides to walk out on his family because he wants to be alone for a while (although the decision, he stresses, is "not irrevocable"). His wife (Geraldine Page) is an interior decorator whose impeccable sense of taste has never been violated either by an idea or by reality. They have three daughters: a witless little TV actress (Kristin Griffith), a would-be photographer (Marybeth Hurt) who is frustrated by the refusal of the family birthright to creativity to make itself manifest in her, and a successful confessional poetess (Diane Keaton) who is married to an unsuccessful novelist (Richard Jordan). Throughout this half of the film, hypersensitivity and intellectual pretentiousness mount casually but unremittingly. Almost every word and gesture is devoted to exploring the mysterious relationship between the creative capacity and the torment of the sensitive human spirit. The ironic tone of this part of the film is least coy when the almost inflectionless gravity with which Allen creates a mood of self-conscious profundity occasionally lapses into absurdity.

The second half of the film becomes even more disquieting. Gradually, Allen contrives to drain it almost completely of any ostensibly comic content, and we detect only very rarely any tinge of irony in his narrative voice. The last major character is also introduced as Marshall informs his daughters that he is going to marry a noisy, unpretentious widow (Maureen Stapleton), whom one of the girls ultimately labels a "vulgarian." Stapleton's ingenuousness and vitality are quite obviously supposed to counterpoint the squalid intellectual pretenses of the family into which she is marrying, and there are times when the counterpoint is developed so explicitly that it seems to become an end in itself. *Interiors* seems to be becoming a straightfaced exercise in dramatic earnestness, growing as importunate as the characters that it has been treating ironically.

There is, however, one particular scene in this part of the film which, while epitomizing the film's increasingly sober tone, is also pivotal in vindicating one's faith in the consistency of Allen's sense of irony. At a dinner party at which the family meets Stapleton, the conversation turns to an unnamed play which everyone present has seen, and the efforts of Hurt, Keaton, and Jordan to plumb the depths of its meaning become so labored and condescending that we actually start to become embarrassed for them. The scene both reinforces the film's overt contempt for (naturalistic) restraint in its dialogue and renews its strategy—developed carefully in the first half—of transparent irony. In addition, the film's most common dramatic vehicle—the conversational exposition of weighty matters—finally coincides quite explicitly with its primary theme: the pretenses of self-conscious sensitivity and intellectualism. Why may we not assume that, like the little playlet that ends *Annie Hall*, the topic of this conversation— an unnamed play of considerable emotional insight and intellectual complexity—also suggests the "play" that we have been watching? We might argue, then, that this scene notes the film's insistence upon collapsing upon itself. The world of the film itself is as hermetic as that of the neurotics who inhabit it. Allen compels such a conclusion, I think, by his insistence upon a few closed sets and, more importantly, by the way the drama unfolds, tightening the familial and emotional bonds upon which every character has grown increasingly dependent and producing a sense of enclosure, of five or six separate cells within the same prison.

This paradoxical feeling—the simultaneous experience of dependence and the desire for isolation and freedom—has in fact been the film's major psychological theme, as well as the source of its dramatic momentum, all along: Page whimpers that she can't live alone and keeps her pathetic faith in the possibility of reconciliation with her husband; Marshall insists at first that the separation is "not irrevocable" but later pleads for his daughters' blessings upon his remarriage; Keaton needs to measure her literary success against her husband's failure, and he needs her success to feed his own self-pity; perhaps most importantly, Hurt needs to establish her sister's success as a measure of her own *relative* failure—as an assurance of the difference between *actualized* and *potential* talent. In each case, the intensity of a character's loneliness and dependence stands in direct correspondence to the severity of his neuroticism.

In fact, we may define neuroticism as it is treated in *Interiors* as follows: It is the paradoxical experience of striving for separation or freedom while acknowledging, in virtually every word and gesture, emotional dependence. We can also summarize Allen's interpretation of neuroticism in *Interiors* in terms of two analogous equations—both of which, in fact, improve upon the sophistic syllogism that we described above and both of which help to clarify what I have characterized as the film's strategy of transparent irony.

The first equation is the fallacy of assuming that the living of life and intellectual sensitivity to it are coextensive activities. For most of the characters in *Interiors*, for example, life seems principally to be disquisition. As people whose main activity is expressing and explaining themselves, they are performers, and other people constitute an audience (pseudophilosophically, an "Other") which validates the performance by letting it take place in the "real" world. The result, of course, is an essentially abstract definition of life itself, for *living* becomes simply an attribute of *performing*. It is not the reality of one's spiritual and intellectual anxieties which the Other substantiates, for these anxieties are real only as "interior" states of being; it is merely the performance which the Other witnesses, so that the relationship between the performer and his audience is always at least one step removed from reality.

The second equation is by far the simpler of the two. It rests upon one of the basic assumptions of intellectual activity—namely, the assumption (also fallacious, in Allen's opinion) that the world in which the intellect finds itself is accessible to it and that sufficient intellectual sensitivity to the world ensures "harmony" or "balance" with it. The common denominator in these two equations is still the phenomenon of *distancing*, for intellectual activity is by its very nature a process of distancing—of "stepping back" from the object of one's contemplation in order to get a better view. When a character speaks in *Interiors*, for instance, he implicitly regards the Other as a member of an audience which represents for him the objective world. But that world exists only insofar as there is an audience. It has been created solely in order that the speaker's persona may exist on its ontological level and so become an object of intellectual self-examination.

In *Interiors*, then, self-examination is primarily talk—verbal performance. Here, too, we find compounded the same ironic consequences which we outlined in our discussion of performance. Enraptured by his own performance, the speaker is led to believe even more firmly in the identity of living and the life of the mind, and his incessant self-serving talk actually works to alienate the Other. Hence the film's gradually escalating mood of petulance and self-pity. The cycle finally threatens to become inescapable. The sense that he has alienated his audience only intensifies the speaker's feeling of isolation and thus reinforces his need to think of himself as superior (or inferior) to another person, so that his dependence upon others as functions in his intellectual constructs only grows.

Only an event of truly dramatic—indeed, melodramatic—proportions can break the cycle of entrapment and dependence, for such an event reminds everyone that the most improbable circumstances in life are not accessible to the intellect. In *Interiors*, Page's final breakdown and suicide result from the shattering of her familial bonds and the sudden and intensified feeling of that isolation which accompanies dependence. Beautifully handled, the climax of *Interiors* is nevertheless melodramatic. Page appears in the beach house in which Marshall has remarried; as Hurt berates her mother with a self-pitying oration on self-delusion, Page walks out of the house and into the ocean; Hurt pursues her screaming, followed by her boyfriend; he pulls her, but not her mother, out of the water, and Stapleton uses mouth-to-mouth resuscitation to save the girl who had once called her a "vulgarian" and an "animal."

Such is the stuff of which drama is made, and the conscientious and powerful rendering of such an event as part of a cinematic narrative, far from convincing us that it is or can be real life, actually heightens our appreciation of it as dramatic artifice. Perhaps this is just another way of saying that, at least on the level on which the story unfolds, the "realism" of a film event corresponds roughly to its approximation of the unfolding of "real" time; otherwise, the fictional event is automatically magnified, regardless of the understatement with which its creator tries to present it. Since fiction is generally governed by principles of ellipsis and selection, few narrative events are truly "realistic" in effect. The realistic aspirations of any narrative art form, then, are predicated on a useful but purely metaphorical assumption about the relationship between real and narrative time. The problem is especially acute in film, which complements the exploitation of self-enclosed space with a movement in time that falls somewhere between the ontology of real time and the abstract temporality of music.

Even more important to the success of the realistic illusion is the *belief* of the characters themselves that their *space*, however self-enclosed, and their *temporality*, however abstract and elliptical, are indeed real. For Woody Allen, however, that belief is perfectly analogous to the illusion which the neurotic suffers when he believes that the exteriorized world in which he has displaced himself is real—that it is a truthful representation of the world which he shares with others and with which he has been trying to strike a psychological balance. In this sense, the heart of all realistic drama beats falsely, and to lay it open is to expose the fallacies of displacement and aesthetic distance. Rather than beat blood into the body of the drama, the false heart gradually blanches the blood of the drama until the drama loses its realistic color entirely and eventually becomes transparent.

Whatever is comic in *Interiors* results from Allen's experimental effort to let an ostensibly realistic drama gradually reveal the fallacies on which it is based. This practice is bound to produce occasional incongruities, some of which Allen himself cannot resist playing for overt comic effect.

VI

Traditionally, comedy has been characterized as a celebrational response to experience, but many of its great theorists have long been at great pains to describe the mean-spiritedness to which its practitioners must momentarily commit themselves when they turn in the direction of satire or parody, for the purpose of these comic forms is frequently nothing less than the annihilation of an entire attitude towards life. What is annihilated is the *ridiculous* or the *ludicrous*. The attack, as Elder Olson puts it, is leveled because the comedian is "concerned" about the phenomenon which strikes him as comic, and it succeeds when it inspires "the laughter emotion"—an affective experience both of freedom from threat and of pleasant equilibrium.[7]

Woody Allen's chief "concern" is the fallacy of believing that intellectual displacement is really a vicarious but valid way of striking a balance with oneself and with the world. He sees this fallacious notion as essentially analogous to neurotic behavior, and because he has seen in his own neuroticism an important analogue of his chief intellectual concern, he has radically interiorized his assault upon the concern which threatens him the most. This much we have said already, but we have emphasized also that Allen's assault has taken the form of a pseudological *reductio*—a sophistic syllogism which, when pursued to its logical end, produces comic results. But Allen himself has engaged consistently in the strategy of displacement. If the *self* is the ground of his concern, then "the annihilation of the concern itself," as Olson puts it, can be accomplished only if the comedian/playwright pretends to believe completely in the consummate displacement of the self in the persona.

How, then, does the comedian/playwright reconcile himself to a faith which he knows to be pretense? Shakespeare's dilemma, Borges has reminded us, resulted from the fact that he was not only a dramatist but an *actor* as well. Such faith is tenable only through the rite of *performance*. In both *Annie Hall* and *Manhattan*, for example, Allen *plays* a comedy *writer*, and the curious onscreen configuration which results reminds us that he insists upon retaining the agency of the *converter* of concern into nothingness while assuming the role of its object at the same time. This strategy accomplishes several things. First, it reconciles the terms of the paradox of false belief, reminding us that willful and systematic belief like that of many "serious" artists and philosophers, is essentially nothing more than intellectual commitment. Second, it justifies a personal posture which, despite Allen's ostensible antagonism towards intellectualism, is unquestionably intellectual in its orientation. Finally, it allows Allen to adopt an honestly cynical stance towards most intellectual activity.

The formula, of course, is by no means new to comedy. For instance, the relationship between the comic and intellectual/moral strategies in Erich Auerbach's description of a farcical eighteenth-century novel—*Manon Lescaut*, by the Abbé Prévost—is much like the one which Allen has developed. According to Auerbach, the novel is both stylistically elegant and realistic. Auerbach is fascinated by the interpenetration of the two styles, particularly as the author "wants us to take his story seriously." To this end, he creates a hero who is a "sharper, a cheat, and almost a pander. [He] never gives up his habit of expressing noble feelings and of allowing himself the pleasure of making moralizing observations which, to be sure, are extremely trite and sometimes dubious but which the author evidently takes quite seriously."[8]

What we find in Auerbach's description is the basis for an approach to the special writer/performer configuration towards which Woody Allen's practice has been leading him and which is most fully realized in *Manhattan*. Even more important, however, is what Auerbach says about the author's belief in his own sentiments. The Abbé Prévost's displacement of his own voice in that of a morally dubious chevalier is certainly more radical than anything Woody Allen would care to attempt, but the peculiarity of the Allen hero's voice results from the same strategy as that which the Abbé Prévost employs in *Manon Lescaut*: the incongruity which exists between the speaker and his announced sentiments simplifies the moral content of those sentiments and lends them, at least in context, an air of self-evidence. Woody Allen *believes* in the intellectual content of his words, even when their thrust is anti-intellectual; his intellectualism, however, is not a faith in the coherence or beauty of systematized ideas, but rather a faith in the self-evident value of intelligence itself, for he believes, like a true man of the Enlightenment, that *intellectual* exercise keeps one in good *moral* condition. The comic power of conversion is an inherently intellectual power, and the comedian exercises it out of a spirit of moral righteousness.

The sentiment in which, as fabulator and comic, Woody Allen believes is, quite simply, the moral utility of the intellect, and it is in this sentiment alone that he asks his audience to share his faith. The simple self-evidence of this posture allows him the expedient of arguing that his belief is different from the willful and systematic belief of the "serious" philosopher-artist. This posture also allows him to argue that his principle of comic conversion is not inspired by the impulse towards destruction, but rather by a mature and well-motivated cynicism. It is the nature of this cynicism which Allen tries to clarify in *Manhattan*.

VII

The case for the intellect and its moral utility is made most explicitly towards the end of *Manhattan*. Allen's persona, an ex-TV writer named Isaac Davis, has been introduced to a woman named Mary, also a writer; she has been having an affair with Isaac's best friend, a married English teacher named Yale; Yale and Mary break up and, partially through Yale's instigation, Mary eventually takes up and moves in with Isaac; one after-noon, however, Mary informs Isaac that she's secretly seeing Yale again; Isaac marches over to Yale's school, takes him from his classroom to what appears to be a biology classroom and berates him with an argument which, while it sounds as if it came from an existentialist's handbook on thoughtful moral behavior, is a fairly accurate assessment of the situation. Yale's reply, meanwhile, reduces to the repeated plea that "We're only human." As they argue, each cut to Isaac reveals the skeleton of a large ape on a stand behind him; while Isaac himself does not refer to the ape or draw any of the obvious moral analogies until late in his oration, the audi-ence cannot help but beat him to it, since the over-explicit presence of the ape is also being played for incidental laughs.

Indeed, the chief difference between Isaac Davis and Alvy Singer is the former's moral earnestness—along with the psychological stability which makes it possible for him to practice it. "You're an island unto yourself," Annie tells Alvy, "like New York City. You're incapable of enjoying life." The truth of what she says is sometimes hard to see, because Alvy Singer is funny enough to be very charming. At film's end, however, it is Annie who has outgrown Alvy, and Alvy himself confesses as much: "Annie and I broke up," he says, "and I still can't get my mind around that, you know. I keep sifting the pieces of the relationship through my mind and examining my life to figure out where the screw-up came."

Annie Hall, despite the direction in which its title points, is about the relationship and its breakup from Alvy's point of view, and as such, it is an exercise in self-examination. Marshall Brickman, who coscripted *Sleeper*, *Annie Hall*, and *Manhattan*, has suggested what direction he and Allen tried to take in examining Alvy Singer, and his remarks also help to sug-gest what progress was necessary to transform him into Isaac Davis: "Face it," admits Brickman, *Annie Hall* "only hints at profound issues, but we asked ourselves, 'Is it neurosis or honesty that makes the character Woody plays so pessimistic? Is it merely maladjustment, immaturity, or is it a relentless philosophical integrity?'"[9] It seems fairly safe to say that, in *Annie Hall*, Allen and Brickman suspected neurosis, maladjustment, and immaturity. When Alvy speaks with "philosophical integrity," he does so almost exclusively in that "ventriloqual" voice that I described above—the voice of the author who believes in his sentiments but who must speak through the character in whom he has chosen to displace himself. The dis-placement causes the voice to be refracted, and the distinction between the author's moral seriousness and the peevishness by which his persona gets laughs is only made more obvious.

In *Manhattan*, however, while the perspective is still that of the Allen persona, that persona is considerably better adjusted and more mature than Alvy Singer; the intellectual and moral earnestness of the author is much more compatible with the attitude of his persona, and his voice is not refracted nearly so badly by any residuum of neuroticism which that persona might have inherited from his ancestors. *Manhattan* still has its share of anti-intellectual jokes, but a significant part of Isaac Davis' emotional stability is his intellectual sincerity. Conversely, Annie Hall's engaging dottiness has in Keaton's Mary Wilke escalated into a neuroticism which, in the moral dubiousness of its consequences, is even more serious than that which Allen normally attributes to his own persona. In *Play It Again, Sam*, for example, Allen and Keaton had compared notes on Darvon and the best airline terminals in which to throw up; in *Annie Hall*, it's Woody's persona who's engaged in a marathon psychiatric session; in *Manhattan*, however, Keaton's character, her self-esteem "one point below Kafka's," is accorded the "Zelda Fitzgerald Emotional Maturity Award." As part of the thorough process of self-examination in which he has been engaged in his films, Allen tries transferring the blame for the breakup to the other party in the relationship, preferring to test the validity of his intellectual integrity without submerging it in the severe emotional muddle that generally governs his persona's behavior. Isaac must, for example, come to the defense of some of his intellectual favorites when Mary and Yale start "trashing" the likes of Fitzgerald, Mahler, and Picasso, and he includes on his list of "things that make life worth living" not only Groucho Marx but the second movement of the *Jupiter* Symphony.

After he had finished *Interiors*, Allen said of *Manhattan* that it "revolves around what I started to do in *Annie Hall*, but this is darker than that. It's got to do with how a person can maintain his lifestyle and integrity, a decent life, in the face of the onslaught of contemporary society, all the temptations and all the terrible stuff that you have to go through. And so again, it's a comedy, but on a more serious level." Admittedly, the assumption which allows Allen to make the transition to his final comment ("And so again, it's a comedy . . .") is not altogether clear in this context. Just what does Woody Allen take to be the relationship between the serious and the comic in *Manhattan*? The answer, I think, lies in his insistence upon associating seriousness with "courage": "In addition to integrity, bravery and courage," he told the same interviewer, "what interests me more personally is more existential. . . . Why are you here? What is the purpose of life? Spiritual meanings." There is nothing, he added, "like having courage . . . , where an act of volition or bravery is required. . . . The real act of courage for me is the guy who acts in spite of an almost paralyzing fear."

The same topic comes up in the very first scene of *Manhattan*: Isaac wonders if anyone at his restaurant table would leap off a bridge to save a drowning man; "I, of course, don't swim," he adds, "so I don't have to worry about it." Since Isaac cannot swim, the issue reduces for him to a purely intellectual exercise; at the same time, the line itself also makes for good comedy—which is also a fundamentally intellectual exercise. Allen is announcing in effect that he has struck a kind of balance, and he has found in that balance between serious intellectual integrity and comic talent a certain mellowness. That mellowness belongs to both Woody Allen the filmmaker and to Isaac Davis the persona, in whom Alvy Singer has ripened without rotting. His most venturesome mixture of the comic and the serious, *Manhattan* also exemplifies Allen's highest professional value: the courage to grow as an artist. *Annie Hall*, he said shortly after the film was released, "isn't so much a sudden need to tell all as a desire to move in more directions. I don't want to keep making the same film over and over again." He was more emphatic in explaining his determination to make *Interiors*: "*Annie Hall* was a big success for me, but . . . I want to depart in some way. I just know that I have to do things I'm not sure I can do and . . . be prepared to fail with them. Even if this movie is a total disaster, I still will have grown. I will have learned more about myself, about my weaknesses, my limitations."

Courage and intellectual integrity also constitute the mellowness of Isaac Davis. Intellectually, Isaac is superior to all the pretentious failures around him, and the fact that he is wittier than they are, his professed anti-intellectualism notwithstanding, is a badge of his intellectual superiority. More importantly, he is morally superior to them. He behaves more honestly in sexual relationships than they do (even his one big error in this respect, breaking off with his seventeen-year-old lover, results from sincere motives), and the single most courageous act in the film—quitting a lucrative job as writer for a schlock TV show—-belongs to Isaac.

What Allen takes to be the relationship between the comic and the serious thus becomes much clearer. Of the two people to whom Isaac's superiority must be developed, one (Mary) is emotionally bankrupt, and the other (Yale) behaves in a way that can most generously be characterized as morally dubious. Their respective shortcomings, like those of the characters in *Interiors*, feed on one another and even interpenetrate. What Allen has come to realize in *Manhattan* is that neuroticism inevitably entails a certain moral failure—-namely, the failure of the courage to be honest, both with oneself and with the rest of the world, one's image of which depends for its accuracy upon the honesty of one's self-image. The neurotic cuts a comic figure (and up through *Annie Hall*, Allen rarely failed to get as many laughs as possible out of his various neurotics), but the moral coward demands more serious treatment—treatment of the sort which Allen's simple philosophical premise about the moral utility of the intellect is able to afford him.

Allen's cynicism——the result of his sensitivity to basic moral shortcomings——has matured at the same time, and by the same process of self-examination, because he himself has matured both psychologically and artistically. In both senses, that maturity has resulted from the gradual discovery of *balance*——a balance which, in turn, has led to an explicit mellowing of his persona's attitude towards life. That mellowness, of course, is reflected in the image of the world which is presented to us in *Manhattan*——an image which, as always, conforms to the Allen persona's image of the world. "He was as tough and romantic as the city he loved," reads Isaac's first voice-over: Isaac's Manhattan is "tough" because it reflects the maturity with which, like Allen himself, Isaac has learned to cope with emotionally and morally crippled people like Mary and Yale, and it is "romantic" because it also answers to the newfound mellowness of the imagination which has fantasized it.

Notes

1. Quotations by Woody Allen come from the following sources: Bernard Drew, "Woody Allen Is Feeling Better," *American Film*, 2, No. 7 (1977), 10–15; Lee Guthrie, *Woody Allen: A Biography* (New York: Drake, 1978); Ira Halberstadt, "Scenes from a Mind. Woody Allen Is Nobody's Fool," *Take One*, 6, No. 12 (1978), 16–20; Eric Lax, *On Being Funny: Woody Allen and Comedy* (New York: Charterhouse, 1975). The scripts for *Annie Hall*, *Interiors*, *Manhattan*, and *Stardust Memories* have been published as *Four Films of Woody Allen* (New York: Random House, 1982).

2. I use the word "fabulator" throughout for much the same reason as Robert Scholes uses it in *The Fabulators* (New York: Oxford Univ. Press, 1967). Noting that it is a "lovely word" which was "dropped out of our language a few years ago," Scholes emphasizes that "fabulation" has the advantage over "novel" or "satire" of asserting "the authority of the shaper, the fabulator behind the fable":

> Delight in design, and its concurrent emphasis on the art of the designer, will serve in part to distinguish the art of the fabulator from the work of the novelist or the satirist. Of all narrative forms, fabulation puts the highest premium on art and joy . . . . For the moment, suffice it to say that modern fabulation, like the ancient fabling of Aesop, tends away from the representation of reality, but tends toward actual human life by way of ethically controlled fantasy (pp. 6–11).

3. Trans. Arvid Paulson, in *Eight Expressionist Plays* (New York: New York Univ. Press, 1972), p. 343.

4. As Diane Jacobs points out (. . . *but we need the eggs: The Magic of Woody Allen* [New York: St. Martin's Press, 1982]), the gags in *Sleeper*, transforming the Allen persona "into some sort of moving vehicle," make it "the most Buster Keatonesque of Allen's films" (p. 79). As a tester of new inventions in *Bananas*, Woody is at one point victimized by a maniacally automated executive desk, but the gag, an obvious homage to Chaplin's encounter with a production-line feeding machine gone awry in *Modern Times*, is no more integral to the film's overall strategy than the shot of a baby carriage careening down some palace steps during a revolutionary battle. In *Sleeper*, however, the *world* in which Woody, as Miles Monroe, awakens after a cryogenic sleep of 200 years conditions both the nature of the

film's gags—which usually involve futuristic gadgetry—and the persona's capacity for survival; the formula, whereby the hero survives by becoming virtually one with a world that seems to alienate everyone else, is vintage Keaton.

5. "Everything and Nothing," trans. James E. Irby, in *Labyrinths: Selected Stories and Other Writings*, ed. Donald A. Yates and James E. Irby (New York: New Directions, 1964), pp. 248–49.

6. *Zelig*, in which the Allen persona effectively and objectively transmutes in order to conform to the world around him, is thus, among other things, an object lesson in the silliness of going about this business backwards.

7. *The Theory of Comedy* (Bloomington: Indiana Univ. Press, 1968), pp. 16, 25.

8. *Mimesis: The Representation of Reality in Western Literature*, trans. Willard Trask (1953; rpt. Garden City, N.Y.: Doubleday, 1957), pp. 347–53. Noted in passing: Auerbach refers to the genre to which *Manon Lescaut* belongs as the *intérieur*.

9. Quoted by Halberstadt, "Scenes from a Mind," *Take One*, 16–17.

Neither Here nor There

GREGG BACHMAN

FOR MORE than twenty-five years I have reserved a special place in my life for the films of Woody Allen. It has been only recently, however, through the perspective that these years offer, that I have been able to fully appreciate how my connection to the films is much stronger than merely an affection for their characters or an affinity for their humor. As I trace the development of Allen's themes across the breadth of his works, I can detect the outline of my own story, the struggle of the hyphenated-American, the assimilated Jew cast adrift between a society not ready to fully embrace him, and a religion and culture he is not fully capable of embracing. I can see the gradual evolution of a spiritual journey not yet complete, from the youthful iconoclast through the dark and troubled agnostic to an emerging, more hopeful pose. If drama, as Hamlet suggests, is but a mirror held up to life, then it is indeed my own life that I see reflected in the works of Woody Allen.

My story is not dissimilar to many first- and second-generation hyphenated-Americans. My grandparents emigrated here in the first quarter of this century. They left behind the rather cloistered society of the European shtetl and found themselves thrust into the roiling melting pot that is America. As their families grew they faced the rather prickly question of assimilation. On the one hand, they could cling to the old ways and desperately build walls to hold the new world in abeyance. For the most part, this was the direction chosen by the Chasidim, the "keepers of the faith," the ultraorthodox sect externally recognized by the men's black frocks, beards, and broad-brimmed hats. Or they could try to go in the opposite direction and attempt to fit into society by becoming "True Americans," a process that would entail a wholesale abandonment of the old ways. Both my paternal and maternal sides chose the latter route: customs were dropped, Yiddish was not taught, goals were altered.

This did not happen all at once, of course; instead, there was a gradual falling away of traditions. The strict dietary laws of kashrut would be maintained in the home, but accommodations would be made for restaurants and eating at the homes of gentile friends. Shabbat, the traditional day of rest and observance, would be acknowledged by the lighting of the candles on Friday nights and attendance at synagogue on Saturday morning,

This essay was written specifically for this volume and is published here for the first time by permission of the author.

but then life would go on, commerce conducted, games played, like any other day of the week.

I was born a baby boomer and raised in a suburb in upper New York state. My house was filled with the latest gimmicks and gadgets, my life, with scouting and camps. Pork and shellfish were served at the family table, milk was drunk with our hamburgers. Friday nights were reserved for football and basketball games, and we attended religious school on Sundays, the gentile sabbath.

There was precious little room for religion. Jewish rituals and traditions become more rote than meaningful, and we followed the Jewish equivalent of the gentile's biannual pilgrimage to church on Christmas and Easter. I remember all too well the interminable holiday meals with older relatives chanting seemingly endless prayers in a confusing language as meaningless and as remote to me as Latin. Bar Mitzvah, the significant ritual marking the crossing of the threshold into adulthood, became an excuse for exotic parties and extravagant gifts.

This is not to say that my family became fully assimilated into mainstream America. We do, after all, live in a predominantly Christian country, where everybody gets days off for Christmas and Easter, while major community events and school tests are held on Jewish holidays. Our status as the other, the outsider, was continually being brought to our attention in a variety of ways. When I was in grade school I was constantly reminded, either verbally or physically, that mine was the first Jewish family on the block. Other ways were less direct. At my private, nonsectarian high school, for example, assemblies were opened by the recitation of the Lord's Prayer, and I was forced to bow my head and pretend to pray lest I draw more unwanted attention. This subtle type of exclusionary practice continues in many other venues to this day, as "our Lord Jesus" is invoked at public gatherings.

Outsiders enter into a rather pernicious cycle. Assimilation, which waters down heritage, leads to insecurity and the attendant fear that we will be revealed as pretenders to the mantle of "True Americans," and that we will suffer the consequence of ostracism or persecution. But once we *are* unmasked and inevitably driven away, where will we turn?

I, for one, had lost any vestige of my own unique sense of culture, and I felt just as out of place with my "own" as I did with gentiles. As a result, I was indeed a classic product of the drive toward assimilation. I found myself in the unenviable position of not only being on the outside of society, but on the outside of my own religion as well. I was constantly being identified as a Jew, but never consciously identifying myself as one; I suffered the pains of exclusion by gentile America, but I found little solace within the culture that made me different.

I was truly neither here nor there.

My attraction to Woody Allen stems from his constant struggle with this same cultural conundrum. His films continually strike the discordant notes of "outsider," "assimilation," "discovery," and all the attending complexities that resonate so clearly with me in my life. We all would like to think that people judge us by who we are and how we behave. However, most Jews cannot escape the reality that once we are discovered to be Jews, people will forever categorize us as Jews. And if we have no strong connection with this affiliation, we then have the makings for a highly personal and difficult struggle.

Although Allen has gone on record saying that being Jewish doesn't enter into his creative consciousness (Pogel, 25), he firmly identifies his characters as Jews. Melish, Stern, Singer, Zelig, Rose, and Kleinman sounds like a Jewish professional association, but all are the surnames of characters Allen has played in his films. "Any character I...play would be Jewish, just because I am (a Jew)," he has noted (Pogel, 25). People simply cannot accept him as anything else (Lax, 165), and, as Mast elaborated, his very success depends upon his Jewishness (Mast, 126). But here is a rather difficult problem: What exactly *is* a Jew? One answer lies in the desperate struggle of the outsider.

From the very beginning, Woody Allen's films were suffused with a preoccupation of being the outsider. In *Take the Money and Run* (1969) Allen is the misfit, the castoff from society who clumsily turns to the life of crime. As the criminal outsider he is constantly under the threat of discovery and arrest. When he is finally caught and incarcerated, he can earn early parole by taking part in an experimental drug program with a dangerous side effect: He is transformed into the ultimate Jewish outsider, a Chasidic Jew.

In *Bananas* (1971) Allen's character, Fielding Melish, in an attempt to find meaning and identity, finds himself instead among revolutionary fighters in San Marcos. Here he is definitely outside of his element in a world filled with bearded, dark-skinned men and tall, virile women, and saturated by Christian symbolism. Indeed, Christianity is so pervasive that it has even invaded Melish's subconscious—he is plagued by the odd, Bergman-inspired dream of being borne on a crucifix by flagellant monks.

Melish valiantly attempts to assimilate with the guerrillas, but significantly winds up getting urinated upon when practicing his camouflage. However, in spite of himself, Melish lives up to the myth of the successful Jew and rises to a leadership role. Then, disguised with a beard that eerily echoes his transfiguration into a Chasid, he returns to the United States to curry favor and funds from the government.

Once back in America, Melish cannot maintain his charade for very long and he is unceremoniously unmasked and put on trial. His prosecution quickly turns into a persecution, as two "expert" witnesses broadly justify an assimilated Jew's uneasiness with being discovered. One is a cop, who bluntly lumps in Melish with other "Jewish intellectual crackpots," while the other, Miss America, the epitome of gentile purity, is disarming but no less intolerant. "It's okay," she warns, "to be different, but not too different." The jury finds Melish guilty, but the judge suspends sentencing provided that Melish not move into the judge's neighborhood, an obvious slap at exclusively gentile enclaves. The extent of the reach of this exclusion is underlined by a mock news bulletin that crawls across the bottom of the screen at the end of the film: The first men on the moon, it reveals, have erected a Protestant-only cafeteria.

Thankfully, segregated neighborhoods are a thing of the past, at least officially. But a Jew, or any outsider for that matter, must still be on guard. When my wife and I first moved into our Gulf Coast neighborhood about five years ago, I was unsettled by a neighbor who noted we were marking a Jewish holiday. "Are you a Hebrew?" he asked, squinting his eyes. "Well...I *am* a Jew," I replied, wondering if I now needed to procure a rather ferocious guard dog for protection. Much to my relief, he was not so much to be feared than avoided. He was a member of a Christian fundamentalist sect that revered "Hebrews" for their part in the story of Christianity, and whenever I subsequently ran into him he would want to explore Scripture with me on the spot, whether we were in the aisle of a grocery store or at a gas station pump. This encounter reminded me of a student I met when I was an undergraduate. Born and raised in the mountains of Pennsylvania, she actually believed that the Jews were a myth of the Bible, an allegorical ancient people whose legacy existed solely to demonstrate particular points in Sunday school lessons and sermons.

In *Sleeper* (1973) Allen confronts this issue in a rather creative way. Just as my schoolmate from Pennsylvania and my neighbor in Florida thought of the Jews as the ancient people of the "Old Testament," Miles Monroe, the protagonist, awakens to find himself out of time and out of step with the world of the future. He is surrounded by those who have been taught to fear contamination by aliens or people like Miles, who follow an ancient and dangerously foreign system of beliefs. As the outsider, Miles futilely attempts to save himself by blending in, this time by masquerading as a mechanized servant. But once again he is discovered and the government sets out to forcibly assimilate him into the prevailing value system. As part of his brainwashing, Miles meets up with a beauty queen, who Allen again portrays as the statuesque gentile vision of what is right and acceptable. To win a pageant one needs to conform to the dominant values and ideals, and Miles is coerced into believing that *he* has won the contest. Reduced to tears, he receives the requisite fur-lined mantle and bouquet, and enters a world of facile people and blind obedience.

With *Annie Hall* (1977), Maurice Yacowar notes that Allen extended his abilities to a more profound place, abandoning parody for a direct voice

(Yacowar, 29). Indeed, almost from the very beginning of this film, the theme of the Jewish outsider in contemporary America is presented with little subtlety. For example, Alvy, the protagonist, tells a friend that he believes he has been accused of being a Jew when someone in fact innocently asked him if he had eaten lunch: "Didchoo eat? Jew? No, not did you eat, but jew eat? Jew. You get it? Jew eat?" And later, Alvy explains why the country won't back New York City: "Don't you see? The rest of the country looks upon New York like we're...left-wing Communist, Jewish, homosexual, pornographers." The coda to this argument is the most telling, for Alvy admits, "I think of us that way, sometimes."

A funny line, to be sure, but very revealing. We must remember that the entire film is presented as a series of Alvy's recollections as he attempts to "get his mind around" his breakup with Annie. So when Annie sets Alvy up by noting that he would be someone her Grammy would call "a real Jew," and we then see Alvy transformed into a Chasid during the disquieting ham dinner at the Halls, we need to keep in mind that it is not others that see Alvy as the outsider, but that *he* sees himself that way. As Gerald Mast observes, this "is an image of Alvy's own self-consciousness (stemming from) his own insecurities and discomfort" (Mast, 132).

If you are abused long enough and are not given an opportunity to develop a strong sense of self-esteem, you begin to believe that maybe you really are deserving of the abuse, and that maybe there is something to your tormentor's attacks. This thought is reflected in a sentiment of Alvy's, which he voices twice in *Annie Hall*: "I wouldn't want to be a member of a club that would have me as a member."

Another response to the abuse might be an ironic variation of the Freudian concept of identifying with the aggressor. Alvy does this when he meets his first wife and reduces her, as she claims, to the stereotype of a New York Jewish Left-wing Liberal Intellectual, thus both reducing his wife to the stereotype he himself fulfills, and turning that self into a redefined aggressor.

This psychopathology can often lead to extremes of self-degradation, as we see in *Zelig* (1983), in which Allen's chameleonlike character wins access to both the Vatican and the Third Reich (Stam, 113). But the mimicry is often incomplete, and the Jew is plagued not only by his own insecurities, but by the continuing fear of discovery as well.

These fears and insecurities achieve their ultimate expression in the Kafkaesque nightmare *Shadows and Fog* (1992). A killer is on the loose and protagonist Kleinman is roused from bed in the middle of the night to take part in "the Plan." But what *is* the Plan? Everyone assumes Kleinman is on the "inside" and knows it, and he wanders the shadowy, fog-filled streets desperately trying to see where he fits in. Ultimately, the mob turns on Kleinman and begins to hunt *him* down, for, as Richard Blake so poignantly observes, the ultimate cost of being the outsider is death, a fact the Jews, living in the shadow of the Holocaust, can never forget (Blake, 63).

In both *Annie Hall* and *Manhattan* (1979) Allen's characters are accused of being paranoid, but with such a history of oppression and anni-hilation, who could find fault in a little Jewish paranoia? Indeed, the Holocaust is an unwelcome poltergeist, haunting even those American Jews who believe their lives were only tangentially touched by this heinous tragedy. For me, a second-generation Jewish-American, a German accent, for example, can stir the oddest knee-jerk reaction of revulsion, mistrust, and fear. The Holocaust, internalized and barely repressed, is hovering just on the other side of consciousness to spew forth at seemingly random times.

Even a cursory look at a number of Allen's films bares witness to this sad and strange phenomenon. Whether it's the swastikas adorning a guest's sweater or a character described as "Mr. White Teeth, Mr. Tall Aryan Nazi Nordic" (*Sleeper*); or California disparaged as a place filled with sycophants who will even stoop to give an award in the name of Adolf Hitler (*Annie Hall*); or Cliff in *Crimes and Misdemeanors* (1989) remem-bering the day his wife stopped sleeping with him because it happened to fall on Adolf Hitler's birthday; or Ike, in *Manhattan*, revealing that he has never had a relationship that lasted as long as Hitler's and Eva Braun's; or Wagner's music being a touchstone for Nazi sentiments (*Annie Hall* and *Manhattan Murder Mystery* [1993]), an Allen film seemingly will not pass without a reference, no matter how fleeting, to Nazi Germany. Even the Volkswagen Beetle, introduced by Hitler as "the people's car," makes a cameo appearance in *Bananas*, *Sleeper*, and *Annie Hall*.

Pushing my point a bit too much, you may say? I, too, was a proud owner of a Bug in my younger days, but my joy was forever tarnished when a Jewish acquaintance looked askance at my car. "Just what *are* those seats made from?" she asked. It was an awful, ugly thought, but painfully on target in its goal of drawing attention to lamp shades, bars of soap, and window curtains.

When confronted with such a legacy of hate and persecution, where do you turn for comfort? Assimilation had so systematically undermined my beliefs that I could find little comfort in my own culture. Woody Allen rec-ognizes these effects of assimilation in *Annie Hall* in the unique conversa-tion he presents across time and space between the Halls of the 1970s and the Singers of the 1940s. Annie's mother asks Alvy's mother how they will be spending the holidays. Mrs. Singer answers that they will be fasting, and Alvy's father explains that this is to atone for their sins. "I don't under-stand," Mrs. Hall complains. Alvy's father sheepishly admits, "To tell you the truth, neither do we."Allen is suggesting here that through assimila-tion, many American Jews have lost touch with the real meaning behind our customs. Our rituals have become empty and our traditions hollow, thus creating room for ambivalence as depicted in such items as the Christmas tree we see in Alvy's apartment as he breaks up with Annie.

In *Sleeper*, the resistance fighters attempt to reverse Miles's brainwashing by making him relive what they call a major trauma in his life. The trauma is a seder, or the ritual meal that marks the beginning of the Jewish Passover, that took place back in the Brooklyn of Miles's youth. That Allen chose this as a traumatic point calls attention in and of itself to the dilemma of Jewish identity in modern America. However, as the gentile actors struggle comically with their Hebrew and Yiddish malapropisms, Miles regresses even further and takes on the persona of the quintessential outsider, Blanche Dubois from *A Streetcar Named Desire*, a character painfully alienated not only from the whole of modern society, but from her own people as well. Blanche is suspended, as are many assimilated people, between the old and the new, and is truly neither here nor there.

The vast majority of the Jews I knew while I was growing up seemed to have a better sense of who they were than I did. They spent more time at the synagogue, went to Jewish camps, and belonged to Jewish organizations. I was never afforded these opportunities, which probably accounts for my discomfort among them as well as among gentiles. The older I grew, the more I sensed something was missing, so I set out to discover what it was.

An obvious course was to reject religion outright and play the youthful iconoclast to the hilt. I didn't need any prescribed system of beliefs. Hadn't the great philosophers of the late nineteenth and early twentieth century declared God dead?

We can see this same response in Allen's earlier films, which befit a younger, more invulnerable person. The premise of *Sleeper* is a wonderful example. The Great Leader (God) is dead and has been dead for some time. Those in control are convinced that if word leaks out of His demise there would be chaos and, worse yet, they would lose their power. The system, then, depends not so much on the existence of The Great Leader, but rather on the illusion of His presence.

If one desires to condemn religious systems in general, one need not look any further than Catholicism, one of the most complex religious systems of all time. Allen seems to save a special barbed enmity for the Catholic church, which he construes as Big Business. The conclusion of *Bananas* is interrupted by a commercial in which a priest pitches God's choice of cigarettes. Allen perceives the act of confession as rote and mechanized, as in *Sleeper*, in which Miles, after his brainwashing, attends an automated confessional and receives a Kewpie doll for absolution. The filmmaker portrays Catholics as fairly simpleminded, because they unquestionably follow doctrine and the concept of papal infallibility; in *Manhattan* Ike reduces Catholics to the level of mindless birds when he observes that they mate for life like pigeons, and the Pope's infallibility is linked with the computer that has run amok in *2001*. The Catholic church is portrayed as corrupt and an instrument of evil, and we are reminded in *Shadows and Fog* of its complicity in the Holocaust when Kleinman (played by Woody Allen) stops in at the Catholic Church to offer a $650.00 donation. Kleinman soon becomes aware that the priest and a Nazi-regime member are drawing up a list of Jewish victims.

In *Interiors* (1978), cathedrals, the monumental symbols of Christianity, are mere edifices, architecture to be admired as pieces of art, but not as places of worship. They are cold, cavernous spaces, void of any solace or love. This idea is underscored as Eve's last hopes of reconciliation with Arthur are cruelly dashed in a vast empty cathedral.

Allen certainly does not feel that the answer lies in the faith of his parents. In the first half of this century, liberal Judaism embraced the insights of twentieth-century science and began to move away from a literal interpretation of an all-powerful God. As the horrors of the Holocaust came to light in the middle of the century, the American Jewish movement continued to move not so much away from God as towards an emphasis on the traditions of social and individual responsibility.

In both *Hannah and Her Sisters* (1986) and *Crimes and Misdemeanors* (1989) characters ask the unanswerable question of where God was during the horror of Auschwitz. Cliff in the latter movie suggests that, assuming the absence of God, the individual is forced to take on the responsibilities of his actions. But the terrible burden of this responsibility is voiced by the almost paralyzed Joey in *Interiors*, when she asks, "How do you figure out the right thing to do? How do you know?"

Finding the basis for an answer can be daunting for some, but for others it is a simple matter of rationalization. For *Crimes and Misdemeanors*'s Judah Rosenthal, whose status and security in life are preserved by the contracted murder of his mistress, God becomes a luxury he simply cannot afford. With time he awakens to birds singing once again, and his guilt-ridden conscience seems to adjust; his father had always warned him that the eyes of God see all, but if the all-seeing, all-knowing God is powerless, what then? End of story.

Contemporary Judaism asks us to consider how we will be remembered before we act. Indeed, one aspect of the Judaic concept of the afterlife is that we will live on in the good deeds we perform in life. For Ike, in *Manhattan*, who stands accused of being too self-righteous, this is a lifelong struggle. In response to Yale's argument that humans are weak and not God-like, Ike's response sounds suspiciously like this basic tenet of contemporary Judaism. Pointing to the skeleton in the classroom in which they are arguing, he asks "What will future generations . . . say about us? . . . It's very important to have . . . some kind of personal integrity. . . . Someday we're gonna be like him . . . and I wanna be sure [that] when I . . . thin out that I'm . . . well thought of."

During the past twenty-five years, many young assimilated Jewish-Americans, who, as Mickey describes it in *Hannah and Her Sisters*, "got off on the wrong foot" with their Judaism, began turning to other religions and philosophies; we had drifted so far from home that we felt we could no longer find safe harbor there. Some chose conversion. I had a cousin who became a Jew for Jesus; a friend's brother became a Southern Baptist. In *Interiors* the Christian Eve turns, as her daughter Renata calls it, to "the Jesus Christ nonsense." Late one night, as Eve watches her televangelist, we hear the televised story of Roy Schwartz, a "Hebrew" who has obviously accepted Jesus and who is there to explain how the Jews fit in to God's plan today. Mickey in *Hannah and Her Sisters*, after dodging a terminal diagnosis, begins his quest for meaning through religion. One of the religions he approaches is Catholicism. He goes out and obtains his interpretations of the external trappings of this religion (a crucifix, a picture of Jesus, a loaf of Wonder Bread), but in the end Catholicism's "die now pay later" philosophy doesn't intellectually appeal to him.

When I was in college, I flirted for a time with Eastern religions, yoga, and transcendental meditation, but Allen shows little tolerance for what he considers mere fads. "I can never subscribe to a religion that advertises in *Popular Mechanics*," Alvy explains in *Annie Hall*. But what *does* he believe in? Alvy describes life as a bleak existence separated into the horrible and the miserable, and he displays, as does Mickey in *Hannah*, an obsessive fear of death. And who fears death more than someone who doesn't have, if not the answer, then at least some faith?

Seeking religion is not so much an intellectual exercise as an emotional journey. This basic struggle between the intellect and the emotions is explored in *Manhattan*. Ike and Mary are shadowy figures wandering through the wonders of the universe re-created in a planetarium and museum. Mary becomes overwhelmed with the availability of information at the museum. She sighs over how she has a million facts at her fingertips and Ike responds by saying that "they don't mean a thing...because nothing worth knowing can be understood by the mind." Mickey echoes these sentiments in *Hannah and Her Sisters*. After reading the great philosophers, he's come to the depressing conclusion that, in the final analysis, they don't know any more than *he* does about the meaning of life. In both these instances Allen's protagonists recognize that the ultimate religious commitment requires that great leap of faith, but they can't quite make the jump themselves. In *Interiors* Allen seems to be suggesting that faith can be found more in the emotions. As the lively character Pearl puts it, if you cannot know the unknowable, than you just have to "feel it."

When I got married I could have very easily turned my back on my Jewish roots and raised my children outside of any particular faith. But I was plagued by the nagging feeling that the Jewish people had withstood more than five thousand years of persecution from without, yet here I was systematically undermining the religion from within. Who was I to say what was right or wrong? My children should have a firm sense of who they are as Jews in America, and the hope and belief that there really *is* a God. As I set out to discover what being a Jew actually entailed, I surprisingly found what was there all along: an emotional and spiritual home not only for my children, but for myself as well.

In Allen's latest films we can see that he has been struggling towards some of these same conclusions. Although we cannot find an affirmation of Judaism, we can, for example, detect at the end of *Shadows and Fog* an almost wistful desire for the ability to accept the illusion of God, an idea suggested much earlier in *Sleeper*, as Kleinman escapes death through the illusionist's magic mirror.

In the same film, Irmy, the sword-swallower (played by Mia Farrow), and the clown, Paul (played by John Malkovich), find renewal and hope, as I have, through a child. But children are not just the hope for what may come; they *are* the reaffirmation of the future itself. The narration that supports the closing images of *Crimes and Misdemeanors* perhaps best exemplifies this emerging optimism: "Most humans keep trying and find joy in simple things like family, work, and in the hope that future generations might understand more."

And perhaps in Allen's future works, he too might come to understand more and ultimately resolve his cultural and religious ambiguity, as I have in my life's journey. I cannot say that my perception of myself as the perennial outsider has vanished completely, but there is something to be said for the old adage that there is safety in numbers.

Works Cited

Allen, Woody. *Four Films of Woody Allen*. New York: Random House, 1982.

Annie Hall. Dir. Woody Allen. Rollins-Joffe/United Artists, 1977.

Bananas. Dir. Woody Allen. United Artists, 1971.

Blake, Richard. "Looking for God: Profane and Sacred in the Films of Woody Allen." *Journal of Popular Film and Television* 19 (1991): 58–66.

Crimes and Misdemeanors. Dir. Woody Allen. Orion Pictures, 1989.

Hannah and Her Sisters. Dir. Woody Allen. Orion Pictures, 1986.

Interiors. Dir. Woody Allen. United Artists, 1978.

Lax, Eric. *Woody Allen*. New York: Alfred Knopf, 1991.

Manhattan. Dir. Woody Allen. UA, 1979.

Manhattan Murder Mystery. Dir. Woody Allen. Tri-Star, 1993.

Mast, Gerald. "Woody Allen: The Neurotic Jew as American Clown." In *Jewish Wry*, edited by Sarah Cohen, 125–40. Bloomington: Indiana University Press, 1987.

Pogel, Nancy. *Woody Allen*. Boston: Twayne, 1987.

Sleeper. Dir. Woody Allen. United Artists, 1973.

Shadows and Fog. Dir. Woody Allen. Orion Pictures, 1992.

Stam, Robert. "A Tale of Two Cities: Cultural Polyphony and Ethnic Transformation." *East West Film Journal* 3 (1988): 105–116.

Yacowar, Maurice. "Woody Allen in the 80's." *Post-Script* 6 (1987): 29–42.

Zelig. Dir. Woody Allen. Orion Pictures, 1983.

Woody Allen and the Jews

SAMUEL H. DRESNER

I N 1985 I published in *Midstream* one of the few critical articles on Woody Allen (born Allen Konigsberg in the Bronx), touching on some of the very same issues that have exploded today. It was met with scorn. How could one cast stones at the icon of the jet set? He was so clever, so funny, so intellectual. Allen has long been among the most glamorous members of the cultural elite that promotes the prevailing paganism.

My concern then and now, however, is not so much with Allen himself. He is a talented, ambitious, Jewishly deprived artist, who does, alas, what so many artists do to gain fame and fortune, irrespective of whom or what he hurts. In addition he uses his work as a kind of free self-analysis (though Allen told *Time* magazine, "The plots of my movies don't have any relationship to my life!"). My concern is rather with his adoring audience, especially his Jewish audience. For that audience, by its adoration, and even by its neutrality, has ipso facto betrayed its faith and its people.

After taking up with Woody (but not marrying him) Mia Farrow appeared in 13 Allen films, and had a child with him in addition to the seven or eight she had already adopted or borne in former marriages. Now, aged 56, Allen has fallen in love, he says, with Soon Yi, Mia's 19–year-old Korean adopted daughter whom she had rescued from the streets of Seoul as an abandoned, emaciated, lice-ridden child, and whom Allen helped to raise.

The affair with Soon Yi seems to have gone on for some time. Mia learned of it when she found a number of spread-leg, nude photos of her daughter in Woody's apartment. They were taken by Woody. Outraged at the photos, Mia accused Allen of violating the deepest family taboos, refused to let Allen see the other children, and permitted evidence to be produced of Allen's alleged sexual abuse of their seven-year-old adopted daughter, Dylan.

"Soon Yi never even dated," says John Farrow, Mia's brother. "Woody got a child. She's not her own woman. It's sad. It's disgusting. How would you like Woody drooling over your eldest daughter?" (Phoebe Hoban, "Woody and Mia," *New York Magazine*, 21 September, p. 35) Child therapist Carole West seems to agree, inquiring, "Does anyone really see Soon Yi as a consenting equal? Would she feel free to say no to the great Woody Allen? Is she intellectually mature enough?"

Reprinted by permission from *Midstream Magazine* (December 1992): 19–23, published by The Theodore Herzl Foundation.

Asked, "Do you consider it a healthy, equal relationship?" Allen replied with the typical cry of the "me" generation, "The heart wants what it wants!"

The affair with Soon Yi, said Allen, posed no "great moral dilemma . . . She's over 18." Mia's friend, Leonard Gershe, commented, "Nobody ever questioned that he did anything illegal. He did something immoral, and that's what he can't understand." (Maureen Orth, "Mia's Story," *Vanity Fair*, November, 1992.)

But if the matter of Soon Yi was immoral but not illegal, Woody's alleged abuse of seven-year-old Dylan, the details of which came to the surface later, may well involve violation of the law. *Vanity Fair* (November 1992) published a shocking article based on numerous interviews of friends and employees describing his intimacies with the child. Allen said he will sue for libel and that the accusation is a conspiracy of Mia's, whom he claimed on "60 Minutes" told him, "You took my child [Soon Yi]. Now I will take yours [Dylan]." The matter is headed for the courts.

In one of Allen's stories in his book *Side Effects*, smartly named "Retribution," he startles us with the remark that the hero hesitates before making a pass at his girlfriends's mother: "Banner headlines in the yellow press formed in my mind. . . . I am in love with two women. Not a terribly uncommon problem. That they happen to be mother and child? All the more challenging!"

The following is a scene from the piece (which I cited in my 1985 article).

The wedding [between Harold Cohen, and Emily, the mother of Connie, with whom Harold had an unsuccessful affair] was held in Connie's apartment and champagne flowed. My folks could not make it, a previous commitment to sacrifice a lamb taking precedence. We all danced and joked and the evening went well. At one point, I found myself in the bedroom with Connie alone. We kidded and reminisced about our relationship, its ups and downs, and how sexually attracted I had been to her.

"It was flattering," she said warmly.

"Well, I couldn't swing with the daughter, so I carried off the mother." The next thing I knew Connie's tongue was in my mouth.

"What the hell are you doing?" I said, pulling back.

"Are you drunk?"

"I have to sleep with you. If not now, then soon," she said.

"Me? Harold Cohen? The guy who lived with you? And loved you? Who couldn't get near you with a 10 foot pole because I became a version of Danny? Me you're hot for? Your brother symbol?"

"It's a whole new ball game," she said, pressing closer to me. "Marrying Mom has made you my father." She kissed me again and just before returning to the festivities said, "Don't worry, Dad, there'll be plenty of opportunities."

I sat on the bed and stared out the window into infinite space. I thought of

my parents and wondered if I should abandon the theater and return to rabbinical school . . . all I could mutter to myself as I remained a limp, hunched
figure was an age-old line of my grandfather's which goes, "Oy vey."

The episode reeks with incestuous overtones, a persistent fascination of
Allen's. There is Cohen's desire for Connie (and her sister) as well as the
mother. Then there is Connie's infatuation with Cohen, at first dampened
by his resemblance to her brother, and later rekindled in anticipation of
his becoming her "father." Connie's desire for Cohen waxes and wanes in
accordance with the two images he projects, each having the opposite
incestuous effect: the brother image repelling her, the father image enticing her. Here we have a snakepit full of incestuous insinuations—much as
in the convoluted real life story of Woody, Soon Yi and Dylan. The concluding words of the story, "oy vey," are, of course, not meant to repudiate
the perversion—again much as the real life Allen does not admit any guilt
for his perverse behavior—but rather to elicit the reader's sympathy for his
nebbish hero, the suffering, almost noble, father/husband who anticipates
the painful sexual demands which both women will thereafter make upon
him (in the same house?).

In *Hannah and Her Sisters* Hannah's husband has an affair with her sister. "She came into my empty life and changed it, and I've paid her back by
banging her sister in a hotel room." In *Manhattan* a Hollywood writer has
his script curtailed because "child molestation is a touchy subject with the
affiliates." He responds, "Read the papers; half the country's doing it."
Allen often plays an older man enthralled with young girls. In *Love and
Death* he is advised by a "sage" that the secret of life can be found in a
steady diet of "two blond 12–year-old girls whenever possible." In
Manhattan he jests about his young conquest, "I'm dating a girl who does
her homework."

In *Annie Hall* his friend considers the mathematical possibilities of having an affair with 16–year-old twins. And in the film that opened the week
after the scandal broke, *Husbands and Wives*, he assumes the role of a
college professor who has an affair with a student one-third his age (her
term paper is "Oral Sex in an Age of Deconstruction"), almost presaging
Soon Yi. "Do you seduce all your students?" Professor Allen is asked.

In these scenes Woody does not use heavy, bold strokes that might
drive the audience off. He prefers the gentle, bantering approach, which
innocently evolves into compromising situations, as if nothing is anyone's
fault. It just happened! One can hardly help sympathizing with the
Chaplinesque nebbish, hero/villain type, usually played by Allen himself.
By portraying middleclass morality—family, faith, patriotism—as consistently hypocritical, he paves the way for his portrayal of the wretched back-
alleys of life. "The heart wants what it wants."

Woody's adoring audience, stunned by the perverse behavior of the real life writer/actor, has not flocked to this last film as to past ones, and has seemed uneasy with the muted enthusiasm which reviewers were offering. Most upsetting was Allen's denial that his actions created any moral dilemma at all—this from one whose purpose was never just to entertain but to pass judgment, to moralize, to instruct the present angst-ridden generation that has revered him as its guru.

This time Allen had crossed the boundary. Many did what they should have done before, considered the moral consequences played out in real life in view of what was portrayed on the screen. In the throes of momentary Allen-stupor, the media have even resorted to a reconsideration of traditional family values, which they found, despite its many failures, to have served as the most effective way to keep the sexual impulse within bounds, even ennobling it.

The accepting Jewish audience of Allen's writings and films has not only contributed to a betrayal of Jewish values, but to a betrayal of the Jewish people. For no one more than Allen has enabled so many to view the Jew, especially the religious Jew, in so corrupt a manner.

A characteristic of Allen is his obsession with Jews. In this he seems a disciple of Isaac Bashevis Singer, depicting snippets of the Orthodox dimension of Jewish life—difficult to locate in America since their numbers are not large—as, almost exclusively, ugly, foolish, and false.

In the story of Harold Cohen mentioned above, notice that his name is not Smith or Jones or even Goldberg, but Cohen, the Hebrew word for "priest," which, apart from being distinguishably Jewish, is religiously so. Cohen, ostensibly a descendant of the biblical priests and a past rabbinical student to boot, marries the mother of his former bedmate on the evening of the Passover Seder, which his parents, along with virtually every other Jew, were attending. ("My folks could not make it, a previous commitment to sacrifice a lamb taking precedence.") It is difficult to imagine any more radical or vulgar denial of one's identity.

Another example from the same collection:

> Brooklyn: tree-lined streets . . . A small boy helps a bearded old man across the street and says, "Good Sabbath." The old man smiles and empties his pipe on the boy's head. The child runs crying into his house.

Here again is a juxtaposition of opposites: piety and perversion. The first contrasts the proper and expected—an old, bearded man greeted by a child's "Good Sabbath"—with the improper and unexpected "emptying a pipe" (on the Sabbath?) on the child's head, reducing him to tears. Religious images—Sabbath, bearded, elderly Jew, as with Cohen, rabbinical student, Passover Seder—are all served up to us, not as a single dish of Jewish piety but tossed by Allen with sadism and incest into one repellent goulash. The concoction is meant to evoke laughter. Tears and rage would be better, for the corruption of the author, and for the obtuseness, and worse, of fawning Jewish critics and patient Jewish admirers who have waited in long lines outside box-offices to be entertained at the expense of their souls.

Finally, two items from Allen's piece, "Hassidic Tales, With a Guide to Their Interpretation by the Noted Scholar":

1. A man journeyed to Chelm in order to seek the advice of Rabbi Ben Kaddish, the holiest of all ninth-century rabbis and perhaps the greatest noodge of the medieval era. "Rabbi," the man asked, "where can I find peace?" The Hassid surveyed him and said, "Quick, look behind you!" The man turned around, and Rabbi Ben Kaddish smashed him in the back of the head with a candlestick. "Is that peaceful enough for you?" he chuckled, adjusting his yarmulke. In this tale [the "noted scholar" explains] a meaning-less question is asked. Not only is the question meaningless but so is the man who journeys to Chelm to ask it. Not that he was so far away from Chelm to begin with, but why shouldn't he stay where he is? Why is he both-ering Rabbi Ben Kaddish—the Rabbi doesn't have enough trouble? The truth is, the Rabbi's in over his head with gamblers, and he has also been named in a paternity case by a Mrs. Hecht. No, the point of this tale is that this man has nothing better to do with his time than journey around and get on peo-ple's nerves. For this, the Rabbi bashes his head in, which according to the Torah, is one of the most subtle methods of showing concern. In a similar version of this tale, the Rabbi leaps on top of the man in a frenzy and carves the story of Ruth on his nose with a stylus.

2. Rabbi Zwi Chaim Yisroel, an Orthodox scholar of the old school and a man who developed whining to an art unheard of in the West, was unani-mously hailed as the wisest man of the Renaissance by his fellow Hebrews, who totalled a 16th of one per cent of the population. Once, while he was on his way to synagogue to celebrate the sacred Jewish holiday commemo-rating God's reneging on every promise, a woman stopped him and asked the following question:"Rabbi, why are we not allowed to eat pork?" "We're not?" the Rev said incredulously. "Uh-oh."

This is one of the few stories in all Hassidic literature that deals with Hebrew law. The Rabbi knows he shouldn't eat pork; he doesn't care, though, because he likes pork. Not only does he like pork; he gets a kick out of rolling Easter eggs. In short, he cares very little about traditional Orthodoxy and regards God's covenant with Abraham as "just so much chin music." Why pork was proscribed by Hebraic law is still unclear, and some scholars believe that the Torah merely suggested not eating pork in certain restaurants.

Consider the image Allen projects of his so-called hassidic rabbi: igno-rance, fraud, adultery, hypocrisy, and violence. What is he getting at by all this? Imagine a rabbi, a hassidic rabbi, no less, with all the visible para-phernalia of intense Orthodoxy, who "likes pork," like a Gentile; strikes people, like a savage; gambles, like a desperado; fornicates, like a libertine; mocks God, like a skeptic; and knows nothing, like an ignoramus. Should we snicker with Allen, or cry? His method is to conjure up the image of piety and then portray the perverse.

In Allen's depiction of religious Jews as adulterers, lechers, and hypocrites, the point separating humor from what is less than humor, and more, is long passed. Why does he do it? Out of concern for them? Sholem Aleichem's stories are satires of the simple Jews of the East European shtetls. Indeed, Jewish humor is typically self-critical. The Jew has historically had the healthy ability to step back and joke about himself. But he has done so out of love. Does one detect a scintilla of love for the Jewish people in Allen?

It should be noted that Allen's one public foray into contemporary Jewish affairs was his infamous op-ed piece in the *New York Times* in which he castigated the anti-intifada tactics of the Jewish State, claiming that "Israel's policies defy belief." Shortly afterwards (23 June 1988), Eli Wiesel responded with a moving review of the tragic situation in which, he said, public opinion has rushed to condemn the Jewish State unfairly, putting Israel in the "place of America during Vietnam, France during Algeria and the Soviet Union during Gulag."

"Many critics," Wiesel continued, now training his sights upon Allen and his crowd, "were outdone by some Jewish intellectuals who had never done anything for Israel but now shamelessly used their Jewishness to justify their attacks against Israel."

Allen projects an ugly picture of the Jew not in some offbeat journal or remote radio program but fleshed out in color and drama on the giant screen for the general public to view. To take but one example, the lusting of the Jew for the Gentile woman. This standard antisemitic canard was part of the devil mythology of the Jew from the Middle Ages to Hitler's Third Reich, incorporated into centuries of anti-Jewish law. Allen's works are replete with such episodes, yet Jewish critics are silent at Allen's defamations. Of course, it will be countered, why the fuss? Allen is merely poking fun. But the average Gentile reader or viewer may be drawing a more serious lesson. And now Allen apparently confirms all that in real life, as the Mia Farrow, Soon Yi and Dylan incidents may be interpreted.

"The heart wants what it wants!" Allen's defense of his personal life is a recurrent message in his dramas. Cleverly packaged, Allen appeals to our savage nature. Once the corrupted heart is the sole arbiter, what objection can be raised to adultery or, more to the point, pedophilia or incest? How, in fact, deny any perverse sexual behavior? The next step would be for Woody to argue, supported by the usual vocal clutch of crazies, that incest, whether by nature or nurture, can be a necessity for which no one is responsible. Woody has summed it up: "The heart wants what it wants."

How, then, shall we deal with the oft-quoted talmudic dictum,"*God wants the heart*"?

Judaism sees the heart as the seat of desire, of both love and lust. (*You shall love the Lord your God with "both your hearts,"* is the reading the rabbis give the commandment based upon an unusual vocalization of the Hebrew). In other words one must conquer the evil by sublimating and ennobling it so that God can be served with "all" our heart. Judaism does not stifle the heart's desire, but trains the spirit through the will to guide it. Allen's acquiescence reminds one of Paul's acceptance of man's helplessness before temptation and his inability to do God's bidding. The difference is that what Paul repents over, requiring "Christ to die for our sins," Woody accepts and in the end delights in.

Judaism offers a third option: man is neither deaf nor impotent; he can hear the Voice and do the deed. But his power to act is not self-generated. Alone, the mind is no match for passion. A central theme of Allen's films is "the titanic, tragicomic struggle between intellect and lust" (*Time*, 31 August 1992). What if the intellect is right? Can it alone control lust? A moment of self-scrutiny is sufficient to tell us. Not often. The fire of passion can only be controlled by another fire, a greater fire: "Thou shalt not!" And, later, "Thou shalt!" To civilize means to moderate desire into acceptable social patterns; it is the internalization of virtue.

Three existential options are always present: exploitation, escape and sanctification. The way of exploitation says nature is holy and thereby unleashes the beast within man: the pagan glorification of our basic drives. The way of escape says nature is unholy and thereby frustrates the natural desires of man; the classical Christian frustration of basic drives. Judaism says nature is neither holy nor unholy but is waiting to be made holy, and thereby the natural desires of man are sublimated through a system of mitzvot in the service of God.

Judaism has achieved the sublimation of impulse through continual nourishment of the spirit and the pattern of the law. Training in the demanding regimen of commandments, regular worship, and the lifelong study of Torah is the Jewish manner of turning "human beings" into "being human" (Heschel). It requires diligence, sacrifice and constancy, but the result is the rarest of beings, moral man. Uncivilized humans were—and are—wont to act like beasts or amoeba, blindly following their impulses. According to Judaism, however, our sexual nature can be hallowed by means of marriage, the home and the family.

For some, it took the tragedy of Mia and Woody to demonstrate the value of marriage. True, the marriage relationship is filled with pitfalls, but it beats the alternatives. Many moderns balk at the marital contract. They yearn to be free of entanglements, to roam, finding momentary pleasure where they chance, to walk in and out of the mysterious process of conception as they wish. There is a male proclivity to behave like insects who deposit their seed and disappear. Over the millennia, one of the elements in educating man meant compelling, persuading, and enticing him, through law, reason and feminine charm, until he acknowledged the value of remaining loyal to a single woman, the mother of his children, and a commitment to do so—marriage. So the notion of the human couple emerged.

Consider the incest taboo, which serves to prevent the power relations and emotional ties of the family from being abused. Proper human growth involves gradually separating emotionally from your family so that you can go off and start one of your own. Incest may permanently disrupt that process. In this age of mass abandonment of marriage, the clear lines of familial relations, however, have been blurred with disastrous consequences. Young girls, for example, are most often sexually abused by their stepfathers. But if it is true that taboos against incest inhibit exploitation of power relations and emotional ties within the family, then those emotional connections which bind the new family may be almost as significant as the "bloodline." Only the future can tell just how deeply Mia and the children, who must deal with a confusion of bondings, have been scarred psychologically and spiritually. Mia's mother, Maureen O'Sullivan, protested that Woody had violated her daughter's soul and her God.

He had violated his own God, too. Judaism stands against the idolatry of the new paganism, and so should the Jew. Allen is guilty of "emotional incest and grotesque disregard for the impact of his behavior on others," writes syndicated columnist Mona Charen in regard to Soon Yi. How, she asks, could a man of Woody Allen's obvious intelligence have the "moral obtuseness" to claim, in an interview, that the fact that his 19–year-old girlfriend was the daughter of Mia Farrow had "no bearing on the relationship"? The answer, she suggests, is found in our morally polluted environment, on the one hand, and, on the other, in the public acclaim with which Woody's every step has been greeted. Charen suggests that had Mia and Woody met before the sexual revolution, in the '40s instead of the '80s, the more traditional mores of the time would have encouraged him to marry Mia, especially if they intended to raise a family. And if the had married, it would have been far more difficult for Woody to justify to others and to himself his sexual entanglement with Mia's daughter whom he had known and helped raise since the age of 10. If the virtues of marital bonds need validation, the sad ending of Woody and Mia has proved it for us.

Marriage and family, which Scripture understands as part of the divine plan, might have prevented the Mia/Woody affair by setting boundaries and establishing responsibilities while providing the threshold for love and companionship. Mia's children require a father and a mother who are married and live together in a home. They need one set of rules, not two. They require the security of permanence as they grow to adulthood and are confronted with ever new problems. They need relationships that are clear and easily comprehended. Fragility, uncertainty, confusion and separation foster instability, inadequacy and sometimes abuse. Marriage, though by no means foolproof, is more likely to produce well-adjusted children.

Because Allen's work has been couched in clever dialogue, sly humor, appealing artistry, and in perverse fantasy, the Jewish public has expressed little dissatisfaction. But since when did art or wit transcend morality for the Jew? If *Mein Kampf* had been written in the style of Henry James, would it be a superior book? The people Israel have been taught to beware of using the measuring rods of art or science to judge a nation. Amos cursed the ivory palaces in Samaria because they represented an immoral society. Matthew Arnold juxtaposed the Greeks' holiness of beauty to the Jews' beauty of holiness. Heine, who abandoned the faith of Israel and worshipped at the altar of Hellenism all his life, recanted on his syphilitic deathbed. "Now I understand that the Greeks were only beautiful youths, while the Jews have always been men, powerful, inflexible men."

Another question is why Woody's lifestyle offended the same audience that extolled his art style. For artist Mapplethorpe to insert a whip into his anus or urinate into another's mouth on TV would repulse the viewer. Why then accept his photos of such acts? It is the action itself, whether performed or described, which should be judged. Outrage was expressed for Woody's behavior. Why not for his films and writings over the years?

Let me suggest some answers. First, there is the tendency to distinguish between the aesthetic and the moral dimensions, modern art's "liberation" from ethics. Then there is the distinction between fantasy and reality: the audience can get its "kicks" by imagining behavior it would not engage in. Further, there is the argument, usually made by producers or writers, that such art does not affect behavior, and, in fact, mitigates the viewer's potentially outrageous impulses by harmlessly draining his desire in the process of watching the film. But if what we see and read does not affect behavior, why are millions of dollars regularly spent advertising on TV in the expectation that a mere 30 seconds will send the viewer off to purchase this or that particular item!

Let us remember that in the American South it was propaganda that defined the Black man as subhuman that made it acceptable to treat him as such, just as in Nazi Germany a step by step process of indoctrination desensitized the German people into accepting the propaganda that Jews were vermin—thus significant elements of America's cultural elite by its example desensitizes this nation about its morality. At first the public was encouraged to fantasize about premarital sex, until it became so accepted that today talk show interviewers commonly ask, "When did you first have sex?"; then about adultery, until many have come to believe everybody is doing it (a Hollywood poll gives 55 percent approval). Allen is now inviting us to fantasize about the next stages, incest and pedophilia, though he denies having committed both. Why not? The heart wants what it wants. Once we abandon the strictures of marriage, family, the home, the bulwarks of Jewish and Christian morality, why not approve pedophilia and incest? Meanwhile, around the corner lurks acceptance of the dark shadow of bestiality, the coupling of animal and human, which we may be told is just another "sexual orientation."

> [Gene] Wilder and the sheep became a torrid item during the filming and had a highly publicized affair, which culminated in his being caught in a Butte, [Montana] hotel room with the sheep, her mother and a teenager who told the judge she was Little Bopeep. (Allen says in *Everything You Always Wanted to Know About Sex*, released in 1972)

Allen has contributed mightily to the whole perverse pursuit to the depths of human infamy. To civilize, as we have noted, has meant first to curb unacceptable behavior, such as robbery, rape or murder; then to so encourage virtue through cultural affirmation, spiritual education and the example of the family, so that even the temptation to perform such acts is muted. To the extent that moral teachings are internalized, so will moral behavior and character change. Further, the process of moral education is never-ending, coming from everything we see, read and hear, on film, in magazines, in the classroom, and at the dinner table. What the heart wants is in large measure what it is *taught* to want.

The Woody Allen craze was, in part, understandable. Gifted, clever, an actor, writer, and director, Allen has a fine eye for the human comedy and the talent to translate it into the contemporary idiom. But Allen's humor is cause for concern. Never before have so many Americans seen so ugly a portrayal of religious Jews as in his oeuvre. For the Gentile, Allen's depiction of religious Jews as pious frauds, and worse, can only confirm the vicious stereotype of the Jew as hypocrite, devil, despoiler of morality, and corrupter of culture. For Jews, the matter is more complicated: Allen has always been a favorite among them, and to many a model of Jewish talent, but almost never a subject of alarm for the Jewish critic or even the Jewish establishment.

The silence of Jews to Allen's attack on their most prized possession, family morality, his celebration of their death through intermarriage, and his demeaning of those with religious commitment is a betrayal both of the Jewish faith and of the Jewish people. In failing to repudiate the perverse behavior advocated by Allen in his writings and his films, his Jewish audience has forsaken elemental Jewish values: the sanctity of marriage and the significance of family. Anchored at the very core of Judaism, these teachings have become the bedrock of Western civilization through the book from which the daughter religions draw nourishment, teachings upon which Judaism itself has built a healthy and joyous community strong enough to endure the maelstroms of history without the benefit of land or army, an achievement unique in human annals.

We stand tremulously near the edge of the precipice, in an age not of some grand successor faith but of a throwback to a more primitive one, Baghdad's totalitarian beast and New York's trousered ape. Talent such as Allen's is too rare to be squandered. Therefore the lament—not only for what Allen has done, but for where his people stand, and for what he could have done.

Self-Deprecation and the Jewish Humor of Woody Allen

MARK E. BLEIWEISS

J UST WHEN The evidence of his public life seemed to imply that Woody Allen is a self-hating Jew, his new film *Crimes and Misdemeanors* opens to shed a fresh light on the comedian's enigmatic spiritual identity. Not only are all of the central characters Jewish—unheard of in Allen's other major works—but the Rabbi, Ben, represents the major ethical figure. With Judaism portrayed positively, Allen appears to have matured significantly from the days when he would only introduce Jewish themes to deride them. Yet *Crimes* still leaves us with many questions about the role of Judaism in Allen's life. To gain a cogent understanding of these questions, we need to survey the history of Allen's career and of Jewish humor.

Sigmund Freud set the precedent for studies of Jewish humor when he suggested that Jewish humorists are the butt of their own jokes. In *Jokes and Their Relation to the Unconscious*, Freud said that Jewish jokes "are stories created by Jews and directed against Jewish characteristics . . . I do not know whether there are many other instances of a people making fun to such a degree of its own character."

Freud observed that the Jews denigrate their own character flaws and not Judaism itself, and that they direct their criticism against the stereotype of the Jew rather than against the actual Judaic system of life. This self-deprecation, while existent in the humor of other ethnic groups, represents the most prevalent feature in Jewish humor.

Many scholars question whether or not humor was a widely accepted characteristic of the Jews before Freud published *Jokes* in 1905. Since Freud's analysis, not only do scholars recognize Jewish humor as an integral part of modern Western culture, but most endorse the basic distinction of Jewish humor as self-deprecatory. Freud defines humor in general as a socially accepted outlet for repressed ideas and that "by the help of a joke, internal resistance is overcome . . . and the inhibition lifted." By studying humor, we find truths about people's identity that their inhibitions otherwise might conceal. If humor can be used to analyze cultural or ethnic identity, what does the self-deprecatory nature of Jewish humor reveal about the Jews? By denigrating their characters, do Jewish humorists, like Allen, actually disclose feelings of self-hatred? We first will explore various interpretations of how Jewish humor reflects Jewish iden-

Reprinted by permission from the *Jewish Spectator* (Winter 1989): 25–34.

tity, and then focus on Allen himself to determine what his humor reveals about his identity as a Jew.

In his book *Jewish Humor*, Avner Ziv distinguishes the main perspectives from which scholars approach Jewish humor as emotional, sociological, and intellectual. While all three approaches overlap—intellectual and social factors directly influence emotions, for instance—Ziv outlines their basic differences. He explains that, in reaction to their tragic history, Jews use humor as an emotional defense mechanism. Rather than cry at the abuse others inflict on them, Jews laugh to ease their pain. Their own foibles provide the best target for their laughter, not only because they are most familiar with the subject, but because by laughing at themselves first, they may prevent others from following suit. Unlike the individual experience of crying, the Jews share their laughter with one another and, through common emotional release, they can look to one another for comfort.

Martin Grotjahn, another early student of Jewish humor, focuses on this emotional component. He develops the idea that Jews indicate their own flaws first in order to prevent others from using these shortcomings as justification for anti-Semitic persecution.

Maurice Samuel has a more sympathetic approach in his focus on the emotional aspect of humor. He sees Jewish self-deprecation as an escape from the tragic realities of Jewish life rather than as a justification for retaining flaws.

Freud's disciple, Theodor Reik, also describes self-deprecation in Jewish humor as an emotional defense mechanism, yet he differs from Grotjahn and Samuel in his analysis. Whereas Grotjahn attributes the pleasure Jews derive from their humor to their natural ability to belittle themselves, Reik affirms Samuel's thesis that self-deprecating humor enables Jews to rise above their tragic history. Yet Reik takes the argument one step further than Samuel by suggesting that this self-deprecation is actually masochistic in its severity. He concludes that masochism, even outside of a humorous context, has been essential to Jewish survival in the diaspora over the last two millennia.

Yet all of the emotionalists remain conspicuously silent about whether or not self-deprecation implies self-hatred. Perhaps this silence itself indicates that Jewish humorists actually reveal their openness toward their Jewish identity. Given the difficulty of identifying as a Jew in a largely anti-Semitic world, the fact that these humorists even discuss Judaism, albeit negatively, shows that they are to some degree self-affirming Jews.

While both the emotional and the sociological approaches to Jewish humor draw from Jewish history, scholars who take the latter approach are more concerned with how Jews express frustration with their precarious social status through humor than with how they use humor as a defense mechanism. Because the majority of Western Jewish humorists trace their roots back to Eastern Europe, scholars focus on the ghetto as the origin of Jewish social identification. The ghetto was traditionally a small, crowded section in the poor part of town in which, because of its claustrophobic nature, conflicts between Jews abounded. When, in their humor, Jews criticize the secluded Jewish life that ghettos represent, they perhaps unwittingly give voice to their disdain for this part of their cultural and ethnic heritage.

In his own study of the social component of Jewish humor, Ziv focuses on the folk characters of the *luftgescheften*, the *schadchen*, and the *schnorrer*, all of whom played a dispensable, yet integral role in the every-day life of the traditional ghetto. Because they were inclined to complain, gossip, beg, and commit other *chutzpadik* acts, they became prime targets for humor. Each character represented a negative Jewish stereotype per-petuated inside as well as outside of the ghetto walls and the rest of the Jews were quick to distance themselves from such objects of abuse. Ziv observes that the Jews from the ghetto did not mean to offend any specific person through their ridicule of these characters—which would have been difficult anyway since few, if any, Jews openly identified as luftgescheftens, schadchens, or schnorrers—but that all Jews shared at least some of their faults. The humor which appeared to be directed outwardly was, in fact, a subtle form of self-criticism. Yet because Jews laughed at their own per-sonal flaws without being abusive, they revealed an admirable form of humility rather than any deep-seated self-hatred.

Although Dan Ben-Amos also denies that Jewish humor reveals self-hatred, he is one of the few students of Jewish humor to reject Freud's thesis on self-deprecation. He agrees with Ziv that many Jews mock nega-tive Jewish stereotypes, but claims that they laugh exclusively at other Jews who embody these stereotypes rather than at themselves. To substantiate his argument, he draws from a study of Jewish dialect jokes by Richard Dorson in which the majority of the American Jewish comedians use a Yiddish accent in relaying their jokes. By using a foreign accent and thus establishing a fictional persona, the comedian distances himself from the subject of his joke. The issue of self-hatred in humor thus becomes irrele-vant to Ben-Amos because the jokes are not ultimately about the narrator himself, but about his invented persona. That the comedian does not iden-tify with his persona is neither a positive nor a negative indication of his own Jewish identity.

While Ben-Amos bases his criticism of Freud on more contemporary data, most modern scholars do not support his conclusions. Stanley Brandes argues that no comedian could distance himself so thoroughly that his persona's beliefs and prejudices do not in any way reflect his own. To be able to mimic the Yiddish accent accurately, as the comedians do in Dorson's study, requires a thorough understanding of Jewish cul-ture, irrefutably linking the supposedly objective comedian with his creat-ed persona.

Even if the narrator could somehow distinguish himself from his persona, the jokes the persona tells must reveal something about the narrator's own identity. After all, by Freud's definition, humor reveals truths that its creators might otherwise conceal. Kurt Schlesinger elaborates Freud's thesis by suggesting that despite the seemingly ambivalent attitude of comedians towards their humor, "hostility is not absent from such wit, but it is . . . expressed . . . with the invocation of indirection, nuance, and intellectuality."

In short, the comedian must express true thoughts with subtlety, allowing the listener to figure out the meaning of the humor. If narrators blatantly mock themselves rather than subtly deprecating a fictional persona, they probably lose their sense of humor in the process. Schlesinger argues that the comedians who mock groups with which they deny cultural affiliation more often than not actually identify as members of such groups.

When Jews indulge in self-deprecation, they attempt to quell their anxiety by keeping their values in perspective. Humor provided the Jew from the ghetto with an opportunity to rise above everyday struggles and realize the absurdity of problems from an objective viewpoint. Even the liberated Jew who is self-mocking, according to Schlesinger, reveals more the desire to retain sanity than any self-hatred through humor.

Though similar to Schlesinger in her analysis, Heda Jason argues that Jews did not mock themselves until after they left the sheltered ghetto community. In the ghetto, the Jew mainly interacted with other Jews, so he had "no need to 'self-efface,' or as we would rather say, to 'justify' [him]self before anyone." He certainly knew of anti-Semitism but, because non-Jews were not a part of his everyday life, he did not feel any awkwardness with his Jewish identity. Once he became a distinct minority outside of the ghetto, prominent cultural traits like his observance of kosher dietary laws made him an unpopular, and even threatening novelty in Central Europe, Western Europe, and America. With external pressure to forget customs and assimilate into Western society, the Jew began renouncing the values of religious tradition. Though embarrassed by misunderstood customs, the Jew does not necessarily hate the Jewish heritage. Instead, Jews remain confused by incompatible cultural ties with both Western society, in which there is at least a legal status of equality, and Jewish background and traditions.

Although most of the sociological scholars of Jewish humor address the subject of self-hatred, none attribute the Jews' self-deprecation to hatred for their Jewish culture. Schlesinger sees the Jew's self-mockery as an attempt to retain sanity, Jason observes that self-mockery reveals the Jew's feeling of cultural ambiguity, and Ziv actually suggests that Jewish self-mockery is a healthy form of humility. Even Ben-Amos, in his rejection of Freud's basic definition of Jewish humor, does not link self-deprecation with self-hatred. Yet none of the scholars go into enough depth to disprove the possibility that Jewish humorists are self-hating. Like the scholars of the emotional aspect of Jewish humor, the sociologists leave the problem essentially unresolved, perhaps relying on the scholars of the intellectual component of Jewish humor to form decisive conclusions on whether the Jews' self-deprecation reveals their self-hatred.

The intellectual approach to Jewish humor, as to other areas of Jewish folklore, is rooted in the Torah—the core of Jewish life—which contains the Jews' monotheistic moral code and principles of justice. While the Torah does not assume that the Jews will live up to all of its rigorous ethical requirements, it does maintain that each Jew must struggle to do the best of his or her ability. Like Christian theologian Paul of Tarsus, many Jews who lived in European ghettos before the enlightenment did not understand that the Torah allowed for the occasional moral blunder, and they criticized the Jewish way of life as untenable with its impossibly high moral demands. When, with increasing tolerance sparked by the Enlightenment, European authorities liberated Jews from the ghettos, many Jews were faced with the seductive opportunity to completely reject the Torah by assimilating into non-Jewish society. These Jews developed humor in order to rationalize their assimilation and to condemn the supposed zealots who maintained tradition. In a sense, humor was a natural outgrowth of the guilt that assimilated Jews felt by accepting the easier route of secularism. At the same time, having rejected Judaism without yet being absorbed into the non-Jewish society left many of these Jews alienated from both cultures. Because their Jewish background was responsible for their feelings of alienation, many assimilated Jews inevitably began to resent their Jewish identity. The intellectual outlet of self-deprecating humor therefore both reconciled their guilt feelings and revealed their "need to search for self-identity," yet most scholars question whether it actually vocalized feelings of self-hatred.

In discussing modern Jewish identity, Sander Gilman defines self-hatred as the outsider's inability to gain acceptance from the majority group. Usually incapable of concealing his distinctive Jewish characteristics and convinced at the supremacy of secular Western culture, the assimilated Jew often concludes that the "contradiction must be within [himself], since that which [he wishes] to become cannot be flawed . . . The fragmentation of identity that results is the articulation of self-hatred."

Professor Alan Dundes of the University of California at Berkeley further points out that the individual, no matter how distinct he may want to appear from his ethnic group, ultimately must define his identity in relation with that group. Yet in identifying as a member of his ethnic group, the self-hating Jew begins to believe that stereotypes attributed to traditional Jewish characters, like those Ziv describes, actually bear resemblance to his idiosyncrasies.

Psychoanalyst Edmund Bergler draws from the sociologists' study of humor when he attributes the Jews' self-deprecatory humor to the sheltered intellectual life of the traditional ghetto. The ghetto's oppressiveness and provincialism so distorted the modern Jew's understanding of Judaism that it was no wonder so many Jews were quick to assimilate after the enlightenment.

The intellectual potential of the Jew was limited to the parameters of his ghetto's physical and psychological walls. Even the sacred Torah, Bergler continues, was of little comfort to the oppressed and impoverished Jew when it relentlessly demanded that he strive harder to improve himself and his community. Jewish humor reveals the Jew's dissatisfaction with life in general, but it does not reveal self-hatred simply because anti-semites, the ghetto, and the Torah—and not the Jew—ultimately cause his misery.

Naomi and Eli Katz concede that the Jew's self-deprecating humor reflects the struggle with cultural identity, yet they differ with Bergler's reasoning that blames the Torah's high moral demands as much as provincialism and anti-semitism for Jewish self-deprecation. For the Katzes, Jewish humor does not mock Judaic values as much as Jewish-American stereotypes. "Rather than being anti-Semitic," the Katzes explain that Jewish humor "is anti-greenhorn, anti-immigrant, and possibly anti-poor." The Jewish American humorist mocks those negative qualities usually attributed to first-generation immigrants who, fresh from the Eastern European ghetto, were less successful in assimilating into American culture. Such self-deprecation does not imply hatred of Jewish ethnicity or of Judaism as much as hatred of the first-generation Jew himself, since the stereotypes being criticized refer to a specific folk caricature rather than to the Jewish system of ethics. In fact, the Katzes note that the Jewish-American caricature has become such a familiar figure that most second- and third-generation Jews "no longer regard [the caricature] as ignorant or embarrassing, but rather as quaint and 'warm.'"

Focusing on the issue of intellectual transition, Salcia Landmann claims that the shift from the mentality of the ghetto to that of the new world has been the only source of self-deprecation in Jewish humor. With the disappearance of the first-generation caricature and the relatively successful assimilation of Jews into America's mainstream culture, Landmann predicts the impending decline of the phenomenon of Jewish humor defined by Freud because Jewish humorists will soon have nothing new to mock. Bernard Rosenberg and Gilbert Shapiro refute Landmann's prediction by indicating a new dilemma for second-and-third-generation American Jews. "Where we previously hated ourselves for being Jews, we now frequently hate ourselves for not being Jews." In other words, whereas previous self-deprecating humor revealed the narrator's rejection of his Jewish identity, modern self-deprecating humor indicates the guilt assimilated Jews feel for not preserving Jewish traditions.

Some scholars take the extremely positive view that self-deprecating humor, rather than revealing any self-hatred, serves to help the Jew improve intellectually. Joseph Dorinson concludes that self-deprecation, without being threatening or humiliating, permits the Jew to deal honestly and openly with problems. Ziv concurs: "Self-disparaging humor makes possible self-criticism, and enables a man to take a more courageous look at his negative aspects. . . . Self-disparaging humor is a sign of maturity and of self insight."

Both Dorinson and Ziv readily admit that the Jew has as many problems as the non-Jew—if not more because of his confused cultural identity—but in the attempt to identify these character flaws, the Jew takes one step closer to improving them.

Elliott Oring best summarizes the views on the intellectual component in Jewish humor as a paradox in the modern Jew's cultural identity. "When a man passionately proclaims his Jewishness and refuses to accept the inferiority that is deemed his, yet secretly or unconsciously reviles his heritage and is utterly convinced of his inferior status, then that man is in a real sense *meshugge*."

Oring identifies the qualities of the modern Jewish mind which are as distinctive as self-deprecation is to Jewish humor—contradiction and confusion. Of the disparate views scholars present on the intellectual component of Jewish humor, all would probably confirm Oring's observation. While most of these scholars note the correlation between self-hatred, as Gilman defines it, and the self-deprecation of the Jew's humor, all heavily qualify what this self-hatred reveals about the humorist's Jewish identity. Where Bergler generalizes by suggesting that the self-deprecating humorist resents his entire Jewish heritage, the Torah included, the Katzes point out that most self-deprecating Jews actually do not hate their own Jewishness as much as the Jewish-American caricature to which their cultural identity links them. Some of this self-deprecation, Rosenberg and Shapiro add, cannot be labeled as self-hatred at all, but as intense guilt which the humorist transforms into apparent self-hatred. Finally, when used correctly, Dorinson and Ziv note the positive value self-criticism can have for the Jew who wants to improve his character flaws.

Perhaps the emotionalists and the sociologists seem to avoid the intellectual issue of self-hatred because such a catch-phrase is too broad to reflect the actual nature of Jewish identity with any accuracy. True, there are elements of Gilman's self-hatred in Jewish humor as there are in other forms of Jewish folklore, but the Jew's cultural identity is more three-dimensional than the two words imply. In the case of Woody Allen, often condemned as a self-hating Jew, his humor reveals that he identifies as a self-affirming Jew in many ways. Nevertheless—whether self-hating, self-affirming, or both—no Jew can be characterized by many of the generalizations made by many of the scholars in this study. Identifying with an ethnic group, Dundes observes, "tends to reduce the individual to a number." Woody Allen's Jewish identity is not only the result of the Jewish-American emotional, sociological, and intellectual experience, but of Allen's complex personal experience as well.

In examining both his persona's attitude towards his Jewish identity and the limited information about the comedian's Jewish background itself, many critics see self-hatred as one of Woody Allen's most distinctive characteristics. While I argue against such a simplistic, and often inaccurate, labelling of the complex subject of cultural and religious identity, Allen's private and public self-deprecation admittedly gives the impression of self-hatred. His persona's *nebbish* appearance and awkward presence send clear signals that he is not comfortable with himself. He seems unsympathetic and occasionally hostile to Jewish causes and institutions. The first time he revealed any interest in Israel was when he publicly criticized the government for the Intifada. He often denigrates his Jewish identity without regard in both interviews and professional work. Many in his audience might even find "self-hatred" too generous a description of a man who seems to deprecate his ethnic culture so maliciously. But, the various scholars of Jewish humor would point out, Allen's self-deprecation does not necessarily imply self-hatred. Ironically, in many ways his humor reveals his self-affirmation as a Jew.

Just as Brandes refutes Ben-Amos' claim that the humorist separates himself completely from his created persona, Maurice Yacowar—in his thorough and insightful analysis of Allen's career, *Loser Take All*—equates much of Allen's identity with that of his persona. Yacowar notes that the two entities are so inseparable that Allen has never ceased playing his persona in any of his movies, written works, or monologues. Of his strong identification with his persona, Allen says that "what I'm really interested in is creating an image of a warm person that people will accept as funny, apart from the joke or the gag."

The real Allen clearly does not share his persona's extreme neurosis and low self-esteem, both of which he exaggerates for the sake of humor. Yet in order to make his persona appear human enough for audiences to identify with him, Allen instills his own personal warmth into all of his roles.

Allen's persona seems to disclose the real Allen's self-hatred by appearing deliberately gawky. Yet if this reflected his true nature, he would probably try to conceal his awkwardness rather than play on it. Allen does not deprecate his appearance out of self-hatred as much as out of the desire to humble himself before audiences who might otherwise idolize him.

Consequently, as Richard Schickel remarks, he forces his audience to identify with him ". . . just by appearing, bent like a question mark, his delivery hesitant, his eye contact with the audience non-existent, looking as if he might bolt and run at any minute."

Allen's intent is neither to mock his Jewish identity nor even the American-Jewish caricature from which he tries to distinguish himself, even though that caricature shares his shifty, hesitant, and clumsy characteristics. Rather, he increases his persona's warmth by stressing his imperfections. His emphasis on the imperfect, far from mocking Jewish values, actually reflects the Jewish notion that we must all learn to accept unchangeable shortcomings so that we can function in our everyday lives.

At an early age, Allen concluded that his sheltered, distorted, and inadequate Jewish upbringing characterizes all of Judaism. He explains that his parents "represent the heart of the Old World: their values in life are God and carpeting." As a result, "only philosophy, magic, and the clarinet became [Allen's] constant avocations," said Eric Lax, because each of these individualistic disciplines were devoid of the hypocrisy of his Jewish community. Through these introverted pastimes he learned to have faith only in himself instead of any higher moral being.

In his short biography, Lee Guthrie observes that although Allen went to Hebrew school for eight years and observed various Jewish customs, Allen "figured out there was no God when he 'first learned to think' at age four or five." Based on his wisdom at age five, Allen essentially rejected Judaism and any other form of monotheism for the rest of his life. As his character Mickey confesses in *Hannah and Her Sisters*, he simply "got off on the wrong foot" with Judaism and God.

While most of his work touches on elements of Allen's life history, his film *Radio Days* is the closest he has come to producing an autobiography. Through a series of anecdotes, Allen recalls various comic incidents that revolved around the most popular American household device of the 1930s and early 1940s, the radio. In the process, the audience has a glimpse of Allen's childhood in the Flatbush community, in which meaningful Jewish observance was virtually non-existent. One particularly telling scene depicts a hypocritical neighbor committing the double sin of sneaking an unkosher pork chop during the Yom Kippur fast. While pointing to the neighbor's blind observance of rituals like kashrut and fasting, which he neither believes in nor understands, Allen also reveals his own ignorance of the meaning of these Jewish traditions. The ritual of kashrut refines the observer's moral discipline by limiting the kinds of foods that can be eaten and requiring those animals allowed for consumption to be killed in the least painful way possible. Fasting during Yom Kippur similarly serves to discipline the observer who, for at least that one day in the year, tries to restrain bodily desires to concentrate on sincerely repenting for misdeeds. To people like the neighbor and Allen himself who do not understand the ethical value of such rituals, both fasting and keeping kosher appear foolish and unnecessary.

Allen reveals not only his contempt for Jewish traditions, but of organized religion in general as an obstacle to rational, decent behavior. In one of his monologues, he recalls a great love affair that did not lead to marriage because of the principles' religious differences—he was an agnostic and she was an atheist, "so we didn't know what religion not to bring the children up in." The one-liner pokes fun at the dilemma of intermarriage between Christians and Jews in America, considered particularly serious in the Jewish community because of the fear of complete assimilation and rejection of Judaism by children of intermarried couples. With enough natural assimilation and intermarriage to dilute the Jewish population, the Jewish system, which tries to encourage the pursuit of morality from generation to generation, may not survive. The concern Jews have for preserving this ethical system of life is not shared by atheists and agnostics who, because they do not affirm any ethical system, usually expect their children to choose their own system of beliefs. Allen's joke responds to what seems an absurd invasion of privacy rather than a concern for preserving morality in the world. As in *Radio Days*, Allen mocks what he does not understand.

Allen best proves his ignorance of Judaism in his response to criticism from a Jewish organization, B'nai B'rith, about a sacrilegious sketch in *Everything You Always Wanted to Know About Sex* in which a Rabbi is guest on a game show called "What's My Perversion?" As contestants look on, the host asks the Rabbi to act out his favorite fantasy, which consists of his being whipped by a beautiful girl while his wife sits at his feet eating pork. This time Allen mocks both kashrut and Rabbis themselves who, Allen maintains, perpetuate an illusion of holiness while they actually experience the same unholy desires as laymen. When B'nai B'rith expressed its disapproval of the scene, Allen responded: "B'nai B'rith complained about whipping the Rabbi . . . I've never considered Rabbis sacred as I've never considered organized religions sacred. I find them all silly. Costumed and bearded just like popes, to me it's all absolutely absurd."

When Allen criticizes Rabbinical self-righteousness, he misunderstands that the Rabbi is not an exalted figure, but an *everyman* who admits experiencing human passions. The word "rabbi" simply means teacher, implying that the Rabbi (hopefully) is a role model for how to live a decent life.

Allen believes that Rabbis are forbidden from indulging in bodily pleasures because such indulgence is simply sacrilegious. If he had any significant knowledge of Jewish life, he could not be so critical. In serving as role models, Rabbis usually try harder not to become slaves to their bodies not only because they fear appearing sacrilegious, but because by giving in to their body's demands, they risk compromising their moral ideals. If Rabbis such as the guest on "What's My Perversion?" occasionally fail to achieve ideal ethical discipline, they merely reveal human shortcomings, and because they make no pretense to exceptional righteousness, they are not hypocrites. The Rabbi's modest clothing symbolizes ethical discipline that he strives to maintain. His traditional beard complements that discipline and serves as a sign of knowledge and observance that befits a traditional Jewish role model. Allen's denigration reveals his superficial knowledge of the role of the Rabbi.

While Gilman attributes self-hatred to ignorance—such as Allen's ignorance of the ethical value of kashrut, the Yom Kippur fast, the Jewish concern about intermarriage, and the role of the Rabbi—Allen nonetheless may have reasons other than self-hatred for criticizing these Jewish institutions. As a popular artist, he needs to remain accessible to all contemporary audiences rather than just Jewish audiences. Allen's harsh response to B'nai B'rith was probably directed against the critics and their comments more than any Judaic ideal or symbol. In criticizing Allen, the leaders of B'nai B'rith indirectly forced him to take responsibility for his Jewish identity in his work, which the non-observant Allen perceived as an unfair demand. In his personal life, Allen feels he has the right to decide freely how he will identify, but his art deserves to remain culturally indistinct. His self-defense is well-justified in many ways. Jews did not become God's "chosen people" in order to conceal Jewish moral values from others, but rather to spread these ideals to the rest of the world. When Allen tries to make the ideals universally accessible, he unknowingly affirms the Judaic ideal of *tikun olam* [repairing the world].

As long as his Jewish identity does not threaten the accessibility of his art, Allen maintains a disinterested attitude towards his background. When film critic Natalie Gittelson noted the predominance of jokes in his work that in some way involve Jewish themes, Allen responds by downplaying the importance of his identity. "When asked, Allen adds the fact of being Jewish never consciously enters his work . . . of course any character I play would be Jewish because I'm Jewish," she wrote. Allen sees his Jewish identity as playing as small a part in his art as his freckled complexion and his scrawny build. He may feel frustrated by all of these traits at times, particularly when they limit his sexual prowess, but he believes that the most important elements of character are talent and hard work. Allen appears to take accusations of Jewish self-hatred lightly simply because, like his complexion and build, he cannot change his Jewish identity.

While Allen downplays the importance of his Jewish identity in his work, not only are many of his characters Jewish, but much of his subject matter deals either with explicit Jewish themes or with general Judaic ideals, from the Japanese characters who speak Yiddish in his first film, *What's up Tiger Lily?*, to the satire on the Jewish American's attempt at social acceptance in *Zelig*, to the scathing portrayal of a Jewish mother in his short *Oedipus Wrecks*. Allen may not consciously admit to the large role his Jewish identity plays in his work—at least compared with the supporting role his freckles and his scrawny build play—but, as Freud would argue, Woody Allen's humor reveals what his conscious mind otherwise conceals.

Far from completely renouncing his Jewish heritage, much of Allen's humor that appears to condemn the Jews and their religion, actually condemns self-hating Jews themselves. In one monologue, he describes an intellectual who "suffered untold injustices and persecution from his religion mostly from his parents . . . they could never accept the fact that their son was Jewish." The joke relies on several ironic twists. First, his parents resent him for being Jewish, something he got from them in the first place, when he should logically resent them. Second, of all the anti-Semitic people in the world, he suffers the most abuse from those who should love and accept him the most. Finally, the stereotype of Jewish parents holds that they cannot accept their children's decision to reject their heritage rather than affirm it which, as the joke implies, Allen does. This third irony suggests that Allen identifies positively as a Jew and, through his subtle criticism, he actually distances himself from self-hating Jews. Allen's joke ultimately makes the issue of self-hatred ridiculous because people cannot change their identity and thus they will only become frustrated by resenting that which they cannot change.

The underlying message in Allen's self-deprecating humor is that, mostly because of his Jewishness, he feels like an outsider. He rarely, if ever, actually refers to himself as an outsider, probably because he assumes that alienation is a natural part of his identity as a member of a minority. Since he blames his Jewish identity for feelings of alienation, Allen logically appears self-hating, yet he is wise enough not to blame his identity alone for feelings of social alienation. The main source of his alienation, like that of most outsiders, lies in our contemporary social framework and not just in his identity as an ethnic minority. Because his humor attracts such large and diverse audiences, most of his fans must also identify as or be empathic to outsiders for them to appreciate his work so much.

Allen's identification as an outsider enables him to look at his life objectively and keep his personal problems in perspective. Guilt and suffering recalls what the sociological scholars of Jewish humor attributed to the ghetto experience. With high moral demands placed on them by their religion, and paranoia caused by anti-Semitic persecution, Allen believes it natural for Jews to identify as outsiders. Feelings of guilt and suffering are not limited to Jews, but belong to all people who aspire to Western culture's impossible ideals of power, status, and financial success. When people inevitably fail to achieve these ideals, they feel guilty and even suffer for not succeeding where so many others seem to have succeeded. They ultimately feel like outsiders. Those exceptions who do not aspire to these ideals also become outsiders simply because of their unusual values. In Allen's world where everyone feels alienated, the only outsider ironically would be those who do not consciously identify as outsiders.

Even the all-American title character in one of Allen's most popular films, *Annie Hall*, suffers as an intellectual outsider, especially when she spends time with the seemingly sophisticated Alvy Singer, played by Allen. Allen the director focuses not just on the problems involved with alienation, but on how the individual deals with these feelings in everyday life. Both of the film's main characters manage to overcome their sense of inadequacy which leads to their alienation. Annie takes literature classes and advances her singing career, and Alvy looks at his life with characteristically Jewish self-mockery.

Like Freud, Allen sees Jewish humor as a paradox. Jews understand their shortcomings—in this case, the inability to accept those who accept them—but often feel destined to retain them. Jews who strive for acceptance into non-Jewish society can never feel satisfied because, as soon as non-Jews accept them, they assume that those non-Jews themselves cannot be social "insiders" or they would not accept Jews.

The figure of the outsider may suffer from feelings of alienation, but he also enjoys a sense of quirkish individuality that an insider often sacrifices for the sake of social acceptance. In an age of technology and uniformity when people try to control characteristics that might distinguish them from what is socially accepted, Allen's uniqueness is a refreshing change of pace. The Jewish robot tailors in the futuristic film *Sleeper* exemplify the importance of the Jewish talent for retaining individuality. The tailors are unique. They even resist conforming to a robot's image of impersonality by retaining their warmth and humor through constant bickering in thick Yiddish accents. When Allen appears to mock the Jewish stereotype of bickering tailors, he actually praises their Jewish individuality for distinguishing them from other robots. The theme of Jewish individuality appears in a later scene in which two of the film's non-Jewish characters try to recreate a Flatbush dinner scene in order to deprogram the brainwashed Miles, played by Allen.

Allen elaborates on the theme of Jewish individuality in *Zelig*, in which a Jewish American wants to be accepted by non-Jewish society so badly that he completely loses his own personality. Through his study of Zelig, Allen mocks those Jews who try to discard their Jewishness. The result of his personality loss is his chameleon-like nature, which enables him to both physically and mentally assume the characteristics of people nearest to him. When he goes into the kitchen of a Chinese restaurant, Zelig becomes indistinguishable from the Chinese chefs. In an all-black jazz band, Zelig appears as a black clarinet player. In the company of Rabbis, Zelig grows a beard and *peot* [curled sideburns]. Allen's comic portrayal subtly jabs those assimilated Jews who imitate non-Jews in order to gain acceptance, and lose their own identity in the process. Allen's criticism is partially self-directed since he himself desires acceptance from non-Jewish society: Zelig's playing of the clarinet, Allen's own trademark instrument, may represent Allen's intention of including himself in his criticism. But at least Allen does not forfeit his individuality, as his quirky persona demonstrates, in his attempt to fit into American society. Although he criticizes the Rabbi's beard in his earlier response to B'nai B'rith, Allen eventually shows his appreciation of such uniqueness in his study of Zelig.

Allen's identification as an outsider also helps him retain his moral integrity. In one of his monologues, he recalls going to a costume party in the Deep South dressed as a ghost when a car of Ku Klux Klansmen mistake him as one of their own. He tries to fit in with the gang by saying "you-all" and "grits," but the Klansmen eventually discover his Jewish identity and prepare to lynch him. As he awaits his death, he sees his life pass before his eyes "as a kid in Kansas, swimmin' in the swimmin' hole, fishin' and fryin' up a mess o' catfish." Suddenly he realizes that this is not his life. He is to be hanged in two minutes and the wrong life is passing before his eyes. Trapped by the alien Klan, Allen cannot even find refuge in his own memory. But his image of a hopeless outsider is not depicted with the animosity of a self-hating Jew. Allen readily accepts his position as an outsider because it places him on a moral pedestal above the vigilante Klansmen. If his being Jewish means he is not guilty of murderous acts of bigotry, Allen gladly accepts his minority status. True, he may have to fear for his safety as an outsider, but Allen's ingratiating wit usually protects him from any harm. In the finale of the story, the Jewish identity which made him an endangered outsider at one time now becomes his ticket to social acceptance as he leaves his newfound friends, the Klansmen, having sold them $2,000 worth of Israel bonds.

Not only does Allen affirm his identity as an outsider, but he has no desire to try to function in any way as a social insider. Mark Schechner points to his unconscious hesitancy to adapt to non-Jewish society, even when he makes a concerted effort. Schechner mentions one scene in *Annie Hall* when "the gourmet in Alvy Singer suddenly yields to the nervous boy from Brooklyn who isn't quite ready to handle the aggressive, snapping traif [unkosher food] that his dreams have conjured up."

Allen may occasionally resent the inferior status his outsider identity forces him to accept, but he cannot be considered self-hating because he recognizes that no matter what his ethnic identity he would still suffer from feelings of alienation in modern American society. While the Jewish culture has its limitations, Allen must finally admit—either consciously or unconsciously—that his humor owes part of its genius to his profound understanding of his outsider identity.

Allen consciously distances himself from the Jewish religion and culture, but his films nonetheless embrace Jewish ideals. Self-deprecation prompts humility and often even self-improvement rather than self-hatred. Allen summarizes his atheistic moral philosophy in which self-improvement serves as a central objective: "We've got to find the transition to a life-style and culture in which we make tough, honest, moral and ethical choices simply because—on the most basic grounds—they are seen to be the highest good."

He does not reconcile the contradiction within his philosophy that, if there is no moral source higher than man, morality is relative to the individual and conflict becomes inevitable. Yet at least Allen tries to pursue the "highest good" in his moral choices by struggling to find the most ethical way of treating other people. Similarly, most of the stories in the Torah can be interpreted as giving the affirmative answer to Cain's question, "Am I my brother's keeper?" in their emphasis on the individual's responsibility to work for peaceful human relationships. Allen unknowingly affirms the Jewish value of tikun olam by struggling to make ethical choices.

Although Allen may appear to have most faith in his artistic or intellectual abilities, especially since he has no faith in God, he realizes that these pursuits are ultimately empty when they are devoid of ethical meaning. In one monologue, he describes how a ballet performance of "The Dying Swan" sold out because of rumors that bookies fixed the performance so that the swan would live. In addition to the absurdity of the idea that criminals would take interest in ballet, Allen subtly suggests that art has the same potential for corruption as any underworld activity. With the same intent, Allen tells the story of two policemen who lose their rationing of tear gas and are forced to perform the death scene of *Camille* in order to coax kidnappers from a house. Allen reduces the sophistication of great literature to the banter of crime stories. Yet Allen values artistic and intellectual pursuits insofar as they provide outlets for his morality plays. In this sense, Allen is even a kind of a Rabbi himself who teaches his audience the importance of striving for integrity in the otherwise morally decadent modern world.

While Allen's persona always struggles to make moral choices, his pursuit is most apparent in his role of Ike Davis in *Manhattan*. Ike is frustrated by the absence of moral decency in his previously cherished urban society. As the film begins, Ike starts to realize that art and intellectualism have replaced morality in Manhattan society by becoming ends in themselves rather than means of expressing moral issues. Most of Ike's peers deny his moral imperatives in their indulgent pursuit of pleasure. In one scene, Ike criticizes his irresponsible, selfish friend Yale for undermining their friendship and cheating on his wife.

> Yale: Well, I'm not a saint, okay?
>
> Ike: But you-you're too easy on yourself . . . You-you rationalize everything. You're not honest with yourself . . .

Yale: You are so self-righteous, you know. I mean, we're just people,
we're just human beings, you know. You think you're God!

Ike: I-I gotta model myself after someone!

Unlike Yale, who uses his human status as an excuse to maintain
immoral conduct, Isaac (Ike) prefers to follow a remote ideal rather than
conform to the corrupt values that surround him. In an earlier scene, Ike
objects to Yale's indulgence in buying a new Porsche, which he claims just
"screws up the environment." Yale defends himself by calling the car "a
work of art," thereby supporting Allen's argument on the emptiness of art
as an ethical ideal. Instead of artists or intellectuals, Ike chooses God as a
role model not necessarily because he believes in the Judeo-Christian
deity, but simply in order to follow the ideal of moral excellence attributed
to that God. The main difference between Ike and Yale is that both accept
their human limitations, but only Ike makes the effort to rise above them
and pursue higher ideals.

His struggle, like any good person's struggle, will last throughout his
life, yet he will conceivably improve with age because he will have learned
from his past mistakes.

Perhaps the strongest evidence of the affinity Allen feels for the Judaic
ideal of ethical struggle appears in his short story, "Remembering
Needleman." The story describes the moronic title character, a self-pro-
claimed Nazi, and his outlook on life. Like Allen, Needleman does not
believe in God, yet he does not share Allen's moral concerns. Allen draws
Needleman as an absurd, yet frighteningly believable character whose
amoral philosophy leads him to the following conclusions:

> After much reflection, Needleman's intellectual integrity convinced him that
> he didn't exist, his friends didn't exist, and the only thing that was real was
> the I.O.U. to the bank for six million marks.

Allen again criticizes the danger of intellectuality when it has no moral
basis, and even points out the potential evil that can result from such
amorality. The six million marks represent the Nazi toll of Jewish lives,
which is also the only element in Needleman's life. Needleman never takes
responsibility for his actions, so he tries to rationalize his evil behavior
instead. When he fell out of his box at an opera he was too proud to admit
his mistake so he "attended the opera every night for the next month and
repeated it each time." He feels guilty for the Nazi's crime of genocide only
as a person feels guilty for not repaying a monetary debt. The story serves
as Allen's most pointed condemnation of immoral people like Needleman
whose distorted values make them lose their sense of moral justice.

Allen goes as far as praising the Jews' often vulgar, yet ethically-minded,
attitude towards life in comparison with Protestant genteelness in his film,

Interiors. The film focuses on how three daughters cope with changes in their family life, told from the point of view of one of the daughters, Joey. Joey's father, Arthur, leaves her mother, Eve, because he can no longer endure her cold and exacting nature. He remarries Pearl, who attracts him with her vibrant and loving nature. Eve clearly embodies Protestant values while Pearl embodies Jewish values, although neither actually identifies her ethnic origins. Eve is obsessed with cleanliness and appearances, as her ice-gray interior design suggests. Like her elegant vases, she has little moral integrity nor even emotions beneath her aesthetically pristine exterior. Similar to Yale in *Manhattan*, she represents the meaninglessness of sophistication as an end in itself. Pearl, on the other hand, has all the vitality, independence of spirit, and vulgarity of Allen's Jewish persona. At her wedding with Arthur, she insists on dancing with all the members of her new family, while they—perhaps under Eve's influence—respond coldly to her affection. Pearl's sensitivity to Joey's awkwardness reveals that she takes nothing for granted, so intense is her appreciation of life. What is vulgar in Pearl's nature can also be seen as life-affirming, especially in contrast with Eve's morbid nature. Allen depicts Pearl's character more sympathetically than any other character in the film, probably because he idealizes her love of life. In an earlier monologue, he explains that "somebody truly close to life will always be regarded as vulgar by cultivated, brainy people." With his praise of Pearl's appreciation of life, Allen elaborates his theme of the importance of morality in our sophisticated, yet decadent modern society.

In the same way he points to the potential immorality in art and intellectualism, Allen pokes fun at philosophical wisdom which does not apply directly to everyday morality. In *Love and Death*, Boris [Allen] attempts a syllogism to rationalize his plan of assassinating Napoleon.

> A: Socrates is a man. B: All men are mortal. C: All men are Socrates. That means all men are homosexual.

Allen reduces the ancient piece of mathematical wisdom to meaningless philosophical banter by his irrelevant conclusion. In Allen's world, philosophy has the same amount of importance to our everyday actions as a junky detective comic book. Yacowar attributes part of Allen's comic genius to his use of bathos, the reduction of the grandiose to the trivial, while Schechner parallels Allen's use of bathos with Yiddish comedy. In addition to revealing his genius through such reductions, Allen reveals his moral skepticism in which he understands that, like art and intellectualism, philosophy itself can lead to evil if it has no moral basis.

Morality for Allen is not just a matter of philosophical speculation, but a way of life grounded in the everyday reality of eating, sleeping, sex, and other forms of human behavior. If Allen was better informed Judaically, he would realize that—far from focusing on any abstract, metaphysical matters—the Torah and the Rabbinical texts that are the core of Judaism concentrate on the ethical regulation of human activities.

Throughout his films and other work, Allen reveals a positive affirmation of the Jewish ideals which his Jewish upbringing must have instilled in him. As a Jew who constantly distances himself from Judaism, Allen would probably deny the influence of Judaism in his life and argue that his morality is the result of his natural goodness. Yet the prevalence of his pursuit of moral integrity, particularly in films such as *Manhattan* and *Interiors*, suggests his Jewishness must have had some influence on him for him to idealize self-improvement as the first step to repairing the world. Despite the commendable objectives of his system of beliefs, he does not affirm any organized system of morality. That has several negative implications. First, because he does not believe in a higher moral source than man, he has no defense against moral relativism in which matters of right and wrong are reduced to each individual's opinion. Second, with no moral system, Allen has no way of transmitting ideals to future generations that may not have access to his artistic works. Finally, Allen's belief in the pursuit of moral integrity in no way obligates him to fulfill all of his moral objectives because he does not have to answer to a higher authority. He may not hate his Jewish identity, but, by not meeting the requirements of his religion, Allen unwittingly reveals his moral laziness.

In January of 1988, Woody Allen wrote an article in the *New York Times* expressing his concern over Israel's controversial policy in treating Palestinian demonstrators. He explains in the article that, as a supporter of Israel, he questions the ethical soundness of the Israeli government's violent, and even "wrongheaded approach." While his article initially seems to reflect his moral conscientiousness, Allen may have had an ulterior motive in writing for the *Times*. Because of his anti-Israel stance, many Jewish and even non-Jewish critics denounce Allen as a "self-hating" Jew. Some mistakenly recall Allen's self-deprecation as a Jew throughout his career as further evidence of his self-hatred, without understanding the true, often self-affirming nature of his Jewish identity which his article reveals. Of all the responses to the article, Charles Krauthammer's observation in *The New Republic* is probably the most accurate in its appraisal. "It is important for Israelis to know that diaspora Jewry will not support a policy of deliberate brutality . . . But it is quite another thing when the protests are designed for the American press and aimed at an American audience . . . Woody Allen was not writing to move Shamir or Rabin. He was trying to reassure his tablemates at Elaine's: not me," said Krauthammer.

Allen's personal statement about his Jewish identity, if not clear in his artistic work, is apparent in his *Times* article. He affirms the struggle for moral integrity in principle, yet is unwilling to follow his ideals in his actual personal activities. He distances himself publicly from Jews and plays the role of voyeur, rather than active participant. As in *Crimes and Misdemeanors* in which he broadly posits that the universe has an arbitrary judicial system, he remains painfully silent in dealing with how decent people like the Rabbi should confront moral crisis. In his outburst about the Arab-Israeli conflict, Allen ultimately reveals what he has tried so hard to conceal about his personal life—that his persona's admirable struggle to become a better human being does not reflect in Allen's personal integrity. In this sense, Freud's idea that humor reveals what the conscious mind otherwise conceals works backwards. Allen's humor, far from revealing any admirable moral strength, actually supplements Allen's otherwise morally lazy actions. Woody Allen is the incarnation of Grotjahn's warning that self-criticism often leads to self-justification and concurrent ethical complacency.

"My Worst Fears Realized": Woody Allen and the Holocaust

MASHEY BERNSTEIN

"For the non-believer there are no answers; for the true believer there are no questions." Wolfe of Zhitomir

"Even if You annihilate us, we shall praise You forever." Biblical commentary by Rashi on Psalm 44:10

THROUGHOUT HIS movies, especially *Shadows and Fog* (1992) and *Crimes and Misdemeanors* (1990), as well as in his seminal essay, "Random Reflections of a Second-Rate Mind," the comedian and filmmaker Woody Allen has joined the ranks of theologians and Jews in the latter part of the twentieth century who ask troubling questions concerning the Holocaust and its implications. The genocide of six million Jews has left many in these categories with a number of queries, especially regarding their relationship with God. How can people believe in God after the events of 1939–1945? Where was God during this dark period in the history of Western civilization? Why did God keep silent? How does one continue to worship a God that let so many die in such a horrendous manner? Is it an act of supreme faith or naive simplicity to continue to believe in God after what occurred? For that matter, how does one continue to believe in humanity when it is capable of such acts of indecency? In recent years, these issues have occupied Allen's mind with ever-growing intensity. As Eric Lax points out in his biography of Allen: "He is consumed with questions of eschatology and a merciful God's existence; with questions of morality and justice, when God may either not care or be absent from worldly life" (Lax, 41). Allen's musings on this topic make him one of the most fascinating of American filmmakers. Few artists, with the exception of Chaplin, to whom he bares some uncanny artistic and personal resemblances, have followed a trajectory so pronounced as Allen has, from the sheer insanity of movies like *Bananas* (1971) to the heartfelt anguish of *Crimes*.

For Allen, the Holocaust serves two purposes. On the one hand, more than any other historical event, it is his most consistent and ongoing referent. He often uses it, without further musings, as the punch line for jokes

---

This essay was written specifically for this volume and is published here for the first time by permission of the author.

or to make a point about a character. On the other hand, and on a far more significant level, it provides him with the lens through which he can examine society and God in the latter part of the twentieth century. The fact that he has chosen this event above all others—with the exception of his love of cinema—may say something positive about his attitude to his Jewish heritage contra those who see him as a self-hating Jew.[1]

That Allen cannot come to terms with the Holocaust is hardly unique. As Nobel laureate Elie Weisel so eloquently put it: "The Holocaust? The ultimate event, the ultimate mystery, never to be comprehended.... Only those who were there know what it was; the others will never know" (Wiesel, 1, 29). Few theologians have been able to achieve what Irving Greenberg has set as the benchmark for a response to the horrors of what occurred: "Let us offer no fundamental criterion after the Holocaust. No statement theological or otherwise should be made that would not be credible in the presence of burning children" (Greenberg quoted in Roiphe, 59). The Grand Inquisitor in Dostoyevski's *Brothers Karamazov* could not have put it better!

In truth, attitudes towards the Holocaust are as many and as varied as the victims themselves. Some respond by justifying the acts of God to humans, thereby providing some kind of rationale for what took place and arguing that God had his private reasons for allowing the Holocaust to occur. This argument is something akin to that provided by the book of Job, the most enigmatic book of the Bible, in which an innocent man suffers without reason or cause yet continues to believe in a God who eventually comes in a whirlwind to offer him "an answer that is also no answer."[2] At one extreme in this group is the orthodox Jewish thinker Bernard Maza, who in his text, *With Fury Poured out* (1986), argues that the Jewish people in some way deserved their fate. The Holocaust was a pouring out of divine fury that would cleanse and redeem the people (Maza, 123–125). The reform theologian Ignaz Maybaum echoes this idea, arguing that the six million were chosen by God to usher in a new era of liberty and global progress (Cohn-Sherbook, 24). Eliezer Berkovitz, in his text *Faith after the Holocaust* (1973), takes up this idea with a vengeance, seeing the creation of the State of Israel in 1948 as the result of this act of "redemption," the state being built, as it were, on the ashes of the martyrs without which its creation would not have been possible (Berkovitz, 144–146). While these apologists are powerful voices, their idea of the sanctification of the State of Israel as the reward for the martyrdom of so many Jews has not found universal favor among Jews, orthodox or otherwise.[3]

The esteemed Jewish theologian Emil Fackenheim, in *God's Presence in History: Jewish Affirmations and Philosophical Reflections* (1970), rebuts the idea that the Jews deserved their fate.[4] Taking up the challenge of Greenberg, he states: "What a sacrilegious thought when among the Nazi's victims were one million children!" (Fackenheim, 73). He also rejects the notion suggested by an anonymous "good Christian" that perhaps "Auschwitz was a divine reminder of the sufferings of Christ" (Fackenheim, 75). Needless to say this idea, when repeated by other Christians, such as Cardinal O'Connor of New York, appalled many Jews (Roiphe, 66).

Fackenheim goes on to present Israel in a different context, not as a reward but as what must become the focus of the Jewish people. He argues that "God's presence in the catastrophe cannot be explained," but that Jews should not hand Hitler a posthumous victory by deserting their faith. "They are commanded to survive...[and] to remember.... They are forbidden to despair of man and his world" (Fackenheim, 84). The notion of not handing Hitler a "posthumous victory" has become something of a battle cry among Jewish leaders in their attack on assimilation.

Fackenheim bridges the gap between those who try to explain God's actions and those who do not understand God's silence. As Arthur Hertzberg succinctly put it: "I have never found a way to absolve God of the crimes of Auschwitz" (Hertzberg, 39). He notes that despite the presence of thousands of volumes on the Holocaust—a number that increases virtually daily—the question remains and it is always the same: What lessons can be learned from it? There is still no satisfactory answer. Hertzberg is one of those who, despite having no answer for what God did or did not allow to occur, has not lost his faith. Nonetheless, he also does not find himself in the camp of Martin Buber, who argues in *The Eclipse of God* (1952) that God is a limited power encouraging people to do good but not responsible for the pain and evil in the world. Buber posits a theory borrowed from the mystical book, the Cabalah, that sometimes God hides his face, absents himself from the world and so darkness rules (Buber, 23, 66, 68). But as Byron Sherwin has pointed out in his article "The Impotence of Explanation and the European Holocaust" (1971), "The eclipse of God is a response but is not a solution to Auschwitz and the theological problems it engenders.... There is no theodicy," no defense of God's goodness and omnipotence in view of the existence of evil (Sherwin, 106). This group echoes the words of Aaron Hass: "The idea of God is not a comfort but a taunt" (Hass, 144).[5]

The final group is made up of those who have lost all faith. Their collective philosophy is best summed up by writer Primo Levi, another Holocaust survivor who, like Elie Weisel, has written extensively and movingly on this topic: "There is Auschwitz, and so there cannot be God" (Levi, 50). The members of this group may originally have been orthodox, or they might have been doubters to begin with, and have had their agnosticism validated; they can barely muster the energy to understand and stumble blindly along in a world that is darker for the occurrence of the Holocaust. For them God either does not exist, or if he does, he is irrelevant. Hass, who interviewed survivors and their offspring, quotes a number of people who presage Allen's questions and attitude in *Crimes*: "If there is a God and he let it happen, he's got to be a pretty sick guy," says one, and "I'm sure that he or she doesn't have anything to do with the workings of the natural world," says another (150–152). Allen would seem to belong in this group: curious, cynical, and skeptical.

Despite his interest in the Holocaust, Allen has had little time for Judaism as a faith: "I was unmoved by the synagogue. I was not interested in the seder, I was not interested in the Hebrew school, I was not interested in being Jewish.... It just didn't mean a thing to me" (Lax, 40).[6] Yet his work reveals a kind of response to life in the second half of the twentieth century that can only be called Jewish. If one were to secularize it, it might be called a New York state of mind, but, for all intents and purposes, that term is really synonymous with Jewish. The world of Allen can only have emerged from a Jewish consciousness. Most of his movies concern characters who are Jews and who live in a narrowly defined world in which all share the same attitude and approach to life. It is a testament to his genius that he has made this world accessible to so many.

At the same time, while this local habitation has given Allen metaphor and language through which to explore his ideas, it may also lead to it becoming somewhat of an irrelevance. As Adam Gopnik notes in an astute appraisal in the *New Yorker*, these two worlds [i.e., that of New York and that of the Jewish sensibility] have in recent years been "either hardened or homogenized. These days jokes about matzo balls and Jewish mothers seem as archival as Falstaff's jokes about sack and cuckhold's horns" (Gopnik, 92). But the problem has long been one that Allen has faced. While, as Mark Shechner argues, Allen's humor is "traditionally" Jewish, embodying "modesty, wit and verbal agility" (Schechner, 102), Allen is caught in an ambiguous situation. He is a comedian "in search of humor who desires to merge with a community and nourish it from within but can find none to merge with. The buoyancy and invention of his humor is darkened by the pathos of his ambition to transcend it and cut deeper into the human condition" (Fischel, 102).

For nearly two decades, ever since *Sleeper* (1973), Allen's cinematic view of the world has—with the rare exception of *Manhattan Murder Mystery* (1993)—grown darker.[7] One's initial hope for a return to the early funny movies has, like the aliens who initially made this request in *Stardust Memories* (1980), gone up into the stratosphere, never to be heard from again. Nowadays Allen's movies, more often than not, reveal a misanthropic view of mankind. Beneath the comic surface lies a belief that life is "short, dark and brutish." His humor is laced with cynicism, his worldview despairing. People will betray each other, love won't last, things never work out for the best. Hope and courage are in remarkable short supply. In a reworking of Murphy's law: what can go bad, will. Characters are prone to existential malaise from which only a love of New York or movies can rescue them.

Concomitant with these feelings have been Allen's increasing references to the Holocaust. As his worldview has darkened, Allen's use of the Holocaust has become more pronounced, resulting in not just one movie that has looked at the event, but a consistent body of work that has unflinchingly probed it, providing philosophical speculation far beyond the norm of American movies. Few writers or moviemakers have been so consistent in their references to one historical event.

I therefore disagree with Desser and Friedman's surprising comment that there are "few overt invocations" of the Holocaust in Allen's movies (Desser and Friedman, 59); I find, in fact, many such references.[8] In movies as diverse as *Annie Hall* (1977), *Manhattan* (1979), *Hannah and Her Sisters* (1986), *Zelig* (1983), *Crimes and Misdemeanors* (1989), *Shadows and Fog* (1992), and *Stardust Memories* (1980) there are explicit references to the Holocaust. Not all the uses to which Allen puts the events have been of the same type. At times, the rise of Nazism, the persona of Hitler, and the facts of the Holocaust are little more than material for jokes—though these themes hardly fall into the category of gallows humor or the offensive. "I haven't had this much fun since the Nuremberg Trials," the protagonist says to one hapless date in *Hannah*, or, as in *Crimes and Misdemeanors*, the Allen persona says, "I remember the last time we had sex, it was April 20, Hitler's birthday." At other times the humor is laced with cyanide, as in the "didyou/jew" sequence in *Annie Hall* in which the protagonist is convinced that a publicity agent is making subtle anti-Semitic jibes. His obsession with the Holocaust is most manifest in *Annie Hall* (1977), wherein he drags dates to see Max Ophul's magnum opus *The Sorrow and the Pity*, a monumental examination of French collaboration with the Nazis. He considers it a mark of his "triumph" when, after they have broken up, he meets Annie with a date coming out of the same movie. Whether true to life or not, Allen's use of this movie can be considered not only fodder for a joke but also revelatory of Allen's own personal interests in the subject.[9]

Over the years Allen has examined in increasing depth the nature of the Jew in the twentieth century, and the image of the Nazis plays a significant role in this exploration. In *Zelig* the title character represents a Jew who assumes the identity of whomever he is with in an attempt to fit in wherever he can, to the point of becoming a chameleon. Desser and Friedman go so far as to consider it "the clearest expression of Jewish fear and paranoia ever produced in the cinema" (Desser and Friedman, 61). In light of this remark, the image of Zelig joining the Nazi party and appearing on the same dais as Adolf Hitler has a peculiar resonance to it. We are presented with, at one and the same time, a Jew who hates himself so much that he joins the enemy, and also the condemnation of a character who would consider such a heinous act in order to escape his heritage.[10]

Nothing has brought out more clearly Allen's attitude toward the Holocaust and its implications than his most significant nonfiction writing to date, the essay "Random Reflections of a Second-Rate Mind" (1991).[11] This basically dour piece of writing is neither random nor second-rate—though some readers thought so.[12] In it Allen recounts a catalogue of reasons why he despairs about modern society. There are comments on women in the Bible, how he feels about being Jewish, and his surprise at the reaction he got from an editorial he wrote that was critical of Israel.[13] (Allen does seem at times to be remarkably naive about how the world perceives and reacts to what he does and says.) The tone of the article is cynical, its message full of despair: Given the slightest opportunity, people will do bad things to one another. Allen offers no solution, no remnant of hope. Humans are bad news: that is a fact of life.

The essay begins and ends with a meditation on the Holocaust. Allen contemplates his relatives' bewilderment over how, during the Holocaust, the friends of their Jewish relatives could turn on them so easily, a fact that did not surprise him at all: "The mystery that had confounded all my relatives since World War II was not such a puzzle if I understood that inside every heart lived the worm of self-preservation, of fear, greed and an animal will to power" (Allen 1991, 8). He prefers the line, "people are no damn good" to the "pandering nonsense" of Anne Frank about "people being basically good" (Allen 1991, 7). In this essay Allen expands on the sentiment of the dour Frederick in *Hannah*: "The fact that a Holocaust happened does not surprise me, the fact that there has only been one amazes me" (Allen 1991). One can only assume that these sentiments reflect not random, but consistent thoughts in Allen's mind and philosophy—a cheery thought from one of our most beloved comedians.

In the light of these remarks, one might wonder if Allen is a cynic for whom the Holocaust is proof of his pessimistic nature, or did his view of the world stem from his (Jewish) reaction to the events of the Holocaust? One may suspect that Allen uses—dare one say, exploits—the Holocaust because it confirms already deeply held beliefs. I doubt this is the case, but it could be argued that the two developed in tandem. After all, Allen, born in 1935, was barely bar mitzvahed by the time the news of the Holocaust was revealed, so it is inevitable that much of his maturing years were full of the news and responses to this event—as indeed the essay implies. It must have become for him, as it did for so many American Jews, the defining moment of their identity. Despite the fact that it occurred in Europe, it stands out as the most significant event in *American*-Jewish life—only to be rivaled by the creation of the State of Israel.[14] Allen, therefore, is typical of many assimilated American Jews whose faith or identity as Jews has been distilled into a response to the Holocaust and the fear that anti-Semitism may precipitate another such occurrence. Ultimately, whatever the uses to which he has put it and whether the Holocaust triggered his cynicism or vice versa, it has been the spur to his discontent.[15]

The ideas in the essay find their clearest cinematic expression in two recent movies by Allen: in the minor key, *Shadows and Fog*, and in the major, *Crimes and Misdemeanors*. While his earlier movies may have had single lines devoted to the topic, none of them can be called a serious or extended study of the Holocaust and its implications. In contrast, the aforementioned movies do address the issues directly and use the Holocaust as their basic thematic material. When *Shadows* appeared, most of the critics either paid the movie little serious critical attention or roundly dismissed it as one of Allen's lesser works.[16] But with a title strongly reminiscent of Alain Resnais's masterful study of Auschwitz, *Night and Fog*, *Shadows and Fog* plays a very important role in an exploration of Allen's response to the Holocaust. In fact, he explores with peculiar insight the deep-seated roots of anti-Semitism. In many ways, it is his most explicitly philo-Semitic (I hesitate to use the word "Jewish") movie.[17]

The plot is simple. One foggy night, a malevolent evil man stalks an unnamed city, strangling random victims. Groups of vigilantes gather to try and capture him. They awaken a nebbish named Kleinman (Allen) and railroad him into their ranks.[18] Never in on their plans, unsure of his own position in the group, Kleinman wanders the city, trying to stay alive. In his search, he encounters the institutions that represent society: a police station, a church, a brothel, and a circus (each peopled by characters portrayed by a vast array of stars, from old Allen standbys like Mia Farrow to trendy newcomers like Madonna). All have answers and yet more questions. Finally Kleinman decides that "illusion" is as good an answer as any to humanity's problems and he settles for what little happiness he can find. Needless to say, with its intermittent dashes of humor and mordant witty lines, the narrative is a typical Allen journey in and out of existential despair. In the space of eighty-six minutes, Kleinman finds the time to question, inter alia, his own sense of reality and the nature of man and God. "Make a leap of faith to believe in God? I can't even make a leap of faith to believe in myself," says the bewildered Kleinman.

Hovering under this plot lurks the theme of the Holocaust. In their attempt to capture the murderer, the townspeople reveal all the fear and greed of people looking for a scapegoat. They are characters out of every Jew's nightmare, incipient anti-Semites and Nazis, every one of them. Perhaps they just embody Allen's concept of evil but Allen loads the script with references that are explicit and referential to the Jewish experience. Innocent people with Jewish names are rounded up under false pretenses and allusions are made to the familiar canards against Jews, including the poisoning of wells. At one point, a character says that Kleinman (obviously the "kleine mensche"—little man—of Yiddish folklore) "is no better than a

piece of vermin, only fit for extermination," a line that resonates with connotations from Nazi propaganda.

Nor does Allen pull his punches. He characterizes the Catholic church
as not only hypocritical, but also as in cahoots with the forces (i.e., the
Nazis) that round up the innocent by means of a list (on which Kleinman
soon finds himself) of those it wants eradicated. With these few strokes,
Allen covers ground well-documented by Rolf Hochhuth in his play *The
Deputy*, which castigated the silence of the Catholic church, and especially
of Pope Pius XII during those terrible years—a silence that rankled Jews of
a certain era, among whom Allen obviously counts himself.[19] Allen's attack
on anti-Semitism and his depiction of this type of mentality could only
emerge from a person deeply conscious of the price that Jews have paid
over the centuries for simply being Jewish. More than *Zelig*, this seems to
me to be the movie that, in the words of Desser and Friedman, is "the
clearest expression of Jewish fear and paranoia ever produced in the cinema" (Desser and Friedman, 61).

Since *Shadows and Fog* borrows from Fritz Lang's *M* (1931), one cannot
help but wonder if Allen deliberately echoed the style of the German
expressionist movement of the 1930s for stylistic reasons or to show off his
knowledge of film lore. In fact, the medium becomes the message. The
epitome of the Germanic 1930s style—which owed a great deal to Jewish
filmmakers who were to be forced into exile or death—forms a neat counterpoint to the themes he is exploring. The movie has the air of a parable in
which characters are more metaphor and symbol than fully developed individuals. The movie seems to spring from the pages of the works of another
writer who wrote with a strong sense of the Jew's precarious place in the
modern world—Franz Kafka. The movie has the Kafkaesque mixture of
realism and surrealism, the same sense of an underpopulated world in
which characters encounter strange forces that they cannot comprehend.
For him, as for the Jewish Kafka, paranoia is the human condition.

At the same time, it must be admitted that *Shadows* is a small movie
and somewhat undeveloped. Though she does not dismiss it as quickly as
some critics, *Sight and Sound* critic Patricia Brett Erens notes that while
the film "resonates" with Holocaust references, the whole is "facile." "The
monstrosity of anti-semitism is not so easily annihilated," she states (Erens,
20). Maybe she was expecting too much from the movie. It might be
enough to have a filmmaker who deals with themes that few have tackled
with success and who presents them without any sugarcoating. Hollywood
can only offer *School Ties* (1992) or *Gentleman's Agreement* (1947),
movies that offer truly "facile" arguments and solutions.

Perhaps *Shadows* frustrated Allen's fans because he had tackled the
same theme, or at least the implications of the Holocaust, far more tren-
chantly just a few years earlier in the film that has to be considered his

masterpiece, *Crimes and Misdemeanors*. Although in the latter movie the theme of the Holocaust is only made in passing, Allen creates a world in which not only can a Holocaust occur, but more to the point, he addresses those very issues that Holocaust theologians have been grappling with since the event occurred. It is a world in which God is seemingly absent. The good have suffered, suffer, and will suffer; the bad triumph and escape without punishment. It is, as James Nuechterlein notes, a world in which "evil, as for Hannah Arendt, comes in the guise of the banal rather than the truly monstrous" (Neuchterlein quoted in Steinfels, 29). The evocation of Arendt is appropriate, for it is she who coined the phrase "the banality of evil" while observing the trial of Adolf Eichman and seeing a "small" person, a "greengrocer," who was capable of masterminding the murder of millions of people; Arendt realized that "evil comes in the guise of the banal rather than the monstrous" (Neuchterlein quoted in Steinfels, 29). In *Crimes* we are dealing with just such a set of mediocre characters who perform heinous crimes, from murder and sexual perversion to corruption of art and betrayal of love.[20] Throughout it all Allen asks, "Where is God? Where is a God who allows such inequality to occur?" It is Allen's most profound exploration of the limits of religion in a world that has seen the worst that people can do to one another. We wait in vain for a God in whom we trust or whom we fear or whom we hope will answer our prayers to appear, or at the very least to answer us out of the whirlwind with "an answer that is no answer." No such luck. In a way, the movie can be seen as a parody of Harold Kushner's popular book, *When Bad Things Happen to Good People* (1981), with its message of hope and comfort.

The plot presents two variations on the same theme: major crimes and minor misdemeanors. In the latter, Allen plays Cliff Stern, a documentary filmmaker given to rather dour subjects like acid rain and leukemia who is currently working on a documentary on a Holocaust survivor, Louis Levy. Cliff is unhappily married to a woman with two brothers who are as different as night and day. One is Lester, a pompous but successful maker of television comedies. Cliff gets hired to make a movie about Lester's life, and while working on the film he falls in love with Halley, a woman who is also working with Lester.[21] The other brother is Ben, a rabbi who is going blind. Ben serves as the bridge to the "crimes" section, which concerns Judah, a successful opthamologist who hires a hit man to murder his mistress, Dolores. Judah, who was raised in an orthodox home in which the idea that "God sees everything" was instilled in him from his childhood, goes through a time of crisis as he waits for God to punish him for his act. In their different ways, Judah and Cliff search for proof that evil will be punished, good will triumph, and that God, who "sees everything," will impose order on the world. At the end of the movie, Cliff and Judah meet and compare notes on their lives and how they have turned out.[22]

While the plot seems to deal with issues far removed from the horrors of the Holocaust, its implications are identical. How can we live in a world in which God takes no action against those who have committed the worst of crimes? Murder is murder, whether of an innocent woman or of an innocent Jew. If a person can murder and get away with it, if a phony like Lester can convince not only America, through his TV comedies, but a person of substance like Halley that he is deserving of her hand in marriage, while the good literally and figuratively are defecated upon, then what is the point of it all? If God exists, argues Judah and wonders Cliff, then shouldn't he strike down the guilty? Does the fact that he doesn't mean that God does not exist, or that if he does it is irrelevant? If that is the case, how are humans to make sense of the universe?

The movie becomes a meditation on the nature of good and evil, and Allen provides a variety of viewpoints that range from the pragmatic to the sentimental, from the religious to the agnostic. All the characters, whether in the crime or the misdemeanors portion, examine the world from a theological point of view. Though none of their answers seems sufficient with regards to the issue, Allen gives each point of view its moment in the sun. Swirling around the questions that Judah and Cliff raise is the cool questioning philosophy of Louis Levy, the warm belief of Ben, the hot credo of Judah's father Sol, and the firebrand philosophy of Sol's sister, Aunt May, who seems to be a stand-in for Allen. In many ways, they fall into the same categories as the theologians who have tackled the Holocaust: those who accept or try to explain the inexplicable; those who accept the irrational and still struggle to believe; and those who see only emptiness, a void where there used to be belief.

Judah follows a path from naive innocence to existential emptiness without really deepening his knowledge in any sort of sophisticated manner. While ostensibly struggling with the notion of an all-powerful God, his God is really rather simple: Do bad and I will punish you. Judah's beliefs recall those condemned by the late Milton Steinberg: "God does not denote an old man on a throne somewhere up in the sky.... [Such a notion] condemns individuals capable of ripe spirituality to the stuntedness...of puerile, unsatisfying and undignified convictions" (Steinberg quoted in Jacobs, 3). At the same time, Judaism does encourage this kind of notion with its emphasis on Yom Kippur and the judgments allotted at that time. Eugene Borowitz makes this connection in his commentary on *Crimes*, noting that the film had particular resonance for him because he saw it "between Rosh ha-Shana and Yom Kippur, the Jewish New Year time when we Jews plunder God's judgement and mercy" (Borowitz quoted in Steinfels, 29).

Judah's beliefs may have been learnt from his father, Sol, whose faith is a gift, "like an ear for music." (Despite the high esteem in which Sol is held, Allen makes him a rather ambiguous character. After all, he sires two sons: one, Judah, is a murderer, and the other an underworld figure who procures a murderer. Is this what comes from unquestioning faith?) Sol has no doubt that God exists. If he has to choose between "God" or "Truth," he will choose the former. But as Rabbi Norman Cohen points out in an otherwise positive appraisal of the movie, Sol's statement is an indication of Allen's "simplistically skewed view of religious faith and Judaism." For the religious person, says Rabbi Cohen, there is no distinction between "God" and "Truth": "In Judaism the two are complementary, not contradictory."[23] Despite this slip, and whatever the faults of Allen's reasoning, he presents Sol as content and secure.

Ben is actually cut from the same cloth as Sol, yet he also echoes the suffering and acceptance of Job.[24] Though struck blind, he never questions his faith. It continues to illumine his darkness: "I couldn't go on living if I didn't feel with all my heart a moral structure with real meaning and forgiveness and some kind of higher power." Given a beautifully modulated performance by Sam Waterston, the rabbi is, as everyone calls him, "a saint." As with Sol, Allen gives us a portrait without cynicism. He shows us his concept of "true" faith. We can reject it or accept it based on our own prejudices, but most of the critics found little to carp about in Allen's depiction of a believer.[25]

Pitted against Sol is his sister, May, who, as one of the characters later says, Judah is most like, though she also seems to express Allen's own belief.[26] Allen places the central argument of the movie, a brief but highly charged philosophical discussion, at a crucial moment in the Passover seder service—the service that commemorates the liberation of the Hebrew slaves from servitude in Egypt.[27] Although a celebration, it is not without moments that recall the horror of what the Hebrews endured. In a flashback, Judah enters the seder at the moment in which his father is making the blessing over the bitter herbs that recalls the hard times that the slaves endured. Despite protesting that he "never was interested in the seder" (Lax, 40) Allen shows at least a familiarity with ritual.[28] Obviously, Allen wants to underline the point: How do we explain the bitter times that have befallen the Jews, whether in Egypt, the Holocaust, or on a more personal level? Seated around the Passover table are family members who represent different points of view, including a religious person who admits to "going through the motions," and a young Judah. The central argument pits Sol, the believer, against his sister, May, the agnostic. Sol opines a very clear—almost simplistic—belief in cause and effect for good and evil: "that which originates from a black deed will blossom in a foul manner." When he argues that "God won't punish me, he punishes the wicked," May is quick to interject with the question "Like Hitler?" Twice she mentions the murder of six million Jews, demanding to know why the Nazis were "able to get away with it." May takes up all the points raised by Allen in "Random Reflections." She is the realist. She denies that there is a moral structure to the universe and that "there is only morality for those who want it." Ultimately, "might makes right." No wonder then that Sol calls her a "nihilist," an idea also taken up by Rabbi Cohen, who says that she sees only "evil and deceit in the world," views that strike me as unnecessarily harsh.[29] At this juncture, Judah interrupts and asks "What if a man kills?" This juxtaposition makes explicit the connection between the crime of Judah and those of the Nazis and the theological implications of both. Desser and Friedman also pick up on this point. For Judah, the murder of Dolores "must ultimately be taken as a test of God's presence, just as on a much larger scale the Holocaust created a monumental rift in Judaic theology" (Desser and Friedman, 97), though the authors seem to be a little heavy-handed when they argue that by making Judah the murderer rather than the murdered, Allen is presenting us with a "disguised" response to the deterioration of Jewish ethical standards. I would argue that the movie does not seem to be an attack on the actions of contemporary Jews, but an examination of ideas. Sol responds to Judah that there is no escape from punishment. May's answer is darker, "If he can get away with it—just like the Nazis—and he chooses not to be bothered by the ethics, then he is home free."

Sol, for whom there are no questions, and May, for whom there are no answers, offer the two extremes of response. Yet there has to be more. These issues cannot be as simple as both May and Sol make it seem from their respective points of view. A third and more complex argument comes from Louis Levy, the Holocaust survivor Allen's character is documenting in a film. It has been suggested by more than one critic that Levy is based on his namesake, Primo Levi,[30] primarily because Louis commits suicide as Levi did in real life. But the situation is slightly more complicated. Louis Levy does not approach the Holocaust from the same point of view as the real Levi, but more importantly, he is played by Martin S. Bergmann, who recently published *In the Shadow of Moloch* (1992), a book built around the themes in the story of Abraham and Isaac, the very ideas he explores in this movie.[31] While Cliff sees Louis as a "positive" influence, the truth of the matter is that Louis is not that far away from May's point of view. In fact, while May is a realist, Levy is a failed romantic. He struggles constantly to create a world that is loving and is dismayed when it cannot be. He finds that we cannot "create a loving image of God," and that the universe is a pretty cold place: "It is we who must invest it with our feeling." While the suicide of Levy comes as a shock, the seeds of his despair were always there, and it is only Cliff's own romantic urgings that painted him in glowing colors.

The two plots converge as Cliff and Judah finally meet at the wedding of the rabbi's daughter where, as he swings the camera from one character to the other, Allen brings all these diverse points of view together in a tour de force cinematic sequence. The scene is rife with ambiguity and has been read as both positive and negative—in its religious implications. When Cliff discovers that his beloved Halley has married the obnoxious Lester, he states that he has had his "worst fears realized." He sits stunned and is joined by Judah, who tells him in the guise of a seemingly fictitious story about a man who commits a murder and not only gets away with it but has had his life enhanced by the experience, as has happened to Judah himself. Since Judah has discovered the veracity of May's theories, and since May seems to be Allen's own voice, it seems that the movie supports this outcome. But Allen is not content with this solution to the problem of God in a post-Holocaust world. He objects to the ending of Judah's story, slightly altering the line he has just uttered to Halley: "The man's worst beliefs are realized," i.e., there is no God. Instead, he offers another solution in which the man assumes the role of God and turns himself in. Judah, in turn, rejects this ending, saying it is only fit for the movies. Of course, the point is ironic. We *are* watching a movie, and for that matter a movie that has just given us the ending that Judah described. But the writer of this movie (Allen) has just said he hates that ending. In this way, Allen has his cake, chews it, and then spits it out.

What is especially interesting in this discussion is the stance that Allen takes vis-à-vis God and morality in this world. Initially it could be argued that Allen is simplistic. No one with any degree of sophistication would be happy with a theology that advocates that the "good will be rewarded and the bad punished," to cite Sol, and indeed, Allen goes much further. For Allen, belief in God is fine for those who want it, but in a post-Holocaust world unquestioning faith seems a luxury and a denial of the facts of life. The philosophy of Judah and May also leaves Allen cold: "I told you the story was chilling," says Judah to Cliff, acknowledging the spiritual emptiness of his life and its total amorality. Allen also certainly rejects the final actions of Primo Levi and Louis Levy, about whose death he makes a cruel joke.[32] Allen explicitly rejected that response in *Hannah*, in which he tried and failed to kill himself. Nonetheless, Allen lets the words—rather than the actions—of Levy speak for him. They offer the most realistic, and in a way, optimistic advice. As different images from the movie punctuate his speech, Levy argues, repeating a speech made earlier:

> We are all faced throughout our lives with agonizing decisions, moral choices. Some are on a grand scale, most of these choices are on lesser points. But, we define ourselves by the choices we have made. We are, in fact, the sum total of our choices. We then unfold so unpredictably, so unfairly. Human happiness does not seem to have been included in the design of creation. It is only we, with our capacity to love, that give meaning to the indifferent universe. And yet, most human beings, seem to have the ability to keep trying and even to find joy from simple things like their family, their work and from the hope that future generations might understand more.[33]

The final image is of Ben, now totally blind, dancing at his daughter's wedding. It is an ambiguous image. One has to wonder if the act is the embodiment of futility, as he blindly goes in circles, or if it is life-affirming, with the rabbi secure in his faith and dancing in joy at a wedding. The movie ends with a burst of applause—whether in response to the rabbi's dancing or to the words of Levy is left unclear.

Ironically, then, Allen carves his own place in this discussion. He rejects the arguments of the doubters as too despairing, yet he also disdains the theological assumptions of those who continue to believe in a benign, though problematic, God. He possesses only a cautious optimism for which he finds a different source. As Lax notes: "For all his questioning and agonizing, Woody Allen is a reluctant (he hopes there is a God) but pessimistic (he doubts there is) agnostic who wishes he had been born with religious faith (not to be confused with sectarian belief) and who believes that even if God is absent, it is important to lead an honest and responsible life" (Lax, 41). Even if God doesn't exist and people are weak, there is oneself and one's own obligation to oneself. As Cliff tells Judah, we have to take on the role of the absent God, and even if we are blind and going in circles and it all seems pointless, somewhere along the line we must live in the hope that it will make sense.

A further indication of the unusual "Jewishness" of this movie lies in Allen's choice of names for the characters in the "crimes" section: Jake (Jacob) and Judah, the sons of Sol (Solomon), Ben (Benjamin), and Miriam, Judah's wife. All of these namesakes played unusually strong roles in the Bible: Judah, "the lion," eventually rose to become the leader of the Hebrew nation, but was not above leading his father into believing that his son Joseph was dead. He also had an unfortunate dalliance with his daughter-in-law, Tamar, which resulted in his being shamed in public—a situation not unlike that almost suffered by the Judah of the film, but without the same resolution.[34] Jake is a rake, not unlike the early Jacob who was got his name from the Hebrew word for heel; Solomon, the wise, saw truth clearly and was able to distinguish between the false and the real; Benjamin was the beloved son of Jacob, and Miriam was the caregiver and protector of Moses. While in other movies Allen's milieu has always been predominantly Jewish, these allusions give their characters an added depth, turning the plot, with its theological ramifications, into something of a parable.[35]

Notes

1. Cf., Dresner, "Woody Allen, Theologian?"
2. This phrase is taken from the script of the television version of Herman Wouk's *The Winds of War*, which also offers a trenchant exposition of the meaning of Job in terms of the Holocaust.

3. Ironically, the ultraorthodox Jewish theologian Joel Tettlebaum, in *On True and False Salvation* (1967), argues that the sin of the Jews was Zionism, for not waiting for the Messiah to appear before moving to Israel (Hertzberg, 39).

4. "At Auschwitz, Jews were murdered, not because they had disobeyed the God of History, but rather because their great-grandparents had obeyed Him. They had done so by raising Jewish children" (Fackenheim, 6).

5. In the same chapter, he goes to a Passover seder where his host, an orthodox rabbi, echoes the sentiment of Maza. Hass is "appalled." Hass's short chapter offers an excellent overview of this subject, of which I have only given a smattering of viewpoints.

6. A very significant aspect of Allen's work and art, Lax makes extremely short shrift of Allen's Jewishness, dismissing it in under four pages.

7. His view may always have been dark. After all, in *Annie Hall* Allen depicts himself as a child who worries that the world will "expand."

8. This discrepancy could be because they define the Holocaust in rather narrow terms. They do not accept, for example, Max Ophul's *The Sorrow and the Pity* as a movie about the Holocaust. Ironically, they see a response to the Holocaust in a movie that has no such explicit referent, *Sleeper*. With its plot about a man from 1973 who finds himself in the world of 2073, and whom the powers-that-be wish to "reprogram," they argue that the movie "stems from the historic situation of Jews in a gentile world." But they are quick to add: "*Sleeper* is a comedy and not an allegory of the Holocaust" (Desser and Friedman, 50). Indeed, it would wrench the movie considerably out of joint to see it as referring in any way towards the Holocaust!

9. Rather than viewing this as an indication of Allen's interest in the Holocaust, Desser and Friedman see his choice merely as revelatory of Allen's obsession with death (84).

10. The fact that this incident happened in real life, as depicted in the movie *Europa, Europa*, gives this idea added irony.

11. The essay was originally published in the July 1992 issue of *Tikkun*. It was reprinted in *The Best American Essays, 1991*, from which all references are taken.

12. Specifically, Rosenbaum, and the slew of *Tikkun*'s readers who responded to the essay.

13. "Am I Reading the Papers Correctly?" *New York Times*, 28 January 1988.

14. Cf., Berenbaum, *After Tragedy and Triumph*, for a comprehensive study of this issue.

15. I admit to speculation on this point, because Allen has revealed very little about his Jewish upbringing. But there can hardly have been a Jewish home that did not react to or discuss the revelations of the concentration camps, and given Allen's current preoccupation with this topic, it would not seem idle speculation to assume that it had its seeds in his upbringing.

16. Typical is Kenneth Turan's review in the Los Angeles Times (March 20, 1992). He calls it "an underwritten tale."

17. Once again, I am surprised when Desser and Friedman say that the movie's references to the Holocaust are "subtle" (101n), when the film positively shrieks with references to this event.

18. This film is based loosely on Allen's earlier play, *Death*, but does not incorporate its downer ending.

19. For whatever reason, Allen has little sympathy for the Catholic church, as is revealed in his none-too-subtle putdown of it in *Hannah*, when in the process of considering conversion the Allen character brings home a cross, mayonnaise, and Wonder Bread. While some have seen this as a joke about *goyishe* taste buds, it could also be a sly reference to the idea of bread being the body of Christ and thus the "wonder" bread (i.e., Jesus), a food considered tasteless and abhorrent to the Jew. Only Mel Brooks in his "The Inquisition" sequence in *History of the World Part One* (1981) tackles the involvement of the Catholic church in the torture of Jews with such explicitness.

20. It could also be said that "Random" is a meditation on this very point.

21. While Cliff would seem to be the character closest to Allen, P. Adams Sitney suggests that Lester, with his successes and academic acceptance, most clearly resembles Allen character, an opinion that certainly puts an interesting spin on Allen's self-perception (Sitney, 61).

22. What seems perfectly organic on the screen was, in fact, the result of many rewrites and compromises (Lax, 365–68). One can only be thankful that given his later troubles, Allen dropped the original last line of the movie: "Little girls are the hope of the world."

23. Quoted from an unpublished sermon given on 5 January 1990 to the Bet Shalom Congregation in Hopkins, Minn.

24. Borowitz suggests Ecclesiastes as the model rather than Job: "Ecclesiastes knew. He said there is no justice, no distinction between the righteous and the wicked, only a world indifferent to our acts" (Borowitz quoted in Steinfels, 29). Sitney, while acknowledging this suggestion as "interesting," says that Allen would never subscribe to the ultimately religious message of the text: "There is a time and a judgement for everything" (64).

25. A noted exception is Sitney, who calls him "coyingly sweet" (46) and "saccharine" (59).

26. In fact, as I intend to prove, he is not like either May or Judah.

27. The use of the Passover seder may be coincidental but it is certainly fortuitous and very appropriate. Ancient commentators like Rashi and Ibn Ezra, for example, while elaborating on the Biblical text in Exodus 1, vs. 8–22, describe circumstances in Egypt that would unfortunately repeat themselves in the concentration camps. With its enforced servitude (under other Hebrew slaves as well as Egyptian overseers), slaughter of male children, and ghettoization of the Hebrews into separate territories, the slavery of the Hebrews in Egypt serves as a paradigm for both anti-Semitic regimes through the ages as well as the Holocaust, to which it bears an uncanny resemblance. The Midrashic commentator Yalkut Shimony, for example, commenting on Deuteronomy 25, notes that the Egyptians kept meticulous records on each slave, again presaging the documentation of the Nazis.

I am indebted to Rabbi A. Gellman of Young Israel in Santa Barbara, California, for pointing out these parallels.

28. Allen has made good use of the seder in his movies. There are references to Passover in *Take the Money and Run* and *Sleeper*, as well as *Crimes* . The only other Jewish holiday to get this much attention is the fast day of Yom Kippur (*Radio Days* and *Annie Hall*). On the secular side, Allen is partial to Thanksgiving (*Broadway Danny Rose* and *Hannah*). The only Christian holiday he mentions is Easter (*Annie Hall*). In this respect, he is similar to many Jewish filmmakers who shy away from Christmas, preferring the more secular holiday of Thanksgiving.

29. Furthermore, Allen presents her as warm, and quick to laugh and respond with amusement to the younger members of the family circle.

30. Sitney and Desser; Friedman et al.

31. To complicate matters even more, the story of Abraham and Isaac has been used by Allen in his writings and in at least one other movie, *Manhattan*. Did Allen write Levy/Bergmann's lines? Did Bergmann write his own lines and agree to Allen's naming him after another, better-known Holocaust writer?

It should also be noted that many theologians who deal with the Holocaust use the Biblical story of Abraham and Isaac as a motif. See, for example, Fackenheim and Sherwin.

32. When Cliff, on hearing the news of Levy's suicide remarks, "[He] always said 'yes' to life,'yes, yes.' Today he said 'no,'" he seems to be making light of Primo Levi, rather than presenting it in a sympathetic manner.

33. In some ways, this ending harkens back to *Hannah*, in which Allen ultimately finds salvation through watching a movie, the Marx Brothers' *Duck Soup*.

34. Not wishing to make this matter too confusing, I repeat Rabbi Cohen's observations that Judah also struggles with his conscience in a dreamlike sequence not unlike the

encounter of Jacob with the angel (Genesis 32: 24–32).

35. I am indebted to Rabbi Cohen for first pointing out the significance of the names and also the point in the seder at which Judah enters, though I have taken the liberty of adding my own interpretation to his readings.

Works Cited

Allen, Woody. "Am I Reading the Papers Correctly?" *New York Times*, 28 January 1988, 22.

—. "Random Reflections of a Second-Rate Mind." In *The Best American Essays, 1991*, edited by Joyce Carol Oates, 1–8. New York: Ticknor & Fields, 1991.

Berenbaum, Michael. *After Tragedy and Triumph*. Cambridge: Cambridge University Press, 1990.

Bergmann, Martin S. *In The Shadow of Moloch*. New York: Columbia University Press, 1993.

Berkovitz, Eliezer. *Faith After The Holocaust*. New York: Ktav, 1973.

Buber, Martin. *The Eclipse of God*. New York: Harper & Row, 1952.

Cohen, Norman. 1990. Unpublished Sermon. Bet Shalom Congregation, Hopkins, Minn., 5 January.

Cohn-Sherbook, Dan. "Life after Death," *London Jewish Chronicle*, 22 December 1989, 24.

Desser, David, and Lester D. Friedman. *American-Jewish Filmmakers: Traditions and Trends*. Chicago: University of Illinois Press, 1993.

Dresner, Samuel. "Woody Allen, Theologian?" *Midstream* (March 1985): Vol. XXXI, no. 3, 73–75.

Erens, Patricia Brett. "No Closer to Eden." *Sight and Sound* 3 (June 1993): 20–23.

Fackenheim, Emil. *God's Presence in History: Jewish Affirmations and Philosophical Reflections*. New York: New York University Press, 1970.

Gopnik, Adam. "The Outsider." *New Yorker*, 25 October 1993, 86–93.

Hass, Aaron. *In the Shadow of the Holocaust: The Second Generation*. Ithaca, N.Y.: Cornell University Press, 1990.

Hertzberg, Arthur. "A Lifelong Quarrel With God." *New York Times Book Review*, 6 May 1990, 1, 39, 40.

Jacobs, Louis, ed. *Jewish Thought Today*. New York: Behrman House, 1970.

Lax, Eric. *Woody Allen: A Biography*. New York: Alfred A. Knopf, 1991.

Levi, Primo. *Survival in Auschwitz*. New York: MacMillan, 1961.

Maza, Bernard. *With Fury Poured out*. Hoboken, N.J.: Ktav, 1986.

Roiphe, Anne. *A Season for Healing: Reflections on the Holocaust*. New York: Summit, 1988.

Rosenbaum, Jonathan. "Notes towards the Depreciation of Woody Allen." *Tikkun* 5 (May-June 1990): 33–35, 98–100.

Shechner, Mark. "Comics and Comedy." In *Jewish-American History and Culture: An Encyclopedia*, edited by Jack Fischel and Sanford Pinsker, 97–104. New York: Garland, 1992.

Sherwin, Byron, L. "The Impotence of Explanation and the European Holocaust." *Tradition*, Vol. 13 (1971): 99–106.

Sitney, P. Adams. "Cinematic Election and Theological Vanity." *Raritan* 11 (Fall 1991): 48–64.

Steinfels, Peter. "Woody Allen Counts the Wages of Sin." *New York Times*, 15 October 1989, Vol. 15–16.

Weisel, Elie. "Trivializing the Holocaust: Semi-Fact and Semi-Fiction." *New York Times*, 29 April 1986, 1, 29.

Selected Bibliography

Allen, Woody. *Four Films of Woody Allen*. New York: Random House, 1982.

Benayoun, Robert. *The Films of Woody Allen*. Translated by Alexander Walkers. New York: Harmony Books, 1985.

Blair, Walter, *Horse Sense in American Humor*. Chicago: University of Chicago Press, 1942.

Blake, Richard. "Looking for God: Profane and Sacred in the Films of Woody Allen." *Journal of Popular Film and Television* 19 (2). 58–66 (1991).

Brode, Douglas. *Woody Allen: His Films and Career*. Seacaucus, N.J.: Citadel Press, 1987.

Desser, David, and Lester D. Freidman. *American-Jewish Filmmakers: Traditions and Trends*. Chicago: University of Illinois Press, 1993.

Doane, Mary Ann. "Film and the Masquerade: Theorising the Female Spectator." *Screen* 23(3–4): 74–87 (1982).

Drew, Bernard. "Woody Allen Is Feeling Better." *American Film* 2(7): 10–15 (1977).

Durgnat, Raymond. *The Crazy Mirror: Hollywood Comedy and the American Image*. New York: Dell, 1969.

Girgus, Sam B. *The Films of Woody Allen*. Cambridge: Cambridge University Press, 1993.

Guthrie, Lee. *Woody Allen: A Biography*. New York: Drake, 1978.

Halberstadt, Ira. "Scenes from a Mind: Woody Allen Is Nobody's Fool." *Take One* 6(12): 16–20 (1978).

Hedges, Inez. *Breaking the Frame: Film Language and the Experience of Limits*. Bloomington: Indiana University Press, 1991.

Hirsch, Foster. *Love, Sex, Death and the Meaning of Life: Woody Allen's Comedy*. New York: McGraw-Hill, 1981.

Hutcheon, Linda. *A Theory of Parody*. New York: Methuen, 1985.

Jacobs, Diane. *. . . but we need the eggs: The Magic of Woody Allen*. New York: St. Martin's, 1982.

James, Caryn. "Auteur! Auteur!" *New York Times Magazine,* 19 January 1986, 25.

Kapp, Isa. "A Cowering Man of Sensibility." *New Leaders,* 58 (26 May 1975): 11.

Lax, Eric. *On Being Funny: Woody Allen and Comedy.* New York: Charterhouse, 1975.

————. *Woody Allen.* New York: Alfred Knopf, 1991.

Pogel, Nancy. *Woody Allen.* Boston: Twayne, 1987.

Rosenbaum, Jonathan. "Notes Towards the Depreciation of Woody Allen." *Tikkun* 5 (May-June 1990): 33–35, 98–100.

Ruben, David. *Everything You Have Always Wanted to Know about Sex* but Were Afraid to Ask.* New York: David McKay, 1969.

Schatz, Thomas. *Hollywood Genres: Formulas, Filmmaking, and the Studio System.* New York: Random House, 1981.

Shechner, Mark. "Comics and Comedy." In *Jewish-American History and Culture: An Encyclopedia,* edited by Jack and Sanford Pinsker. New York: Garland, 1992: 97–104.

Sitney, P. Adams. "Cinematic Election and Theological Vanity." *Raritan* 11, no. 2 (Fall 1991): 48–64.

Stam, Robert. "A Tale of Two Cities: Cultural Polyphony and Ethnic Transformation." *East West Film Journal* 3 (1): 105–116 (1988).

Wetzsteon, Ross. "Woody Allen: Schlemiel as Sex Maniac." *Ms.* 6, no. 5 (November 1977): 14–15.

Yates, Norris. *The American Humorist: Conscience of the Twentieth Century.* Ames: Iowa State University Press, 1964.

Yacowar, Maurice. *Loser Take All: The Comic Art of Woody Allen.* New York: Frederick Ungar, 1979.

An Allen Filmography

1965

What's New, Pussycat?

Screenplay: Woody Allen

Director: Clive Donner

Director of photography: Jean Badel

Editing: Fergus McDonell

Music: Burt Bacharach

Producer: Charles K. Feldman

Distributor: United Artists

Cast: Peter Sellers (Fritz Fassbender); Peter O'Toole (Michael James); Romy Schneider (Carol Werner); Capucine (Renee Lefebvre); Paula Prentiss (Liz Bien); Woody Allen (Victor Shakapopolis); Ursula Andress (Rita); Edra Gale (Anna Fassbender); Catherine Schaake (Jacqueline); Jess Hahn (Perry Werner); Nicole Karen (Tempest O'Brien); Jean Paredes (Marcel); Jacqueline Fogt (Charlotte); Jacques Balutin (Etienne); Annette Poivre (Emma); Sabine Sun (Beautiful Nurse); Tanya Lopert (Miss Lewis); Colin Drake (Durell); Louise Lasser (The Nutcracker); Richard Saint-Bris (The Mayor); Francoise Hardy (Mayor's Secretary); Richard Burton (Man in Bar)

Running time: 106 min.

1966

What's Up, Tiger Lily? (Original Japanese version)

Screenplay: Hideo Ando

Director: Senkichi Taniguchi

Director of photography: Kazuo Yamada

Editing: Unknown

Music: Unknown

Producer: Tomoyuki Tanaka

Production company: Toho

Cast: Tatsuya Mihashi (Phil Moskowitz), Mie Hama (Terry Yaki), Akiko Wakayabayashi (Suki Yaki), Tadao Nakamaru (Shepherd Wong), Susumu Kurobe (Wing Fat)

1966

What's Up, Tiger Lily? (American version)

Sreenplay: Woody Allen, Frank Buxton, Len Maxwell, Louise Lasser, Mickey Rose, Julie Bennett, Bryna Wilson

Director: Woody Allen

Director of photography: Kazuo Yamada

Editing: Richard Krown

Music: Jack Lewis, Lovin' Spoonful

Producer: Ben Shapiro

Distibutor: American International Pictures

Cast: Woody Allen, Frank Buxton, Len Maxwell, Louise Lasser, Mickey Rose, Julie Bennett, Bryna Wilson

1967

Casino Royale

Screenplay: Wolf Mankowitz, John Law, Michael Sayers; suggested by a novel by Ian Fleming

Directors: John Huston, Kenneth Hughes, Val Guest, Robert Parrish, Joseph McGrath

Director of photography: Jack Hildyard

Editing: Bill Lenny

Music: Burt Bacharach

Producers: Charles K. Feldman, Jerry Bresler

Distributor: Columbia

Cast: Peter Sellers (Evelyn Tremble); Ursula Andress (Vesper Lynd); David Niven (Sir James Bond); Orson Welles (Le Chiffre); Joanna Pettet (Mata Bond); Deborah Kerr (Widow McTarry); Daliah Lavi (The Detainer); Woody Allen (Jimmy Bond); William Holden (Ransome); Charles Boyer (Le Grand); John Huston ("M"); Kurt Kaznar (Smernov); George Raft (Himself); Jean-Paul Belmondo (French Foreign Legion Soldier); Terence Cooper (Agent .007); Barbara Bouchet (Miss Moneypenny); Angela Scoular (Buttercup); Gabriella Licudi (Eliza); Tracey Crisp (Heather); Jacqueline Bisset (Miss Goodthighs); Anna Quayle (Frau Hoffner); Bernard Cribbens (Taxi Driver); Tracy Reed (Fang Leader); Percy Herbert (First Piper); Man in Bar (Peter O'Toole)

Running time: 131 min.

1969

Don't Drink the Water

Screenplay: R. S. Allen, Harvey Bullock; after a play by Woody Allen

Director: Howard Morris

Director of photography: Harvey Genkins

Editing: Ralph Rosenblum

Music: Pat Williams

Producer: Charles Joffe

Production company/Distributor: Avco Embassy

Cast: Jackie Gleason (Walter Hollander); Estelle Parsons (Marian Hollander); Ted Bessel (Axel Mayee); Joan Delaney (Susan Hollander); Michael Constantine (Krojack); Howard St. John (Ambassador Mayee); Danny Meehan (Kilroy); Richard Libertini (Father Drobney); Pierre Olaf (The Chef); Avery Schreiber (The Sultan); Mark Gordon (Merik); Phil Leeds (Sam); Howard Morris (Pilot of Escape Plane)

Running time/Rating: 98 min./G

1969

Take the Money and Run

Screenplay: Woody Allen, Mickey Rose

Director: Woody Allen

Director of photography: Lester Shorr

Editing: Paul Jordan, Ron Kalish

Music: Marvin Hamlisch

Producer: Charles H. Joffe

Production company: Palomar Pictures

Cast: Woody Allen (Virgil Starkwell); Janet Margolin (Louise); Marcel Hillaire (Fritz); Jacqueline Hyde (Miss Blair, the Blackmailer); Lonny Chapman (Sake); Jan Merlin (Al); James Anderson (Chain Gang Warden); Howard Storm (Fred); Mark Gordon (Mince); Micil Murphy (Frank); Minnow Moskowitz (Joe Agneta); Nate Jacobson (The Judge); Grace Bauer (Farm House Lady); Ethel Sokolow (Mother Starkwell); Henry Leff (Father Starkwell); Don Frazier (The Psychiatrist); Mike O'Dowd (Michael Sullivan); Louise Lasser (Kay Lewis); Jackson Beck (The Narrator)

Running time/Rating: 85 min./M (Mature)

1971

Bananas

Screenplay: Woody Allen, Mickey Rose

Director: Woody Allen

Director of photography: Andrew M. Costikyan

Editing: Ron Kalish

Music: Marvin Hamlisch

Producer: Jack Grossberg

Production company: Rollins-Joffe/United Artists

Cast: Woody Allen (Fielding Mellish); Louise Lasser (Nancy); Carlos Montalban (General Parkas); Natividad Abascal (Yolanda); Jacobo Morales (Esposito); Miguel Suarez (Lois); David Ortiz (Sanchez); Rene Enriquez (Diaz); Jack Axelrod (Arroyo); Howard Cosell (Himself); Roger Grimsby (Himself); Don Dunphy (Himself); Charlotte Rae (Mrs. Mellish); Stanley Ackerman (Dr. Mellish); Dan Frazer (Priest); Martha Greenhouse (Dr. Feigen); Axel Anderson Tortured Man); Dorthi Fox (J. Edgar Hoover); Dagne Crane (Sharon); Conrad Bain (Semple); Allen Garfield (Man on Cross); Princess Fatosh (Snakebite Lady); Hy Anzel (Patient); Sylvester Stallone (Street Hood)

Running time/Rating: 81 min./PG

1972

Play It Again, Sam

Screenplay: Woody Allen, after his play

Director: Herbert Ross

Director of photography: Owen Roizman

Editing: Marion Rothman

Music: Billy Goldenberg

Producer: Arthur P. Jacobs

Distributor: Paramount

Cast: Woody Allen (Allan Felix); Diane Keaton (Linda Christie); Tony Roberts (Dick Christie); Jerry Lacy (Bogey); Susan Anspach (Nancy); Jennifer Salt (Sharon); Joy Bang (Julie); Viva (Jennifer the Nymphomaniac); Suzanne Zenor (Disco Girl); Diana Davila (Suicidal Museum Girl); Mari Fletcher (Fantasy Sharon); Michael Green and Ted Markland (Motorcycle Hoods)

Running time/Rating: 85 min./PG

1972

Everything You Always Wanted to Know about Sex* (*but were afraid to ask)

Screenplay: Woody Allen, after the book by David Reuben

Director: Woody Allen

Director of photography: David M. Walsh

Editing: Eric Albertson

Music: Mundel Lowe

Producer: Charles H. Joffe

Distributor: United Artists

Cast: Woody Allen (Fool, Fabrizio, Victor, Cowardly Sperm); John Carradine (Dr. Bernardo); Lou Jacobi (Sam); Louise Lasser (Gina); Anthony Quayle (King); Tony Randall (Operator); Lynn Redgrave (Queen); Burt Reynolds (Switchboard); Gene Wilder (Dr. Ross); Jack Barry (Himself); Erin Fleming (The Gorgeous Girl); Elaine Giftos (Mrs. Ross); Toni Holt (Herself); Robert Q. Lewis (Himself); Heather McRae (Helen); Pamela Mason (Herself), Regis Philbin (Himself); Titos Vandis (Milos); Stanley Adams (Stomach Operator); Oscar Beregi (Brain Controller); Alan Caillou (Fool's Father); Geoffrey Holder (The Sorcerer); Jay Robinson (Priest); Ref Sanchez (Igor); Baruch Lumet (Rabbi Baumel); Robert Walden (Sperm)

Running time/Rating: 87 min./R

1973

Sleeper

Screenplay: Woody Allen, Marshall Brickman

Director: Woody Allen

Director of photography: David M. Walsh

Editing: Ralph Rosenblum

Music: Woody Allen, Preservation Hall Jazz Band, New Orleans Funeral Ragtime Orchestra

Producer: Jack Grossberg, Executive Producer: Charles H. Joffe

Distibutor: United Artists

Cast: Woody Allen (Miles Monroe); Diane Keaton (Lana Schlosser); John Beck (Erno Windt); Mary Gregory (Dr. Melik); Don Keefer (Dr. Tryon); John McLiam (Dr. Agon); Bartlett Robinson (Dr. Orva); Chris Forbes (Rainer Krebs); Marya Small (Dr. Nero); Susan Miller (Ellen Pogrebin); Lou Picetti (Master of Ceremonies); Jessica Rains (Woman in Mirror); Spencer Milligan (Jeb Hrmthmg)

Running time/Rating: 88 min./PG

1975

Love and Death

Screenplay: Woody Allen

Director: Woody Allen

Director of photography: Ghislain Cloquet

Editing: Ralph Rosenblum, Ron Kalish

Music: Sergei Prokofiev

Producer: Charles H. Joffe

Distributor: United Artists

Cast: Woody Allen (Boris); Diane Keaton (Sonia); Frank Adu (Drill Sergeant); Lloyd Battista (Don Francisco); Olga Georges-Picot (Countess Alexandrovna); Harold Gould (Count Anton); Jessica Harper (Natasha); Jack Lenoir (Krapotkin); James Tolkan (Napoleon); C. A. R. Smith (Father Nikolai); Georges Adet (Old Nehamken); Patricia Crown (Cheerleader); Harry Hankin (Uncle Sasha); Alfred Lutter III (Young Boris); Denise Peron (Spanish Countess); Zvee Scooler (Father); Beth Porter (Anna); Henry Czarniak (Ivan); Despo Diamantidou (Mother); Florian (Uncle Nicolai); Brian Coburn (Dmitri); Luce Fabiole (Grandmother)
Running time/Rating: 85 min./PG

1976

The Front

Screenplay: Walter Bernstein

Director: Martin Ritt

Director of photography: Michael Chapman

Editing: Sidney Levin

Music: David Grusin

Producer: Martin Ritt, Executive Producer: Charles H. Joffe

Distributor: Columbia

Cast: Woody Allen (Howard Prince); Zero Mostel (Hey Brown); Herschel Bernardi (Phil Sussman); Michaz Murphy (Al Miller); Andrea Marcovicci (Florence Barrett); Marvin Lichterman (Myer Prince); Lloyd Gough (Delaney); David Margulies (Phelps); Norman Rob (Howard's Attorney); Charles Kimbrough (Committe Counselor); M. Josef Sommer (Committee Chairman); Danny Aiello (Danny La Gattuta); Marilyn Sokol (Sandy); John "Jack" Slater (TV Director)
Running time/Rating: 94 min./R

1977

Annie Hall

Screenplay: Woody Allen, Marshall Brickman

Director: Woody Allen

Director of photography: Gordon Willis

Editing: Ralph Rosenblum

Producer: Charles H. Joffe

Executive producer: Robert Greenhut

Distributor: United Artists

Cast: Woody Allen (Alvy Singer); Diane Keaton (Annie Hall); Tony Roberts (Rob); Carol Kane (Allison); Paul Simon (Tony Lacy); Shelley Duvall (Pam); Janet Margolin (Robin); Colleen Dewhurst (Mom Hall); Christopher Walken (Duane Hall); Donald Symington

(Dad Hall); Helen Ludlam (Grammy Hall); Mordecai Lawner (Alvy's Dad); Joan Newman (Alvy's Mom); Jonathan Munk (Alvy, Age 9); Ruth Volner (Alvy's Aunt); Martin Rosenblatt (Alvy's Uncle); Hy Ansel (Joey Nichols); Rashel Novikoff (Aunt Jessie); Russell Horton (Man in Theatre Line); Marshall McLuhan (himself); John Doumanian (Coke fiend); Bob Maroff and Rick Petrucelli (Men outside Theatre); Dick Cavett (himself); Johnny Haymer (Comic); Lauri Bird (Tony Lacy's Girlfriend); Jeff Goldblum (Party Guest); Humphrey Davis, Veronica Radbum (Analysts); Shelly Hack (Pretty Girl on Street); Beverly D'Angelo (Star of Rob's TV Show); Sigouney Weaver (Alvy's Date at End); Walter Bernstein (Annie's Date at End)
Running time/Rating: 93 min./PG

1978
Interiors
Screenplay: Woody Allen
Director: Woody Allen
Director of photography: Gordon Willis
Editing: Ralph Rosenblum
Producer: Charles H. Joffe
Executive producer: Robert Greenhut
Distributor: United Artists
Cast: Kristen Griffith (Flynn); Marybeth Hurt (Joey); Richard Jordan (Frederick); Diane Keaton (Renata); E. G. Marshall (Arthur); Geraldine Page (Eve); Maureen Stapleton (Pearl); Sam Waterston (Mike); Missy Hope (Young Joey); Kerry Duffy (Young Renata); Nancy Collins (Young Flynn); Penny Gaston (Young Eve); Roger Morden (Young Arthur); Henderson Forsythe (Judge Bartel)
Running time/Rating: 93 min./PG

1979
Manhattan
Screenplay: Woody Allen, Marshall Brickman
Director: Woody Allen
Director of photography: Gordon Willis
Editing: Susan E. Morse
Music: George Gershwin
Producer: Charles H. Joffe
Executive producer: Robert Greenhut
Distributor: United Artists
Cast: Woody Allen (Isaac Davis); Diane Keaton (Mary); Michael Murphy (Yale); Mariel Hemingway (Tracy); Meryl Streep (Jill);

Anne Byrne (Emily); Karen Ludwig (Connie); Michael O'Donoghue (Dennis); Victor Truro, Tisa Farrow, Helen Hanft (Party Guests); Bella Abzug (Guest of Honor); Gary Weiss (TV Director); Karen Allen (TV Actress); Damion Sheller (Ike's Son); Wallace Shawn (Jeremiah); Mark Linn-Baker (Shakespearean Actor); John Doumanian (Porsche Owner)

Running time/Rating: 96 min./R

1980
Stardust Memories
Screenplay: Woody Allen
Director: Woody Allen
Director of photography: Gordon Willis
Editing: Susan E. Morse
Producer: Robert Greenhut
Executive producers: Jack Rollins, Charles H. Joffe
Distributor: United Artists

Cast: Woody Allen (Sandy Bates); Charlotte Rampling (Dorrie); Jessica Harper (Daisy); Marie-Christine Barrault (Isobel); Tony Roberts (Tony); Daniel Stern (Actor); Amy Wright (Shelley); Helen Hanft (Vivian Orkin); John Rothman (Jack Abel); Anne DeSalvo (Sandy's Sister); Joan Neuman (Sandy's Mother); Ken Chapin (Sandy's Father); Leonardo Cimino (Sandy's Analyst); Eli Mintz (Old Man); David Lipman (George, Sandy's Chauffeur); Robert Munk (Sandy as a Boy); Sharon Stone (Pretty girl on train); Jack Rollins (Studio Executive); Howard Kissel (Sandy's Manager); Judith Crist (Critic); Louise Lasser (Sandy's Secretary); John Doumanian (Armenian Fan).

Running time/Rating: 89 min./PG

1982
A Midsummer Night's Sex Comedy
Screenplay: Woody Allen
Director: Woody Allen
Director of photography: Gordon Willis
Editing: Susan E. Morse
Producer: Robert Greenhut
Executive producer: Charles H. Joffe
Distributor: Orion

Cast: Woody Allen (Andrew); Mia Farrow (Ariel); Jose Ferrer (Leopold); Julie Hagerty (Dulcy); Tony Roberts (Maxwell); Mary Steenburgen (Adrian); Adam Redfield (Student Foxx); Moishe Rosenfeld (Mr. Hayes); Timothy Jenkins (Mr. Thomson); Michael

Higgins (Reynolds); Sol Frieder (Carstairs); Boriss Zoubok (Purvis); Thomas Barbour (Blint); Kate McGregor-Stewart (Mrs. Baker)
Running time/Rating: 94 min./PG

1983
Zelig
Screenplay: Woody Allen
Director: Woody Allen
Director of photography: Gordon Willis
Editing: Susan E. Morse
Music: Dick Hyman
Producer: Robert Greenhut
Executive producer: Charles H. Joffe
Distributor: Orion
Cast: Woody Allen (Leonard Zelig); Mia Farrow (Dr. Eudora Fletcher); Ellen Garrison (Older Dr. Fletcher); Mary Louise Wilson (Sister Ruth); Stephanie Farrow (Sister Meryl); John Doumanian (Greek Waiter); Erma Campbell (Zelig's Wife); Jean Trowbridge (Dr. Fletcher's Mother); Deborah Rush (Lita Fox); Contemporary Interviews: Susan Sontag, Irving Howe, Saul Bellow, Bricktop, Dr. Bruno Bettelheim, Prof. John Morton Blum (Themselves); Announcers: Ed Herlihy, Dwight Weist, Gordon Gould, Windy Craig, Jurgen Kuehn (Themselves); Narration: Patrick Horgan
Running time/Rating: 79 min./PG

1984
Broadway Danny Rose
Screenplay: Woody Allen
Director: Woody Allen
Director of photography: Gordon Willis
Editing: Susan E. Morse
Producer: Robert Greenhut, Executive Producer: Charles H. Joffe
Distributor: Orion
Cast: Woody Allen (Danny Rose); Mia Farrow (Tina Vitale); Nick Apollo Forte (Lou Canova); The Carnegie Deli Comics: Corbett Monica, Howard Storm, Morty Gunty, Sandy Baron, Will Jordan, Jackie Gayle, Jack Rollins (Themselves); Milton Berle (Himself); Howard Cosell (Himself); Joe Franklin (Himself); Craig Vanderburgh (Ray Webb); Hugh Reynolds (Barney Dunn); Paul Greco (Vito Rispoli); Frank Renzulli (Joe Rispoli); Edwin Bordo (Johnny Rispoli); Gina De Angelis (Johnny's Mother); Gloria Parker (Water Glass Virtuoso); Bob and Etta Rollins (Balloon Act); John Doumanian (Waldorf Manager); Leo Steiner (Deli Owner)
Running time/Rating: 85 min./PG

1985

The Purple Rose of Cairo

Screenplay: Woody Allen

Director: Woody Allen

Director of photography: Gordon Willis

Editing: Susan E. Morse

Music: Dick Hyman

Producer: Robert Greenhut, Executive Producer: Charles H. Joffe

Distributor: Orion

Cast: Mia Farrow (Cecilia); Jeff Daniels (Tom Baxter, Gil Shepherd); Danny Aiello (Monk); Irving Metzman (Theatre Manager); Stephanie Farrow (Cecilia 's Sister); David Kieserman (Diner Boss); Ed Herrmann (Henry); John Wood (Jason); Deborah Rush (Rita); Van Johnson (Larry); Zoe Caldwell (The Countess); Eugene Anthony (Arturo); Ebb Miller (Bandleader); Karen Akers (Kitty Haynes); Annie Joe Edwards (Delilah); Milo O'Shea (Father Donnelly); Dianne Wiest (Emma); Helen Hanft (Movie Viewer)

Running time/Rating: 81 min./PG

1986

Hannah and Her Sisters

Screenplay: Woody Allen

Director: Woody Allen

Director of photography: Carlo di Palma

Editing: Susan E. Morse

Producer: Robert Greenhut, Executive Producers: Jack Rollins and Charles H. Joffe

Distributor: Orion

Cast: Woody Allen (Mickey); Michael Caine (Elliot); Mia Farrow (Hannah); Carrie Fisher (April); Barbara Hersey (Lee); Lloyd Nolan (Hannah's Father); Maureen O'Sullivan (Hannah's Mother); Daniel Stern (Dusty); Max Von Sydow (Frederick); Dianne Wiest (Holly); Sam Waterston (The Architect); Tony Roberts (Mickey's Friend); Helen Miller, Leo Postrel (Mickey's Parents); Bobby Short (Himself); John Doumanian (Thanksgiving Guest)

Running time/Rating: 106 min./PG-13

1987

September

Screenplay: Woody Allen

Director: Woody Allen

Director of photography: Carlo di Palma

Editing: Susan E. Morse

Producer: Robert Greenhut, Executive Producers: Jack Rollins and Charles H. Joffe

Distributor: Orion

Cast: Mia Farrow (Lane); Elaine Stritch (Diane); Denholm Elliott (Howard); Dianne Wiest (Stephanie); Sam Waterston (Peter); Jack Warden (Lloyd); Ira Wheeler (Mr. Raines); Jane Cecil (Mrs. Raines); Rosemary Murphy (Mrs. Mason)

Running time/Rating: 82 min./PG

1987

Radio Days

Screenplay: Woody Allen

Director: Woody Allen

Director of photography: Carlo di Palma

Editing: Susan E. Morse

Producer: Robert Greenhut

Distributor: Orion

Cast: Julie Kavner (Mother); Wallace Shawn (Masked Avenger); Seth Green (Joe); Michael Tucker (Father); Josh Mostel (Abe); Joy Newman (Ruthie); Hy Anzell (Mr. Waldbaum); Dianne Wiest (Bea); Kenneth Mars (Rabbi Baumel); Mia Farrow (Sally); Tito Puente (Latin Bandleader); Danny Aiello (Rocco); Jeff Daniels (Biff Baxter); Kitty Carlisle Hart (Radio Singer); Tony Roberts (Emcee); Diane Keaton (Singer)

Running time/Rating: 91 min./PG

1988

Another Woman

Screenplay: Woody Allen

Director: Woody Allen

Director of photography: Sven Nykvist

Editing: Susan E. Morse

Producer: Robert Greenhut, Executive Producers: Jack Rollins and Charles H. Joffe

Distributor: Orion

Cast: Gena Rowlands (Marion); Mia Farrow (Hope); Ian Holm (Ken); Blythe Danner (Lydia); Gene Hackman (Larry); Betty Buckley (Kathy); Martha Plimpton (Laura); John Houseman (Marion's Father); Sandy Dennis (Claire); David Ogden Stiers (Young Marion's Father); Philip Bosco (Sam); Harris Yulin (Paul); Frances Controy (Lynn); Caroline McGee (Young Marion's Mother); Margaret Marx (Young Marion)

Running time/Rating: 84 min./PG

1989

Oedipus Wrecks (short film in omnibus *New York Stories*)

Screenplay: Woody Allen

Director: Woody Allen

Director of photography: Sven Nykvist

Editing: Susan E. Morse

Producer: Robert Greenhut

Distributor: Touchstone Pictures

Cast: Woody Allen (Sheldon Miles); Mia Farrow (Lisa); Julie Kavner (Treva); Mae Questel (Sadie Millstein); Marvin Chatinover (Psychiatrist); Jessie Koesian (Aunt Ceil); George Schindler (Shandu the Magician); Bridgit Ryan (Rita); Mayor Edward I. Koch (Himself)

Running time/Rating: 45 min.

1989

Crimes and Misdemeanors

Screenplay: Woody Allen

Director: Woody Allen

Director of photography: Sven Nykvist

Editing: Susan E. Morse

Producer: Robert Greenhut

Distributor: Orion

Cast: Martin Landau (Judah Rosenthal); Woody Allen (Cliff Stern); Mia Farrow (Halley Reed); Alan Alda (Lester); Sam Waterston (Ben); Anjelica Huston (Dolores Paley); Joanna Gleason (Wendy); Caroline Aaron (Barbara); Jerry Orbach (Jack); Daryl Hannah (Starlet); Claire Bloom (Miriam); Jenny Nichols (Jenny); Martin Bergmann (Levy); Stephanie Roth (Sharon Rosenthal); David S. Howard (Sol)

Running time/Rating: 104 min./PG-13

1991

Alice

Screenplay: Woody Allen

Director: Woody Allen

Director of photography: Carlo di Palma

Editing: Susan E. Morse

Producer: Robert Greenhut

Distributor: Orion

Cast: Mia Farrow (Alice); Joe Mantegna (Joe); William Hurt (Doug); Keye Luke (Dr. Yang); Alec Baldwin (Ed); Blythe Danner (Dorothy); Judy Davis (Vicki); Bernadette Peters (Muse); Cybill

Shepherd (Nancy Brill); Elle Macpherson (Herself); Patrick O'Neal (Alice's Father); James Toback (Professor); David Spielberg (Ken); Judith Ivey (Alice's Friend); Bob Balaban (Sid Moscowitz); Julie Kavner (Decorator)

Running time/Rating: 106 min./PG-13

1992

Scenes from a Mall

Screenplay: Roger L. Simon, Paul Mazursky

Director: Paul Mazursky

Director of photography: Fred Murphy

Editing: Stuart Pappe

Music: Marc Schaiman

Producer: Paul Mazursky

Distributor: Touchstone Pictures

Cast: Bette Midler (Deborah); Woody Allen (Nick); Bill Irwin (Mime); Daren Firestone (Sam); Rebecca Nickels (Jennifer); Paul Mazursky (Dr. Hans Clava); Jack Brodsky (Pharmacist); Patrick Ferrelly (Santa); Kamarr (Magician)

Running time/Rating: 87 min./R

1992

Shadows and Fog

Screenplay: Woody Allen

Director of Photography: Carlo Di Palma

Editing: Susan E. Morse

Producer: Robert Greenhut, Executive Producers: Jack Rollins and Charles H. Joffe

Distributor: Orion

Cast: Woody Allen (Kleinman); Kathy Bates (Prostitute); John Cusack (a john); Mia Farrow (Irmy the Sword-Swallower); Jodie Foster (Prostitute); Madonna (Circus Fortune-Teller); John Malkovich (Paul the Clown); Kate Nelligan (Prostitute); Lily Tomlin (Brothel Madame).

1992

Husbands and Wives

Screenplay: Woody Allen

Director: Woody Allen

Director of Photography: Carlo Di Palma

Editing: Susan E. Morse

Producer: Robert Greenhut

Distributor: TriStar

Cast: Mia Farrow (Judy Roth); Woody Allen (Gabe Roth); Judy Davis (Sally); Blythe Danner (Rain's Mother); Juliette Lewis (Rain); Liam Neeson (Michael); Sydney Pollack (Jack); Cristi Conaway (Shawn Granger)

Running Time/Rating: 108 min./R

1993

Manhattan Murder Mystery

Screenplay: Woody Allen

Director: Woody Allen

Director of Photography: Carlo Di Palma

Editing: Susan E. Morse

Producer: Robert Greenhut, Executive Producers: Jack Rollins and Charles H. Joffe

Distributor: TriStar

Cast: Alan Alda (Ted); Woody Allen (Larry Lipton); Anjelica Huston (Marcia Fox); Diane Keaton (Carol Lipton); Jerry Adler (Paul House); Joy Behar (Marilyn); Ron Rifkin (Sy)

Running Time/Rating: 107 min./PG

1994

Bullets over Broadway

Screenplay: Woody Allen, Douglas McGarth

Director: Woody Allen

Director of photography: Carlo Di Palma

Editing: Susan E. Morse

Producer: Robert Greenhut

Distributor: Sweetland

Cast: John Cusack (David Shayne); Jennifer Tilly (Olive Neal); Dianne Wiest (Helen Sinclare); Chazz Palminteri (Cheech); Tracy Ullman (Eden Aungenu); Mary-Louise Parker (Ellen); Jack Warden (Julian Marx)

Running Time/Rating: 105 min./R

Index